God Is My AdventureA Book On Modern Mystics Masters And Teachers

GOD IS MY ADVENTURE

books by the same author

*

GOD
IS MY ADVENTURE

a book on modern mystics
masters and teachers

by

ROM LANDAU

FABER AND FABER
24 Russell Square
London

Gratefully to

B

*who taught me some of the best
yet most painful
lessons*

*First published by Ivor Nicholson and Watson
September Mcmxxxv
Reprinted October Mcmxxxv
November Mcmxxxv
November Mcmxxxv
February Mcmxxxvi
September Mcmxxxvi
December Mcmxxxvi
June Mcmxxxix
Transferred to Faber and Faber Mcmxli
Reprinted Mcmxliii, Mcmxliv, Mcmxlv and Mcmliii
Printed in Great Britain by
Purnell and Sons Ltd,
Paulton (Somerset) and London*

PREFACE TO THE FIRST EDITION

'There is something sacrilegious in your intention of writing such a book,' said a friend—and yet I went on with it.

Since I was a boy I have always been attracted by those regions of truth that the official religions and sciences are shy of exploring. The men who claim to have penetrated them have always had for me the same fascination that famous artists, explorers or statesmen have for others—and such men are the subject of this book. Some of them come from the East, some from Europe and America, some give us a glimpse of truth by the mere flicker of an eyelid, while others speak of heaven and hell with the precision of mathematicians.

I have met them all, and some I have watched in their daily lives. For years now I have sought their company, questioned them and watched them closely at work. I have tried to dissociate the personality from the teaching and then to reconcile the two. I have included some of those whom now I cannot view without mistrust. Since thousands of other people believe in them, they are at any rate most interesting figures in contemporary spiritual life, however little of ultimate value their teaching may possess.

There are people who know the heroes of this book more intimately than I, but my aim has never been to identify myself with any one teacher. On the contrary, I have always been anxious to discover for myself through what powers they have influenced so many people.

This attitude will warn the reader not to expect an impersonal survey of contemporary spiritual doctrines. I have limited myself to writing of those men with whom I have been in personal contact. I approach them not as the scholar but as the ordinary man who tries to find God in daily life.

This book is the confession of an adventure and the story of my friendships with those men whom a future generation may possibly call the true prophets of our time. The core of the adventure is a search for God. I leave it to the reader to decide whether such a search can be sacrilegious.   **R. L.**

MOCKBRIDGE HOUSE
HENFIELD, SUSSEX
Summer, 1935

5

PREFACE TO THE NEW EDITION

(Ninth Impression)

It is an agreeable duty for an author to express his pleasure when one of his books has enjoyed public favour sufficiently to call for yet another edition seven years after its first publication. In the present case, to the author's pleasure must be added his gratitude to his readers. For I have greatly profited from the thousands of letters received from people previously unknown to me, and even more so from the many valuable personal contacts which have often resulted from such correspondence. I should be false to my real feelings if I refrained from giving utterance to my gratitude for the enlightenment which I have thus derived.

When the manuscript of *God Is My Adventure* was first submitted to its original publishers, four of the five readers to whom the book was sent for a professional opinion, turned it down. The fifth pointed out that, whatever merits the book might possibly possess, it hardly justified publication since not more than a handful of people were ever likely to be interested in it. The five readers were unanimous in thinking that for a 'philosophical' book *God Is My Adventure* was not sufficiently orthodox, and for one purporting to explore the by-ways of modern esotericism, not pronounced enough in its allegiance to any individual one of the teachers and systems which it described.

Nevertheless the book has had to be repeatedly reprinted during the last seven years, and I assume this has mainly been due to two facts: people are always eager to learn from the spiritual experiences of a fellow seeker: many others, disillusioned by the Churches, were only too willing to delve into the ways and methods of unorthodox schools of thought, yet without at the same time feeling compelled to accept this or that method as the only valid one. In spiritual research the utmost personal freedom is a *sine qua non*. The seeker may, and indeed does, demand that those of whose findings he reads, should have a definite viewpoint of their own. But he will draw back as soon as he suspects that he is being pontifically forced by the author into accepting a certain point of view.

If in *God Is My Adventure* no effort was made to impose dogmatic opinions upon the reader, this was not because of undue modesty

7

on the part of the author, but rather because of his belief that none of the doctrines expounded by him had the monopoly of the 'whole' truth. In his opinion both the knowledge and the methods of the men under review were complementary to, rather than exclusive of, one another. And is it not a truism to say that a system which to-day perfectly fulfils our spiritual needs, may easily prove inadequate at some future stage of our search? Living truth cannot possibly be static. Though truth is one, its facets differ, as do our means of comprehending it.

Unless I completely misread the signs, I believe that there are reasons far beyond the possible merits of the present book which make its re-issue necessary in war time. I am only one among those who are convinced that the present war is mainly the expression of a spiritual conflict. The armed struggle is merely the visible reflection of something far more fundamental. Most of our spiritual conflicts can manifest themselves only by means of struggles on the material plane. But surely no-one imagines that the establishment of conditions propitious for victory and the right Peace afterwards is a purely material task, concerning economists and politicians alone. Is it not in reality a task incumbent upon every individual, however far he or she may be removed from the actual prosecution of the war? And does it not therefore follow that it is the spiritual effort of the individual which ultimately counts? But such efforts are doomed to frustration unless they are inspired by an intense inner urge. Routine and habit will not take us very far. Equally, this inner urge will lead us into blind alleys if we remain ignorant of the means by which it can be translated into practical action.

Books obviously cannot create a sense of spiritual urgency. But by demonstrating the reality and the power of what is spiritual in man, they can certainly intensify it. The response to *God Is My Adventure* leads me to believe that something of the burning urge responsible for the writing of the book, may possibly have been reflected in its pages. Moreover, many of the men described in it were concerned with methods of transforming spiritual ardour into practical action. Thus, though *God Is My Adventure* hardly touches upon subjects directly related to war, it does deal with some of the permanent verities of life which 'cannot be separated from the problems confronting us to-day.

No-one can solve the problems of his neighbour: how much less

8

can books achieve this. Yet what they can do, is to indicate the way in which others have tried to meet their own problems. All faith and all search for truth share a common denominator. If our own vision of God finds confirmation in the visions of our fellow seekers, we cannot but help feeling strengthened.

I believe more than ever to-day that every book or work of art which helps us to realize that the great events in the outside world are not independent of ourselves, but magnified projections of something within ourselves, has a useful function to perform. Whether our individual awareness grows through study, suffering, religion or personal relationships, is immaterial. What matters, is that we should become more acutely conscious of our responsibility in regard to those bigger events which appear to be beyond our own control. Division, like space, is a relative entity whose existence is limited to the material world alone. In the spiritual world neither of these have any existence. And since in the spiritual world it is the individual who counts, his motives and the workings of his mind are the forces that ultimately may have the power to tip the scales of historic events.

If this war-time edition of *God Is My Adventure* can succeed, in however imperfect a way, to help a few individuals to become more aware of their spiritual responsibility, then this new reprint would seem to be fully justified.

. . . . .

The eight or nine years which have elapsed since *God Is My Adventure* was first written have not made me change my original assessment of the men of whom the book treats. Those who at that time appeared to me genuine and significant have since increased in both these qualities. Those, on the other hand, whom I could not help viewing with a certain reserve, appear to me to-day even more dubious Thus, except for a number of minor corrections, it has not seemed necessary to introduce alterations into the text.

ROM LANDAU

THE MANOR
STOUGHTON, CHICHESTER
1942

9

ACKNOWLEDGEMENTS

I wish to acknowledge the following permissions and to express my thanks to the various authors and/or publishers and editors: Messrs. Basil Blackwell for quotations from *Oxford and the Groups*; Messrs. Jonathan Cape for quotations from *Introduction to Keyserling*, by Mrs Gallagher Parks; Mr. Harry Collison for quotations from his various translations of the books by Rudolf Steiner; Messrs J. M. Dent for quotations from the article 'More about the Perfect Master' in *Everyman*; The Hogarth Press for quotations from essays by Mr. C. Day Lewis and Mr. Michael Roberts in *New Country*; Messrs. John Lane, the Bodley Head, for quotations from *Saints Run Mad*, by Marjorie Harrison; The Oxford University Press for quotations from *What is the Oxford Group?*; Messrs. Kegan Paul for quotations from *Mrs. Annie Besant* by Theodore Besterman; Messrs. Rider and Mr. Paul Brunton for quotations from the latter's *A Search in Secret India*; Messrs Martin Secker for quotations from *Lorenzo in Taos*, by Mrs. Mabel Dodge, and *The New Statesman and Nation* and Mr. Bensusan for quotations from the latter's article 'Mother Earth and the Husbandman'; *The Sunday Chronicle* for quotations from the article 'This New Religion', by J. B. Priestley; *The Sunday Express* and Mr. James Douglas for quotations from the latter's article 'Shri Meher Baba'; *The Evening Standard* for quotations from the article 'Dr. Buchman', by Alva Johnstone; *The Times* for quotations from the leading article 'The Oxford Group Movement'.

CONTENTS

CONTENTS

PART THREE: FULFILMENTS

ILLUSTRATIONS

PART ONE

THE UNKNOWN CONTINENT

'God is a Spirit: and they that worship him
must worship him in spirit and in truth.'
· St. John iv. 24.

INTRODUCTION

TRUTH IN KENSINGTON GARDENS

'I am not sure that the mathematician understands
this world of ours better than the poet and the
mystic.'
Sir Arthur Eddington.

I

It began like this. one day in May, during an exceptionally cold
spell, I was walking through the deserted Kensington Gardens,
and it suddenly occurred to me that had it not been May, but January, we should not have thought the weather very cold. Instead of
cursing our treacherous climate, we should have enjoyed the Park
even without overcoats. I found the idea attractive, and I began to
make myself believe that it really was not May but January. The
atmosphere around me seemed to change. The air no longer appeared
to be cold, and the icy wind had the pleasant mildness of one of those
occasional breezes which distinguish an English from a continental
winter.

I now remembered an earlier experience. I had been travelling
through China, and once for a whole day it had been impossible to get
any food. To pass the time, I began to imagine the perfect meal, thinking of it not in an abstract way but as though I were actually eating it.
I went solidly through it, taking two helpings of each of the many rich
courses, and eating more than was good for me. The intensity with
which I gave myself up to it made me feel quite ill.

The experience in China, like that in Kensington Gardens, illustrates the power of one's mind. Belief in the power of the mind over
the body does not, however, imply advocacy of mental healing.
Modern civilization has been concentrating on the development of

B   17

our bodies while neglecting our minds. We sleep with our windows wide open in winter; we consult doctors about our diet; we visit expensive spas, and examine, at the slightest provocation, the colour of our tongues—but we do not bother about finding the best exercises for our mind or the right diet for our mental system. The various forms of mind healing drew our attention to the fact that for the cure of illness our mind may be as important as doctors and medicines; but we cannot pretend that our mental equipment has reached a stage at which it could replace the highly specialized apparatus of modern medicine.

There may come a time when we shall heal every disease through the power of the mind, and when we shall communicate with our friends in the other hemisphere through mental processes. We cannot, however, expect humanity to evolve a therapy of mental healing within one or two generations.

II

After the war of 1914–18, wherever I went, no matter whether in England, on the Continent, in America or the Far East, conversation was likely to turn to supernatural subjects. It looked as though many people were feeling that their daily lives were only an illusion, and that somehow there must somewhere be a greater reality The urge towards it lay constantly at the back of their curiosity, and they were trying to satisfy that urge whenever they were able to get away either from their daily round or from solitude. For most people can employ their thoughts only when stimulated by company and conversation. There were also those men and women who were trying quite methodically to find the reality behind the illusion of daily life; and they would attend special schools and follow special teachers.

Slowly I began to understand that the quest for God is nothing but the desire of discriminating between illusion and reality. It is the longing for that ultimate truth which Blake described when he wrote:

> *To see a world in a grain of sand,*
> *And a heaven in a wild flower,*
> *Hold infinity in the palm of your hand,*
> *And eternity in an hour.*

Though the problem of truth is as old as the world, yet few things are more difficult than to define its limits. and the further we advance

18

in the search for truth, the more those limits recede. It is not truth itself that varies, but only conceptions of it. The green apple is no longer green when I look at it in a dark room. Its greenness disappears if I give myself up to the enjoyment of its flavour, forgetting all about its looks; it vanishes, too, if I concentrate on another object near by; it changes according to its surroundings, according to the colour of the object placed beside it. Yet there must be means of seeing the essential oneness of the apple instead of its superficial multiplicity.

To-day one of the main difficulties in seeing truth lies in our incapacity for thought. Our work has become specialized and simplified, our travelling quick and effortless, even our amusements are transmitted to our homes. There is neither time nor apparent need for thought. Yet the most natural way of finding truth is through thinking.

For most people it is easier to look at an apple—to smell, to touch, to eat—in short, to perceive it through their senses, than to contemplate it. To think, in a way that would allow us to record truth as clearly as the eye records colour and the palate taste, we must know how to think. Few people can do this, and it might be well if every one of us were forced to spend half an hour a day in a quiet room, utterly bereft of radios, telephones, newspapers, magazines—even of good books. There, out of sheer boredom, we should perhaps begin to think, and after a few months we should begin to discover that during those thirty minutes we had been able to accomplish more of significance than during the rest of the week.

III

It was only in the last two centuries that intellectual truth was considered alone acceptable and spiritual truth merely a doctrine of the various religions. And yet truth in its spiritual sense is, as compared with purely intellectual truth, like the day as compared with its image seen through the spectacles of night. During a sleepless night little everyday dangers seem insuperable, and each difficulty is magnified beyond recognition. Every one of us has felt at some time or other during the nightmares between sleeping and waking that his problems were too complex to be solved by any other means than that of a dive through the bedroom window into the street below. When the morning arrived, the problems resumed their correct proportions, and likewise when seen with the eyes of spiritual truth those of our instincts and motives that seemed full of mystery become natural.

There are, however, other reasons for searching after truth. The idea of such a search lies very near the idea of living according to standards consonant with ethical laws, for to live ethically means to do instinctively the things that are spiritually right.

Here it may be remembered that there would probably have been fewer attempts of a transcendental kind after the war of 1914–18 if modern leadership had been based more firmly on spiritual truth and thus have had deeper ethical roots. Surely conditions to-day would be different if the men who directed our destinies had been driven more by a conscious faith than by the forces of scepticism, of national ambitions and of racial prejudice. For who were the leaders who directed the life of Europe in the last few decades? Emperors, kings, politicians, financiers, industrialists and demagogues of various kinds. Do we find in many of them the sign of mystical power which the late Czar of all the Russias or the Emperor of Germany pretended to possess by simple virtue of his office? Or did such 'realists' as the Bulows, Czernins and Isvolskys see the problems of their time as a 'reality in the final and highest sense'? Shrewdness, talent for debate, memory of fact were the main qualifications required It will be an interesting task for future historians to show how far the disasters of the last twenty-five years are due to the lack in the responsible men of Europe of real ethical foundations.

For the people at large, driven into losing faith in former ideals, there was some excuse for their seeking after truth along new channels For truth reveals itself in many ways: through thought, through vision, through clairvoyance, through religious experience.

IV

This book is 'not intended to disturb the serenity of those who are unshaken in the faith they hold'. Neither is it meant for those people who sweep aside anything that cannot be explained in terms of the matter of fact. This book is meant neither for them nor for those who believe in the destruction of the individual for the glorification of an abstract State or a political doctrine. It deals with men who profess to have unveiled 'some Divine truth which we could not have discovered for ourselves, but which, when it is shown to us by others to whom God has spoken, we can recognize as Divine' (Dean Inge). Many of the activities of the men described in this book would (in the nineteenth century) have been called supernatural; but men, when seeking truth, have always studied the supernatural. Whether we read *Prometheus Bound, Hamlet, Faust* or the works of Homer, Dante, Milton, Shelley, we always find in them a preoccupation with the hidden powers that direct man's destiny from lands unknown.

There are more signs than one that we no longer live in a period in which to seek truth in supernatural regions would be considered as verging upon insanity. Are the waves generated by a little electric instrument and those produced by our minds so different as to exclude the possibility of similar results? Is the one more 'real' than the other?

Higher mathematics and physics have reached a stage of such intellectual differentiation that soon it will become impossible to refer to them as to rational sciences, and they might find themselves one day in the unusual company of such a scientific bastard as occultism. Many scientists admit that the new wave parable rather than the former theory of the structure of electrons or the theory of transformation of matter into energy has brought science to a point where the word 'matter' becomes somewhat out of place. The difference between certain processes within the atom and the process, say, of creative thought or emotion may, after all, not be very great. A man of science such as Sir James Jeans admits in his *Mysterious Universe* that science is not yet in contact with 'ultimate reality'. If a leader of scientific thought admits that science does not provide ultimate reality, then people with less circumscribed vision simply have to venture into those lands that science feels shy of entering. 'No science,' says Dean Inge in his admirable Book on *English Mystics*, 'which deals with one aspect of reality . . exhausts what may be truly said about things. The world as projected by the ethical . . . faculties has as good a right to claim reality as that which the natural sciences reveal to us.'

Science has begun to admit that the world of the spirit and the world of matter are not two antipodes. The same applies to the natural and the supernatural worlds, and it is again Professor Jeans who confessed that the scientific conception of the universe in the past was mistaken, and that the borderline between the objective world, as it is manifested in nature, and the subjective one, as it expresses itself through the mind, hardly exists. In his presidential address at the

21

annual meeting (1934) of the British Association at Aberdeen, he said: 'The Nature we study does not consist so much of something we perceive as of our perceptions; it is not the object . . . but the relation itself. There is, in fact, no clear-cut division between the subject and object.' Twenty years ago such a statement would have been thought madness.

What matters more than this new 'spiritualization' of science is the fact that there have always been men who believed in those unknown lands and who tried to investigate them even though science, philosophy and at times official religion denied their existence. The names these people attach to their researches are of no importance. What matters is to know that we are pursuing something that brings us nearer to God—whether in China, Aberdeen or Kensington Gardens.

CHAPTER I

WISDOM IN DARMSTADT

Count Keyserling

I

In no country after the war could the desire for new ideals have been stronger than in Germany. Germany had become the melting pot of so many contradictory tendencies that some spectacular results were bound to follow. The Nazi Revolution fifteen years later was only one of them. In 1919 Germany was a country whose ideals had been destroyed. The paradox of a nation situated, both in the geographical and spiritual sense, in a critical position between the Western and the first outposts of the Eastern world; a nation intellectually keen, full of an exaggerated pride and of a burning desire for power, yet in the throes of an unparalleled defeat; bursting with a talent for organization, yet limited in her activities and stifled in her aspirations by an indecisive Peace Treaty; betrayed by an Emperor who for thirty years had been the idol of sixty million all too docile people—such a paradox was bound to create conditions in which the most extraordinary movements could flourish.

Though life in Germany in the period after the war was anything but pleasant, I do not regret having spent several years there at that epoch. The experience was not always edifying but it never failed to be enlightening.

It may strike one as incongruous that a search for God should have begun in a country which seemed further removed from Him than any other. Yet it is mainly under such conditions that a strong reaction can originate. In Holland, Switzerland and the Scandinavian countries there had been no dangerous upheaval, and there was no need for an establishment of new values. In the Latin countries spiritual research, outside the paths prescribed by the Roman Catholic Church, has hardly ever existed. Russia, in the depths of its fermentation, had replaced all deliberate spiritual activities by the deification of the State. The new countries were too preoccupied with organizing their new existence and too absorbed in their national ambitions to bother about purely spiritual issues.

23

THE UNKNOWN CONTINENT

Besides a native inclination it needs a great national catastrophe to account for the popularity of a supernatural movement. Germany had that inclination, and had experienced such a catastrophe. All values in German life had shifted; such words as 'faith' had but little meaning, and the few existing beliefs had solely an intellectual character. Serious problems were mostly treated with cynicism. The poorer classes knew nothing but resignation and bitterness, and the upper classes followed any fashion and craze that made them forget their unreal existence. This was especially evident in Berlin. In many places of entertainment, men dressed up as women and women in masculine attire added to the sense of the unreality of sex. The price of a body was as low as the price of cocaine or some newer drug which would destroy for a few hours the last vestige of reality. Yet in most cases cynicism and flippancy were but a mask concealing the anxiety which at times assumed proportions of real terror. People were constantly preoccupied with such questions as: What were the realities of German life? What of the stability of the German Republic? What of the German mark, of the power of finance and industry, of the to-morrow?

Certain sections of the younger generation tried to find new values in life through movements built on the pattern of the English Boy Scouts. In some of these one could find vague metaphysical, homosexual and above all political elements, many of which found unmistakable realization fourteen years later in the Nazi Storm Troops and the Nazi Movement in general. One might say that it was the moment of a darkly occult and a sexual awakening of German youth. The body with all its functions came into its own; the world of the spirit did not come into its own, but it was discovered by people who formerly would have denied its very existence

II

In the provinces there was much less cynicism than in Berlin. and values had not shifted with the same rapidity. Serious spiritual efforts could only be expected in the smaller German towns. They still enjoyed even now an atmosphere conducive to serious thinking, Stefan George, whom experts consider Germany's greatest poet since Goethe, lived in Bingen on the Rhine; Rudolf Steiner, the teacher for whom occultism was becoming as precise a science as mathematics, had settled just across the frontier at Dornach near Basle; Oswald

WISDOM IN DARMSTADT

Spengler, author of *The Decline of the West*, was pouring out his pessimistic philosophy in voluminous tracts from a prussianized Munich. None of them, however, had gained such a spectacular success as Count Hermann Keyserling, who had just opened a 'School of Wisdom' in Darmstadt, the small capital of the former Grand Duchy of Hesse. Keyserling's fame spread over the spiritual horizon of Germany overnight, and this fame was due to his origins and to his looks at least as much as to his uncommon philosophical attitude. People compared his narrow eyes and high cheekbones with those of Ghenghis Khan, and they talked of him as though he were an Eastern autocrat. The name of the 'School of Wisdom', situated conveniently in a former grand-ducal residence, impressed the simple and amused the intelligent. This academy was said to promise the delivery of spiritual products that would enable the pupils to climb the ladder of a new human order. This new 'élite' was to absorb Eastern and Western wisdom and thus to obtain a proper understanding of its own duties and powers. Slowly a new civilization would come into being, replacing one that was founded on scientific creeds and that was purely materialistic. This would be achieved mainly by attaching a new value to old problems.

It all sounded most promising. It was the sort of school that would appeal to eager intellectuals of post-war Germany. The future of the school was not romantically left in the hands of fate, it was virtually assured by the considerable and even sensational success which Count Keyserling had just achieved with his *Travel Diary of a Philosopher*, for this book was more widely read than either travel books or books by philosophers. There was something irresistible in the spectacle of a philosopher who, instead of brooding over books in his study, travelled the world *en prince*. Count Hermann tried to draw out the spiritual essence of most countries outside Europe, mainly in Asia. He had absorbed the soul of nation after nation with magic rapidity. Though the significant truths about those countries may not always have fitted into the mould which the imperious Count had shaped for them, the book still contained enough truth about India, China, Japan, Hawaii and America to satisfy Germany's thirst for knowledge.

The success of the two large volumes was not surprising. There had always been a large public in Germany for new intellectual manifestations. The disappointment caused by a lost war had produced both mental hunger and the wish to escape everyday realities. Intellectual

25

achievement coupled with an aristocratic name was bound to exercise a strong fascination over the citizens of the new Republic, in which the glamour of a monarchic past was already beginning to be remembered. Another reason for the great success of this book was that the Germans themselves had not been able to travel for nearly five years, and few nations travel with greater enthusiasm than the German. Their love for travel is composed of a strong 'Wissenshunger', a thirst for knowledge, a romantic idealization of the Faraway, and the worship of everything foreign, no matter whether it be the columns of a Greek temple or the pattern of a Scottish tweed. The German frontiers had remained more or less closed since 1914, and the country had been reduced in size. The German mark was losing its value, and travelling abroad was becoming a luxury that only the very rich could afford. The word 'abroad' shone with a tempting aura of its own. The exotic atmosphere of the *Travel Diary*, with its descriptions of remote countries, supplied at the time a very real need among a people thirsting for travel. You could not enter a drawing-room without noticing on a table the two volumes of the *Diary*, bound in black cloth, their paper showing all the poorness of a product manufactured in a country in which the war had hardly ceased to be a reality.

I, too, read the book, and felt stimulated by its sparkling thoughts and daring conclusions. The author's dogmatic pronouncements and his repeated contradictions antagonized and irritated me; but there were enough new and surprising aspects of the spiritual to excite the curiosity of any student of spiritual truth.

I decided to join the 'School of Wisdom'.

III

Count Hermann Keyserling comes from one of those Russo-German families which lived on the Baltic between East Prussia and Finland. Most of them were Russian citizens and spoke German with a Slav accent. Count Hermann's English biographer, Mrs. Gallagher Parks, traces her hero's ancestors back to the Middle Ages when certain German nobles settled in those eastern provinces. One of his ancestors, Caesar Keyserling, could pride himself on being one of the closest friends of Frederick the Great; Count Hermann's own grandfather was an intimate friend of Bismarck, and there were family connections with Immanuel Kant and Johann Sebastian Bach.

26

WISDOM IN DARMSTADT

A relationship of a different kind brought Tartar blood into the family: Count Alexander, the friend of Bismarck, married a Countess Cancrin whose mother, a Mouravieff, had Tartar blood in her veins.

Hermann Keyserling was born on the family estate of Konno in 1880. He was given a very strict and secluded 'aristocratic' education by private tutors. He hardly mixed with other boys till, after the death of his father, he was sent at the age of fifteen to a school at Pernau. He studied at the University of Dorpat; but the boisterous life of youthful excesses was cut short by a duel in which Count Hermann was seriously wounded. Keyserling himself tells us that this experience turned him from an easygoing student into a pure intellectual; and certainly he soon left Dorpat to take up more serious pursuits at Heidelberg, where he plunged into the study of natural sciences. He chose to study geology, as his grandfather Alexander had done. His biographer aptly remarks that one might call Keyserling a psychological biologist. Keyserling was not altogether satisfied with his study of biology nor indeed with that of philosophy, which in nine cases out of ten would become the spiritual haven of most serious-minded German students. Keyserling's outlook was finally shaped by Houston Stewart Chamberlain, a writer who, strangely enough, had also a fundamental influence on the 'philosophy' of Adolf Hitler and his Baltic 'Kultur-Diktator', Herr Alfred Rosenberg. Keyserling came under the spell of Chamberlain's *Foundations of the Nineteenth Century*, a book in the origins of which Richard Wagner, a pseudo-mysticism, an English upbringing, and a fanatical devotion to the Teutonic spirit of Bismarckian Germany, played equally important parts. Chamberlain, who had married one of the daughters of Richard Wagner, was then living in Vienna, and in order to be near him, Keyserling went there to study. He lived from 1901 till 1903 in Vienna, where the influence of Chamberlain and the Viennese 'mystic' Rudolph Kassner moulded Keyserling into an aesthete, an 'inactive dilettante'.

The following ten years were spent mainly between Paris, Berlin and London; and the social life of these capitals of Edwardian Europe played in Keyserling's life as important a part as private studies, reading and preoccupation with the arts. The Paris and London of those years must have been fairly full of young gentlemen with impressive bank balances, undefined spiritual ambitions and social pursuits. Slowly, however, Kant, Schopenhauer and Flaubert

27

replaced Mr. Chamberlain in Count Hermann's esteem; and this inner readjustment, together with a great personal disappointment, was responsible for Keyserling's first philosophical book, *Das Gefuege der Welt* ('The World in the Making'). Keyserling began to occupy himself with the serious sides of life, delivering a number of lectures in Berlin and Hamburg and by these and his writings obtaining a success in certain scientific circles in Germany.

In 1905, after the Russian Revolution, Keyserling believed he had lost his fortune. By 1908, however, the fortune was restored and he could settle down on the estate Raijkull, 'dividing his time between his literary activities and the life of a Russian agricultural nobleman'. In 1911 Keyserling set out on the momentous journey round the world which was the material for his *Travel Diary*. He took a whole year to complete the journey, and he worked on his diary till the beginning of the war He was not able to join the Russian army during the war on account of his old wound, and these years were spent at Raijkull, in 'the writing and rewriting of his book', while he drowned 'his profound disillusion and discouragement in the depths of self-analysis and spiritual self-control'.

The Russian Revolution finally deprived Keyserling of his property, and when in 1918 he moved to Berlin he was entirely dependent upon the results of his intellectual labours. A year later he married a grand-daughter of Bismarck, Countess Goedela von Bismarck, and his biographer remarks: 'This marriage is perhaps one of the clearest proofs of a certain unexpected sense of reality which runs like a foreign element through the strain of mysticism and almost disorderly imaginativeness which is Keyserling's. No choice that he could have made could possibly have been happier.' She completes her account of her hero's private life by mentioning his children: 'There have been born of the marriage two boys who, whatever gifts they may develop in maturity, already possess clearly defined and original personalities.'

IV

Though the name of the magic carpet on which Count Hermann Keyserling journeyed from obscurity to fame was, almost symbolically, *Travel Diary of a Philosopher*, this book was by no means his first essay in literature. It was preceded by several geological monographs, and one or two philosophical books. In 1907 *Unsterblichkeit* ('Immortality') appeared, a book which Dean Inge described as the finest on the subject written in modern times. In a number of his statements Keyserling shows that even at that early date he possessed a better brain for detecting new truths in old wisdom than most living people. Belief is, for Keyserling, the most central form of knowledge, and religious belief its highest variety. Such a statement coming from a man who fifteen years later still called himself a philosopher, was surprising. Even more surprising is the statement that it is always belief that creates reality. This suggests that those sections of the German public, especially the younger ones, who were trying to find truth outside mere intellectual knowledge, seemed justified in concentrating on 'the new light that shone' from Darmstadt.

It was not till 1919 that the success with the *Travel Diary* enabled Keyserling to found an academy with the strangest of all names that any teacher has ever dared to give to his own creation.

V

By 1922 the 'School of Wisdom' had achieved such fame that people throughout Europe were asking themselves what exactly it stood for. It was the continuation of a Philosophical Society formed a couple of years earlier by Keyserling and sponsored by the former Grand Duke of Hesse, Ernst Ludwig. Intellectual young Germans flocked to Darmstadt; yet, as will be seen later, it was not so much they who were responsible for the most striking aspect of the new movement; it was rather the more conspicuous social world that descended upon the quiet town in south-western Germany. For, though there was a constant nucleus of activities in Darmstadt, they did not reach their climax until the one or two yearly congresses, called 'Tagungen'. A Tagung lasted a week, and was attended by hundreds of people from all over the world. Officially it consisted of lectures.

For Keyserling the school was to be 'a radiator of spiritual influence with no institutional character but with international membership'. This was absolutely in keeping with his ideas about himself. He did not look upon himself as a scholar and a philosopher but as the 'apostle of a new spiritual era'. The fundamental idea of the school was 'to deepen a man's nature, to readjust his intellectual point of view'. The school tried to mould its pupils through personal influence rather than abstract teaching, and it aimed at showing its pupils 'the eternal beyond the temporal'. Keyserling's idea was also

29

to make his followers take a new and stronger interest in things that had interested them before, but that were losing their importance or their attraction.

Keyserling was eager to create by degrees in society an élite class that, by its higher intellectual and moral standards, would set a potent example to the people at large. It was due to this conception that Keyserling had an exaggerated opinion of English life and of the English idea of the gentleman. When asked about the aims of the school, he answered that it was 'an organism for transferring rhythm'. Friendship, discussion, meditation were among the means for this 'rhythmical transference'.

It may be that Keyserling's ideas were not academic enough for his German followers, accustomed to a more systematic method of education. It may be that the quickness and the versatility of his intellect bewildered people used to more comfortable methods of education. Whatever the reason, it was obvious to me from the very beginning that the school as it actually presented itself during the Tagung hardly corresponded to its creator's high ideals. Even if there were individuals who gathered from Keyserling enough spiritual knowledge to readjust their inner attitude towards life, the general impression was less promising.

VI

It was not difficult to guess what prompted many members to come to the Tagung. The few hotels in the town were packed, and at breakfast one imagined oneself sitting in an hotel *de luxe* in a fashionable spa rather than in the modest hotel of a sleepy provincial town. Certainly, during breakfast the names of Buddha, Plato and Laotse formed the centre of most conversations; but they were manipulated as though they belonged to social celebrities of the moment.

Most of the morning was given up to lectures. I was impressed by the names of the lecturers, whose addresses invariably maintained the expected standard. The lectures illustrated Keyserling's ideas with examples of Eastern and Western wisdom. Among the lecturers was the German sinologist, Richard Wilhelm, a man who had spent thirty years of his life in China and who had translated some of the profoundest Chinese thought into German. There was an impressive German Rabbi, Leo Beck, whose presence at this gathering showed that the organizers had been anxious not to give any signs of racial or religious prejudices. There was Leopold Ziegler, a man with a searching mind and a tortured body. When, assisted by his wife, he mounted the platform, the fight between spirit and flesh and the victory of the former became apparent in a moving way. But no speaker was more stimulating than Keyserling himself, who delivered a lecture almost every day, and who acted as an, at times, impatient and autocratic 'spiritus rector' of the whole Congress.

Platform and audience, however, seemed far apart, and the rays cast from the one illumined the other but rarely.

Though the passionate personality of Keyserling focused the general attention—at times even during the lectures of others—it was mainly two white chairs covered with red silk that exercised a magnetic influence over the eyes, and presumably the minds, of many members of the audience. They occupied the centre of the front row, and they were almost more responsible for the atmosphere during the Tagung than anyone or anything else. They were the seats of Ernst Ludwig and his consort.

In becoming the patron of Keyserling, Ernst Ludwig, the former ruler of Hesse, the grandson of Queen Victoria, the brother of the Russian Empress, the nephew, cousin or uncle of most of the crowned or ex-crowned heads of Europe, continued the policy which he had been pursuing even in the days before the war. Though he was no longer the ruler of his country, he still lived in his Palace, situated in a distinguished residential street in Darmstadt. His cousin, the Emperor William II, is reported to have remarked one day that, though Ernst Ludwig was his best friend, he was undoubtedly his worst soldier. By this criticism he probably meant that he did not approve of the stories circulated about his cousin. Some of them reported that Ernst Ludwig preferred milking cows behind the trenches to attending meetings of his Staff, and that he was leading in France an altogether more rustic life than the martially minded Emperor considered in keeping with the standards of a Royal prince. Yet even now the Grand Duke was more popular with the citizens of the Hessian Republic than his cousin at Doorn had ever been with the citizens of his Empire. The Grand Duke was a dilettante *par excellence*: he painted pictures, made beautiful embroideries, wrote poems and dramas of much feeling; he encouraged new artists to come to work in Darmstadt; he was an amusing conversationalist and an altogether delightful personality. He was also

31

deeply interested in mysticism. It must have been attractive to this alert and intelligent man to become the patron of a philosopher who might one day develop into the spiritual teacher of a new Germany. On the horizon of Ernst Ludwig's mind there may have appeared the vision of another Grand Duke· Karl August of Weimar and his protégé Johann Wolfgang Goethe.

The Grand Duke never missed a lecture and, considering the time of the year and the excessive heat, this alone was an achievement. Though he was now only a private individual, the consciousness of Royal presence and the atmosphere of Court could hardly have been stronger in pre-war days. The people, who before a lecture had been sitting about and chatting, would jump up from their seats like soldiers the moment the ducal couple appeared in the doorway. The Grand Duchess, by birth a member of one of the smaller princely families, was a shy but stately lady, kind and rather self-conscious. She used to arrive with ropes of pearls falling down to her knees, but on her face there was the homely expression of a typical *Hausfrau.* The ducal couple walked slowly along the path between the chairs All eyes followed them, and nobody uttered a word. Here and there they would smile at people they knew. The Grand Duke liked stopping between the rows, making jokes to friends. He was always immaculately dressed in a double-breasted suit, with a winged collar and a bow tie, and he approached the silk-covered chairs with the easy elegance of a man who is used to making his entry under the rapt eyes of hundreds of spectators. Only after the Grand Duke and his wife had taken their seats would the rest of the audience sit down.

VII

The Grand Duke and his consort were only partly, and in fact passively, responsible for the courtly atmosphere during the Tagung. This was created far more by the ladies and gentlemen who often by their very clothes distinguished themselves in this philosophical gathering. The men wore dark suits and stiff collars the excessive height of which presumably corresponded to their own elevated position. The dresses of their wives and daughters had an old-fashioned correctness which brought visions of courtly procedure and well-studied ceremonial. They were ladies and gentlemen formerly connected with the Court in official or private capacities, but now left stranded and forlorn. They seemed, however, eager to follow their former master even in his spiritual footsteps, and so they spent long mornings and afternoons fighting bravely against the heat and the boredom of lectures. Beads of perspiration would appear on their faces, and their heads would droop like those of weary travellers journeying through a hot summer night in a third-class carriage.

There was apparently some logic in the presence of so many members of the aristocracy. The Grand Duke was only one, and the less important, reason for their enthusiasm for philosophy More important was the presence of Count Keyserling himself. Though intensely intellectual and only half German, Hermann Keyserling was a member of their caste. In his autocratic and self-centred mind over and over again he displayed his social origin. While for the time being the German aristocracy as a whole had lost its influence, Keyserling the aristocrat was increasing his power as an individual. He was becoming a vital force, and attained to his position without sacrificing his aristocratic attitude or trying to flatter the new régime. This was bound to impress the old but powerless aristocracy, even though many members of it disapproved of Keyserling's advanced ideas, and called him the 'Socialist' or the 'Red Count'. It was very important, however, to most of them that Keyserling seemed to be creating a new aristocracy: a new caste in which their own ancient traditions would be invigorated by his spiritual reform. For the old nobility there must have been something very satisfactory in the promise of a new aristocratic order, essentially German, which was likely to carry its influence far beyond the frontiers of a diminished Fatherland

The aristocratic world contrasted in appearance somewhat with the smarter air of a number of visitors, mainly women, from Berlin, Vienna and other capitals. There were also a few Americans for whom the combination of philosophy and royalty must have been irresistible. It was this world that was most visible during the whole Tagung. As the lectures proceeded, the eyes of the audience were focused more and more on the two white chairs. It would have been pleasant to meet some of these often cultured people had one arrived in Darmstadt for entertainment. It was, however, somewhat disappointing to young enthusiasts who, like myself, had not come to Darmstadt for that purpose, but to be enlightened, uplifted or at least instructed.

I realized on the first day that it would not be easy to find answers to the various questions a great many of the younger generation were asking themselves. The main difficulty in the way of a satisfactory solution to our problems lay no doubt in ourselves. It consisted in the impossibility of formulating the questions clearly. Perhaps I should—reporter-wise—have had them ready beforehand, expecting Keyserling to give unconditional and explicit answers. Yet the problems themselves were not precise and it was not a matter of intellectual curiosity. We wanted an indication as to a right way of thinking, a right discipline of feeling. Some of us had indefinite ideas on the necessity of celibacy. We had all dabbled in Yoga and similar exercises, but we were vague about them; we pretended that we knew more than we actually did, and we hoped that someone would give us clear rules. We were too young to know that general rules can be issued much more easily in a factory than in such an assembly. Meditations were held for a certain group of people, but meditations held collectively on hot summer days and in European clothes seemed even to my inexperienced mind somewhat unconvincing. It appeared to me as though Keyserling was trying to give us the very fare we were looking for. Yet somehow it was impossible to break through the courtly apparatus of the Tagung.

Nevertheless there was one piece of advice which remained alive long after the Tagung was forgotten—that it was not the things and the ideas in themselves that had to be changed but the accents we put on them. One day I asked Keyserling what he really meant by this phrase. The answer must have been so omnipresent in his mind that, even without stopping in his walk towards the exit, and without looking at me, he answered: 'We cannot solve problems by destroying them or by working them out in elaborate systems, but merely by re-ordering their accents, by robbing them of their former weight. If we begin to neglect a problem, minimizing its previous importance, it will begin to disappear from our consciousness; it will soon die and thus solve itself.' The conversation of no-one else gave me so strongly the impression of written rather than spoken words: it was as though the mouth could not follow the tremendous pace of the brain and was forced to leave the words only half finished; they were thrown into the listener's ear at a bewildering speed, and they left behind the vision of a quite uncommon nervous energy.

WISDOM IN DARMSTADT

VIII

There was no means of escaping the atmosphere of the provincial court. In pre-war days this courtly character must have been delightful. Now, deprived of its significance, and placed in the midst of a philosophical gathering, it had become quite irrelevant. The social interludes, which were meant to establish the contacts of one with another on a basis of deeper understanding, were in keeping with the general character of the Tagung. Keyserling had been right when he had planned these social gatherings. Unfortunately a great many of the members put the accent on the outer framework only. Most conversations held in the presence of women—and as usual on such occasions there were many more women than men—only rarely allowed one to come nearer to the understanding of the problems for the elucidation of which the Tagung had been organized. They deteriorated into gossip, and ended generally with some remarks about the wife of a powerful banker from Berlin. The ladies taking part in a conversation would suddenly find it shocking that the banker's wife appeared three times a day in different clothes and, what is more, in clothes that had obviously come from Paris. One's own mental accent became so focused on the lady from Berlin that on the third morning even I could not help my attention wandering in an effort to locate the lady and verify these accusations.

One night we were asked to a party by a very rich nobleman whose house was famous for its magnificent collection of works of art. In Germany collections of such a kind can never be seen unless one knows the owner personally. It was a very rare occasion, and I was grateful for the opportunity of seeing a masterpiece by Van Eyck and a number of hardly less famous pictures and statues placed in perfect surroundings. I expected to find great eagerness on the part of the other members of the Tagung. With very few exceptions, however, they were entirely absorbed in watching the arrival of the Grand Duke and his wife, whose backs they had been admiring for an almost unlimited number of hours in the last few days. And when the handsome wife of the banker from Berlin arrived with ropes of pearls more magnificent than even those of the Grand Duchess, the topic of conversation seemed decided for the remainder of the evening.

The picture of the Tagung would be incomplete without the mention of an occasion at which Keyserling's ideal combination of

35

social intercourse and spiritual stimulation was to be realized at last. It was the visit of the Indian poet Rabindranath Tagore, whose European fame had just reached its zenith. In Germany he was considered one of the greatest poets of the age. Like myself, some of the younger members of the Tagung had by now become critical and hypersensitive to little details. In honour of Tagore the Grand Duke issued invitations to a garden party in his hunting castle outside Darmstadt. It was a hot sunny day, and the invitation was accepted with enthusiasm. After a lovely walk through the old park, we had tea in the castle. During tea a small incident took place which in my hypercritical state of mind seemed to become symbolical of the whole Tagung.

I had been introduced by a cousin of the Grand Duke to his two sons, who were then still at school. We had tea together and were joined later by several guests who were staying during the Tagung at the Grand Duke's palace in Darmstadt. Among them was 'Auwi', prince August Wilhelm, the fourth son of the Kaiser. My friend, who was his cousin also, introduced me to the prince, remarking that though by profession a sculptor I was very much interested in Keyserling's teaching. The prince looked at me for a second or two as though trying to find a suitable remark or to realize the meaning of his cousin's explanation. Then he said: 'Oh, you are a sculptor. A sculptor? Does that mean that you have to do so, so?' The last words were accompanied by a gesture of both hands indicating the movements of a hammer striking the chisel. It was presumably the only way in which the prince was able to express his comprehension. As his face remained serious, I had no reason to suspect a joke. My friend blushed for his cousin's remark, but for me it seemed to sum up my personal impression of the Tagung. Even in later years, whenever someone mentioned the name of Tagore, I used to blush at the recollection of the prince, anxious to be agreeable to a friend of his cousin, and trying hard with both hands to show his comprehension of the profession of a sculptor.

After tea we went into the neighbouring fields, and grouped ourselves on the slope of a hill, on the top of which stood Keyserling and Tagore. Their dark silhouettes were sharp against the pale gold of a perfect summer sky. The Indian poet was wearing long silk robes, and the wind played with his white hair and his long beard. He began to recite some of his poems in English. Though the majority of the listeners hardly understood more than a few words—

36

it was only a few years after the war, and the knowledge of English was still very limited—the flush on their cheeks showed that the presence of the poet from the East represented to them the climax of the whole week. There was music in Tagore's voice, and it was a pleasure to listen to the Eastern melody in the words. The hill and the fields, the poet, the Grand Duke and the many royal and imperial princes, Keyserling and all the philosophers and philistines were bathed in the glow of the evening sun. It was a very striking picture.

CHAPTER II

EPISODES IN MODERN LIFE

Stefan George and Bô Yin Râ

I

I was beginning to wonder whether the mission of a teacher was to give us final proof, or merely to act as a stimulant and to show us that it is only ourselves who have the power of applying a new teaching in our lives. Often even our daily life would act as such a stimulant.

I had not a scholar's interest in metaphysical subjects and theosophical or Buddhist schools attracted me as little as monasteries or Eastern *ashrams*. And yet I was asking myself constantly the same questions that most younger people around me seemed to be asking themselves, and to which our ordinary knowledge could supply no satisfactory answers. Was our earthly life a complete whole or was it merely a stage in a much longer journey? Was the belief in *karma*[1] and in reincarnation more satisfactory than that in the Paradise and Purgatory of the Christian Church? Had our sex instinct to be regulated according to some hidden plan, or to physical necessity, or to conventions in which we had been brought up? Were our actions the free expressions of our free will or merely the results of habit and education? Ought we to follow the conventional ethics of our day or try to discover ethics that might have a more spiritual significance?

Acquaintances who had hitherto appeared materialistic in outlook suddenly seemed animated by the same spiritual urge.

One day during conversation at lunch in the house of a woman who was known to me only as a popular hostess I happened to use one of those silly adjectives such as 'heavenly' or 'incredible'. My hostess interrupted me suddenly, and said in a low voice so that nobody else could hear: 'You should not use words that you cannot possibly mean. I am sure you know that words have a deeper meaning in themselves than the one which we thoughtlessly give them'. I was impressed by her honesty; her remark was indeed the beginning

---

[1] *Karma*—conditions into which man is born as the result of his good and bad deeds during his former life on earth.

38

of a deep friendship which was cut short only by her death. In the few years of our friendship I discovered that her own, at times extremely successful, way of getting at the roots of things consisted in always trying to avoid the use of words in their wrong sense. She never used them irreverently, but was always anxious to remember that a word is both a symbol and a centre of spiritual power in itself. I began to watch myself and to be careful in the use of adjectives; the 'most incredible' and 'heavenly' were eliminated from my vocabulary. I no longer answered invitations by saying, 'I shall simply adore' to come I noticed that the feminine fashion of the exaggerated use of adjectives—and not only of adjectives—was not confined to the younger, frivolous set, but was equally popular with older and more serious people.

In the following weeks, during which I was beginning to treat words with some of the respect due to them, life became more real; problems appeared simpler, and I seemed to see them in their right proportions. It was as though I were becoming more honest. The slipshod employment of words and the use of exaggerated expressions put you into an atmosphere of artificiality, making the ground on which you stand seem insecure.

II

It can hardly have been an accident that I came across the work of Stefan George exactly at a moment when some of the lesser mysteries of life were beginning to reveal themselves to me through the medium of words. While I was staying in Germany, a friend gave me for Christmas a book of poems by George. The binding, with its faintly Gothic character, was self-conscious, the type and setting reminiscent of William Morris; there was no punctuation, and the use of capital letters was arbitrary. These external details made reading difficult. In former days I should merely have skipped superficially through the decorative pages: in my present state I was absorbed from the very beginning; the poems impressed me so deeply that I bought George's other four volumes; and I spent weeks in a state of exhilarated study of George's poetry.

I was beginning to understand why the anagogic personality of George was so much admired, nay worshipped, by some of the most serious-minded Germans. They approached the poet in a spirit of almost mystical veneration.

THE UNKNOWN CONTINENT

Stefan George, the descendant of peasants from Lorraine, the son of an innkeeper in the Rhenish vineland, had been living for years in an impenetrable seclusion. This was responsible for the many fantastic stories circulated about him. The critics called him an aesthete and a highbrow; and indeed there was little doubt that in his earlier days he had exhibited a certain artistic precocity. He would be mentioned by people—who knew little more than his name—in connection with Rossetti, Oscar Wilde, Beardsley and William Morris. An apocryphal story was told of George at a big dinner, sitting behind a screen so as not to be seen by the other guests, and consuming during the meal no more than three grapes. Gossip was invented because hardly anyone knew or had ever seen George, in no directory of any kind was his address or even the district in which he lived to be found, he was enshrouded in mystery; he never compromised, or descended to the level indispensable to the attainment of worldly success. George had never subscribed to any popular movements; he had not belonged to any literary school; he had always worked in a personal and independent way—but the number of his admirers grew from day to day, and almost against his will.

George was a poet and nothing else. He did not try to be either critic, dramatist, journalist or politician. He followed only the commands of his Art, which he kept pure and free from all alien elements. He considered that his mission as a poet was that which is open to none but the poet: that is to uncover truths, to disseminate wisdom and to create beauty. He was never unfaithful to these principles, and this accounts perhaps for the prophetic quality of many of his poems. It also explains a part of his influence upon the more serious-minded sections of German youth. And yet neither the subject matter nor the form of his poems was modern. They contained, side by side, pagan sensuousness and classic severity of tone, and they glittered with a richness of texture that induced superficial readers to call him an aesthete. No-one since Goethe had possessed such a mastery of the German language, nor had any other German poet created more magnificent new words. His words always seemed to give the only possible picture of that 'higher reality' which before him had been known under many different names.

George was becoming his country's most important poet, sage and teacher. Young Germany was finding in his poems a truth that had hitherto been but dimly apprehended, and a stern, manly beauty that contrasted strongly with the life around ·The irretrievable past had not been replaced by a satisfactory present, and the lost war had left behind a deep bitterness. The result was the growth among some of the young men of a vague internationalism which, rarely creative, was in the main limited to criticism and retrospect. Under George's influence such positive values as 'friendship', 'earth', 'homeland', 'leadership' became desirable once again.

The small group of people who belonged to George's immediate circle exercised a far wider influence than seemed justified by the smallness of their number and their insignificance in the world. They held no office, their names practically never appeared in the news-papers, they were hardly ever heard of at internal congresses. Never-theless, their spiritual superiority had a growing influence. A few of them, such as Friedrich Gundolf, the professor of literature at the University of Heidelberg, or E. Kantorowicz, lectured, and thus in-fluenced youth directly. Others such as the critics, poets and histor-ians, Karl Wolfskehl, Friedrich Wolters, Ludwig Klages, Berthold Vallentin, Ernst Bertram, were felt through their writings and their personal contacts.

George received but a very few people into his immediate circle, but having once accepted a disciple, he shaped not only his intellect but his whole character. He was, for all his artistic exclusiveness, not a mere dreamer, and his influence touched all practical sides of life. This saved his followers from that sentimental idealizing, which was so typical of all intellectual efforts in Germany.

George's most lasting force lay in his poetry. Though many Ger-mans had succumbed to it, George had not yet become a national property like Goethe and Wagner. His claim to fame rests on his purification and enrichment of the German language. Experts re-garded this work as of an almost magical significance. Like most modern languages, German had become cheapened. But the lan-guage and the people of a country are so closely connected that the cheapening of the one involves a similar deterioration of the other; purification of the language can be followed by a subsequent and automatic regeneration of the people, and George was fully conscious of this fact. In his work of over forty years' duration he tried to give back their language to the Germans. Many serious minded Germans imagined that his legacy would solve many German problems more easily than all manner of political programmes could do.

It was not George's poetry alone that had impressed the Germans so deeply: it was also that inner attitude which can only be described by the German word *Haltung*. The word does not exist in English. The Englishman possesses an inner dignity by nature; in English the term becomes therefore almost meaningless. In Germany this is not so. *Haltung*, or the strength of one's poise, is such a rare phenomenon that it is always impressive. George's attitude of proud seclusion, of silence, of loyalty and devotion to his ideals, of avoidance of publicity, of a stern responsibility towards his work—in short, the whole magnitude of his *Haltung*—impressed the Germans as something truly superior. For forty years they had heard about the uncompromising poet from Bingen on the Rhine, who had never given an interview; who had never appeared on any public platform; who had never published an article in a newspaper; who had never accepted the titles or the invitations of an academy, a university or a government; and whose Dantesque face seemed the very symbol of an inner strength and of a pre-eminent *Haltung*.

For many of the younger men George had become a sort of ever-present conscience urging us to live up to his high standards. Though only a very few knew him; though by his very seclusion and distance from ordinary life he had become to his followers almost an abstract power, his purifying and dignifying influence was stronger than that of those men we had been taught to admire. It is but rare in modern life that spiritual influence becomes real without personal contact, and merely through the power of the word and the *Haltung* of the teacher.

III

Unfortunately, such is our mental laziness that even the noblest influence begins to lose its stimulating power when confronted by economic worries and by the constant rush of new impressions. Both the enthusiasm and the impatience of youth make it difficult for it to remain for long faithful to the same self-chosen message, and so every new spiritual experience becomes only a passing stimulant.

But life went on creating excuses for new efforts. The purifying influence which had unexpectedly come through the casual remark at luncheon, and the acquaintance with Stefan George which followed, were only two of various events which pushed me along new paths.

The editor of a newspaper to which I was a contributor one day handed me a slender volume, bound in red paper, and asked me whether I would care to write a review of it. He thought that I might be interested in 'that sort of thing'. One or two other people in the editorial office had refused to write the review, and the editor himself felt that he could not deal with it. The book had been sent personally to the editor by its author, Felix Weingartner, the celebrated composer and conductor The editor had a greater admiration for Herr Weingartner's musical gifts than for his spiritual and literary activities, which left him slightly bewildered. The book was called *Bô Yin Râ*, and I took it home to read

IV

The three syllables Bô Yin Râ meant nothing to me at the time, but Herr Weingartner's name was a guarantee that some quality might be expected. The book contained the story of the conversion to a new creed of one of the most distinguished musicians of the day, together with an enthusiastic account of that creed and of its founder, hidden behind the exotic name Bô Yin Râ. Even before I had finished the book I knew that I should not forget it easily, and I bought several of Bô Yin Râ's own books. Instead of writing the usual notice I asked the editor if I might write a review of four columns, though even that length I thought at the time inadequate, and I was therefore not surprised when within a year after I had first come across the name of Bô Yin Râ I learned that his books had become best sellers.

Most people were intrigued by the exotic name, while others were puzzled by the semi-mystical and very modern pictures with which some of the books were illustrated. It was plain from these pictures that the author was also a painter of some distinction. It was impossible to verify who he was, and though Herr Weingartner wrote to me at great length he would not disclose anything about the identity of his hero.

There was no school, Church or movement that bore the name of Bô Yin Râ. His message was contained in his little books, read with eagerness by thousands of Germans. *The Book of the Living God, The Secret, The Book of Man*—all of them were variations on a theme. They were meeting more than halfway the spiritual needs of a disillusioned nation, eager to forget the misery of daily life.

Bô Yin Râ's gospel might not have been accepted so willingly had it not contained various statements that suggested in his case the

43

possession of esoteric knowledge.[1] The promise or even the possibility of such knowledge never fails to interest people. The more serious student hopes to find in it the core of certain teachings, hidden from the layman but apparently in existence since time immemorial; in the masses it evokes visions of supernatural power. Bô Yin Râ claimed that his store of knowledge came from the same source as did some of the most ancient wisdoms. In several publications he was referred to as a 'Master', and he was supposed to be in constant spiritual communication with certain other 'Masters' who transmitted their secret knowledge to him These 'Masters' were referred to as 'Sages of the East' or the 'Inner Helpers'.

Though it was impossible at the time to understand fully what all such claims entailed, Bô Yin Râ at least seemed an honest man who believed in the truth of his statements.

His teaching was neither new nor startling, but it was sound, and it contained certain fundamental truths. Its main thesis was that we can find true and lasting happiness only within ourselves, and that we must abandon the search for it in the world without. The moment we begin to listen with greater attention to ourselves we uncover those spiritual powers that create happiness. Although happiness was a definite command in Bô Yin Râ's doctrine, he did not base it on any asceticism or self-denial, but on a sensible and deliberate acceptance of life, on honest and decent living and on the absolute elimination of fear.

Bô Yin Râ did not consider himself a new prophet or messiah, but the 'mediator' between higher powers and man, who cannot find happiness in life. His object was not to persuade people but merely to stimulate those faculties in them that are needed for the establishment of an inner harmony.

Bô Yin Râ's success was not surprising. In an existence with little material security and with just as little hope for immediate improvement, his gospel was bound to find many adherents. Most of the other new gods—Freud with his sublimations and complexes, Keyserling with his 'sense of life' and 'replacement of accents', Einstein with his incomprehensible relativity, Spengler with his intellectual pessimism, George with his poetic visions, Steiner with his startling scientific perceptions—could not be enjoyed without intellectual preparation. Bô Yin Râ was easy to understand. The style of his

[1]Esoteric—having a secret meaning Esoteric teaching is only given to initiates or specially prepared disciples.

44

books was almost that of books for children; no religious or intellectual conversion was required; his kind of happiness could be achieved by the rich and by the poor. Above all, he appealed to the emotions. In a way Bô Yin Râ did for many Germans what Dr. Frank Buchman tried to do ten years later for certain sections of the British public.

It did not come as a surprise to me when I found out later that Bô Yin Râ was a Bavarian painter with the prosaic name of Herr Joseph Schneiderfranken.

Joseph Schneiderfranken was born in 1876 at Aschaffenburg in Bavaria. After various manual occupations he found the means to study painting in Munich and in Paris. He lived for a while in Greece, married, became the head of a large family, and settled down in Switzerland. He did not begin writing till he was forty, and he based his whole teaching solely on personal experience without any relation to existing doctrines or religions He claimed that his name was not arbitrary, but that it was given to him by his 'Masters' for reasons connected with its esoteric meaning.

Though the majority of his admirers suspected behind his name a rather picturesque mystic, they responded in the first instance to that honest and unsophisticated ring in his words that never fails to appeal to the expectations common in all men. Even in his appearance Bô Yin Râ inspired confidence. He was big and heavy, rather rough cut, of peasant features and yet of gentle expression. One easily believed that he loved few things better than climbing high mountains, planting trees in his garden, or performing manual work.

In the artificial, hectic life of post-war Germany the simple message of Bô Yin Râ was like a refreshing breeze It satisfied certain emotions that had not found realization in any of the other creeds. We all have a first awakening in life when we turn away from our youthful egotism and feel the desire to be decent and unselfish, to help others and to create harmony within. Bô Yin Râ appealed to those instincts.

But such instincts soon lose their power if the foundations of the message that satisfies them are solely emotional. After a period of enthusiasm I felt, like many others, that Bô Yin Râ's doctrine was of too general a kind and that it did not satisfy the intellectual thirst. An inner transformation that touches the emotions without affecting the intellect cannot last.

Nevertheless I was grateful for the laziness of my colleagues which brought me into touch with the Bavarian peasant painter Bô Yin Râ.

V

And this is the last incident. A friend of mine who was the legal adviser of an old mercantile firm asked me one day to come over to Hamburg, where he lived, to advise him as to the production of a new monthly review which his firm had decided to publish I thought there was some misunderstanding: I could hardly imagine myself the right person for a job that would require knowledge of finance and economics.

Nevertheless on the following Saturday I took the train to Hamburg, and by lunch time I was sitting between my friend and the owner of the firm. Before long I realized that the review was to be dedicated to 'cultural, literary and artistic matters', and that I was to become one of the three editors. The task seemed interesting and I accepted the offer

After two numbers of the review had appeared, its owner decided that it could not fulfil its purpose in its present form. It was meant to appeal to serious-minded people, who had grown tired of the usual academic and literary monthly publications produced mainly to satisfy the vanity of their contributors and editors. The review had therefore deliberately to deal even with thos subjects that most people still called supernatural, and the proprietor considered that the right treatment of these matters might disclose more truth than had the conventional methods hitherto employed.

An exciting correspondence now began with new collaborators, and the review in consequence included articles about the more serious side of graphology and astrology, symbolism in ancient art, the relationship between religion and language; it also published fiction in which the invisible background of life was seriously treated. As far as editorship was concerned, we were all amateurs; the review was amateurish, and it changed its face almost from number to number. Most of our decisions as to the contents were based on guesses, and yet the review's circulation grew with each month of its publication; and though it received much abuse, it inspired some praise from unexpected quarters.

It is only to-day that I comprehend why we introduced supernatural matter into the review. The obvious reason was, of course, the apparent demand of our readers. The main reason had a more selfish origin, for the three of us felt that we could come nearer to grasping truth only if we were forced to deal with certain problems in a more serious manner than we had done before. The new professional responsibilities forced us to order, read, accept, refuse and at times even write articles on subjects that dealt more with the background than with the obvious things of life, with hidden rather than with visible connections. Our professional preoccupation with these subjects disclosed certain truths that had hitherto been hidden from us.

At first the directors and presumably most of the many employees of the firm looked at the new attempts of their 'boss' with suspicion and bewilderment. At the end of a few months most of them read the review. Many of them approached the editors with questions which showed how deeply interested they were in the problems with which it dealt.

VI

The recorded experiences of the last few years were perhaps nothing more than unimportant episodes. Nevertheless they seemed to suggest to me that even an apparently insignificant event has its meaning, and that it may help us to perceive truth no less than do the larger events of our lives. Each experience opens up a new path, just as each teacher acts as a new stimulant, and it is by no means merely restlessness or lack of faith that compels us continually to try to travel along new roads.

CHAPTER III

OCCULT TRUTH

Rudolf Steiner

I

I go back now to the days of the war.

I was a student in Warsaw, which was then occupied by the German troops. One day a German officer told me a most unusual story. He had been suffering from a rather exceptional illness of which he had only quite recently been cured. His affliction was a form of second sight which operated in one particular direction. Baron V was the descendant of an old family, was a scholar, and a traveller. He was a member of a flying corps on the Western Front. Every time his colleagues were ordered on a flight Baron V could foresee exactly who would return and who would be killed. On several of these occasions he communicated his forebodings to his superior officers, and each time his presentiment was borne out by the event. Baron V.'s situation became unbearable the nervous strain produced by this gift of prophecy increased to an alarming extent, and he anticipated a breakdown. He decided that if he were to stay in the service he must rid himself of his fatal talent. He wrote to a friend at home and was advised to see an Austrian, a certain Dr Rudolph Steiner, who lived in Berlin, and who was said to possess extraordinary powers.

Dr. Steiner was the leader of a movement known as Anthroposophy He was not a physician but was reported to be a man of learning and scholarship Though Baron V had become rather sceptical, he was feeling so worried that he telegraphed to Dr. Steiner, and two days later he took the short leave he had been promised and left the front for Berlin.

He drove from the station straight to Dr. Steiner's flat, where he was shown without delay into a big sitting-room. In his frock coat and his large black bow tie Dr. Steiner suggested both a scholar and a poet, his face with its deep-set eyes was expressive, but his manner was simple and quiet. A faint and pleasant accent betrayed his Austrian origin He gave Baron V. no promises, but he advised him to practise certain mental exercises which he thought would be helpful.

48

Baron V. had to admit that the natural manner of Dr. Steiner had impressed him. He had never read any of Dr. Steiner's publications, but he left Berlin with a suitcase filled with them, and read some of them on his way to the front Though they seemed less simple than the manner of their author had led him to expect, Baron V. was struck by their logic and their scientific precision, and it appeared to him that they were distinguished by these attributes from the generality of writings on occult subjects. Baron V. began the mental exercises immediately, and after a short time his second sight disappeared

Had Baron V. remained only a casual acquaintance, whose trustworthiness had not been tested, I might have considered this story apocryphal. In repeated contacts stretching over many years, however, I have never found any reason to doubt his truthfulness.

II

The man, who had meant nothing to me until then, was now suddenly constantly talked about in my presence When I visited Germany after the war. it was almost impossible not to hear the name of Rudolf Steiner. Violent attacks and 'revelations' were appearing in many newspapers—not concerned with scholarly subjects but with politics. The authors of these articles were mostly army officers and politicians, and the commonest accusations held Rudolf Steiner responsible for one of the biggest German defeats, and thus for the death of thousands of soldiers. I found it by no means easy to find my way through this labyrinth of statements and counter-statements.

What was the crime that put the scientist and scholar Rudolf Steiner into the very centre of a military-political battle? Jules Sauerwein, the distinguished editor of the Paris *Matin*, summed up these accusations when he began an interview with Steiner with the following words: 'Do you know that your enemies say that, if it had not been for you, neither the German Chief of Staff nor the German Headquarters would have lost their heads and consequently the Battle of the Marne?'

Steiner had indeed been on terms of intimate friendship with Frau von Moltke, the wife of General von Moltke, the German Chief of Staff, for many years. He did not know the general intimately, and yet he was accused of having influenced Moltke's decisions in the first weeks of the war, and was thus made responsible by many people for the overwhelming defeat of the German armies. The accusers spread legends that he had exercised his influence over Moltke and Frau von Moltke through mediums and in even more sinister ways. As both Moltke and his wife admitted that they had the highest regard for Steiner, the stories about his influence over them were believed even in responsible quarters. The truth became known only later, when Moltke's *Memoirs* appeared and when, after the collapse of the German Reich, Steiner felt entitled to publish all the evidence of his connection with Moltke. Only then was it realized that Steiner had not seen Moltke during the preparations for the Battle of the Marne, and that the two men never spoke of purely military matters The truth was that the Emperor William in one of his irresponsible moods withdrew his confidence from Moltke and that the Chief of Staff was left in bewildering uncertainty as to his own position. In her anxiety Frau von Moltke begged Steiner to go and see her husband, who felt the necessity of some spiritual comfort. Steiner went to Coblenz to see Moltke, and the two men spent several hours in a philosophical conversation. This meeting became known. No officer in the German Army liked the idea that the Chief of Staff should spend important hours in mystical conversation with a philosopher, and the fact that he had done so was in itself sufficient to provide the calumniators with their material.

These attacks were almost all the news of Steiner that I could glean from the daily press. Yet the newspapers were no longer the only source of information. Though my interest in Steiner was still detached, I met more and more people who knew or were studying Steiner's teachings. His followers seemed to belong to nearly all professions: there were engineers, doctors, artists, journalists, business men, theologians. Whilst the followers whom I had met at the 'School of Wisdom' at Darmstadt had treated spirituality rather as a topic of smart conversation, the followers of Steiner were serious, and many of them seemed experts in the most varied subjects. While the majority of Keyserling's followers seemed to have read only his *Travel Diary*, the majority of the people whom I met in connection with anthroposophy appeared to have read a great many of the more difficult of Steiner's books.

Steiner's teaching was evidently the most widespread and, by the quality of its followers, the most important of its kind on the Continent.

OCCULT TRUTH

III

Rudolf Steiner was born in 1861 at Kraljevic, a small town within the Habsburg Monarchy on the frontier of Hungary and Croatia. His father had formerly been in the employment of a Count Hoyos, but had afterwards become stationmaster at a small provincial station. The boy spent his childhood not only in the fields and woods near the railway line but also in everyday contact with such realities as trains, timetables, and the mechanics of earlier telegraphy. At first he was educated partly by his father, partly at the local school. The high school his father chose for him was a so-called 'Real Schule', and this meant that mathematics and the sciences were emphasized much more than were the classics.

From his earliest days the boy was given up to the contemplation and enjoyment of inner sensations as much as to external pleasures, and he was trying to understand the background of life through a fuller knowledge of nature. He was gaining that knowledge through the usual channels and through a form of observation which in later years he was able to diagnose as second sight. The boy felt dimly that it was not 'normal' to view the world in such a way, and he tried to fight against his visions. The study of mathematics reassured him, however, and in geometry he experienced for the first time the existence of a real world which is not visible to the bodily eye. The triangle he learned about in geometry was not a particular triangle that he himself might draw but the essence of all triangles. This ideal triangle could be seen with the 'inner eye', but could not be reproduced, and this absolute idea of a geometrical figure showed the boy that it was not wrong to 'see' things which are not visible to our physical sight.

On leaving school, he began to study at the University of Vienna, but as his parents were too poor to help him he had to support himself by giving lessons. In later years he was grateful for this necessity. As it happened, most of his pupils had to be trained in classics; and Steiner, who was studying natural sciences and mathematics, was forced to go through the whole of a classical education. Through an accidental meeting with an aged expert on Goethe he stepped into the world of literature and philosophy, and these subjects were added to mathematics and the sciences. During his years in Vienna he seldom worked for fewer than fifteen hours a day; and he had trained himself to do with only a few hours' sleep.

THE UNKNOWN CONTINENT

Even after he had taken his degree Steiner went on studying both his old and his more recent subjects, and he was still earning his own living by giving lessons, by writing articles in periodicals, and later on by giving lectures His thorough scientific education and his preoccupation with Goethe enabled him to accept a commission for editing the latter's scientific works, and this subsequently procured him a much-coveted situation at the famous Goethe-Archive in Weimar, where he was put in charge of Goethe's scientific writings.

During these days an incident took place which was to leave a very deep impression on Steiner. This was his meeting with Nietzsche. Frau Foerster-Nietzsche, the philosopher's sister, invited Steiner to reorganize her brother's private library, and Steiner spent many weeks of absorbing work at the Nietzsche-Archive. This spiritual intimacy with Nietzsche culminated in the one and only meeting between the two men.

An understanding—if any—between them could only be achieved on a plane where material incidents play no part. Nietzsche's name was at that time one of the most famous in European letters, and Steiner entered Nietzsche's room in a state of intense excitement. It was in the afternoon and a soft light fell upon the man lying on a sofa. His eyes were wide open and he was staring at the young man at the door. Steiner could see at a glance that the man with the vast forehead and the sad eyes almost covered by his thick eyebrows no longer beheld the world around him. Yet Steiner did not feel that he was confronted with a man who was, soon afterwards, to die insane. The picture of the resting giant who had abandoned the world of physical realities had moved Steiner deeply in more ways than one. Later he described his impression of that meeting in the words: 'His eyes were fixed upon me but they did not find me; their blankness seemed to rob my own eyes of their normal power of sight ' Steiner believed that now, released from the necessity of physical contact with Nietzsche, he could behold and meet him in a purely non-material world.

Already at the age of thirty-six Steiner had formed his conception of the world. He was no abstract philosopher but a realist brought up on science. Spirit was for him not something outside nature, but something within it. Man was the only being that could act, feel and think in full consciousness of what he was doing. But Steiner demanded from man that he should use these faculties to view the world not from an intellectual but from a spiritual centre. This would disclose the hidden powers that direct life. He never tried to approach those powers through unconscious trance or exaltation—the practice of most people possessing supernatural gifts. All visions obtained in occult experience had to be controlled by full consciousness, and Steiner was anxious that the connection between occult and our common experiences should be established in a purely objective way. Thus he was striving towards a knowledge that would be deeper than any knowledge offered by modern science. Hitherto it had only been found scattered here and there in various religions and in ancient and mediaeval secret doctrines.

Steiner's road to the final establishment of his knowledge led through an association with Theosophy when he became Secretary-General of the German section of the Theosophical Society. The theosophical idea of the reincarnation[1] of the 'World Teacher', in the body of the young Indian boy Jiddu Krishnamurti, compelled Steiner in 1913 to adopt an antagonistic attitude that forced the Theosophical Society to expel him. In the eyes of Annie Besant and Charles Leadbeater, as well as in those of most theosophists, Krishnamurti was to become the vehicle for a reincarnated Christ. For Steiner it was sinful to claim authority for anyone solely on the grounds of reincarnation. Besides, he believed that Christ could descend to earth only once and that the expectation of a 'second coming' of this kind was mistaken. He had the greatest contempt for any amateurish or flippant treatment of the belief in *karma* and reincarnation, and he saw such treatment in the Krishnamurti affair.

IV

When Steiner's association with the Theosophical Society ceased, the time came to establish his own doctrine—anthroposophy—as a separate teaching. This creed had for years been held by a distinct section of the German Theosophical Society. The word 'anthroposophy' means 'wisdom under the aspect of man'. The name appeared for the first time in an English book of the sixteenth century by Thomas Maughan, but it seems that Steiner took it from a book by Immanuel Hermann Fichte, the son of Johann Gottlieb Fichte, the philosopher. In a short time the meagre beginnings developed into the vast Anthroposophical Society, with its thousands of members all over the world, and with activities ranging from purely

[1] Reincarnation: Eastern doctrine of the rebirth of the soul in a new body.

occult and religious study to work in scientific laboratories and art studios.

Steiner's own activities were ever increasing. Besides giving lectures and teaching private pupils, he was not only preparing the establishment of the headquarters for the society, but also writing plays and experimenting in various artistic media.

Steiner's leading idea was still that truth can best be proved through physical things. Though he demanded that ordinary experience be always transformed into an act of thought, he was antagonistic to abstract thought. In fact he disliked the word 'thought' and only used the word 'thinking'. He repudiated the usual method of abstract thought in which one becomes so absorbed by the object that one forgets that one is thinking. He wanted the thinker to remain conscious all the time of what he was doing. And he wanted man to think in 'pictures' instead of in abstractions.

Such a process can best be explained by a comparison with Plato's ideas. Plato was the last great representative of an epoch which had the gift of 'seeing' the world in visions. In the words of Edward Schuré, the French writer and mystic, the Greeks had from earliest times 'an intuitive awareness of the direct and intimate communion that exists between the outer life of the world and the inner life of the soul. The Greek genius did not separate the human soul from the cosmos, but conceived them as an organic whole. . . .' The images that were evoked during a vision were not thoughts but spiritual pictures called by a later period 'Platonic ideas'. It was only Plato's pupil Aristotle who began to think of the world, instead of 'seeing' it. While Plato was the great Greek 'seer', Aristotle was the 'thinker' of truth. Plato cared for truth as contained in spiritual ideas, whilst Aristotle was concerned with truth as expressed in the physical world.

No-one expressed that difference between the two philosophers more strikingly and yet more simply than Raphael, who perceived their individuality with the peculiar clarity of genius. In his picture of 'The School of Athens' he painted Aristotle pointing down towards the earth, and Plato pointing up towards the heavens.

Steiner, as we shall see later, tried to combine their wisdom—by assimilating truth as a spiritual reality and by translating it afterwards into physical reality.

Though Steiner had a number of personal pupils, he never tried to impress upon them his individual knowledge, and he gave his

54

personal opinions only when asked for them. Though he never imposed his teaching, he answered every question put to him.

At his lectures he spoke without notes. Generally he focused his attention on those listeners whom he could help in particular, and his whole lecture would be adjusted to those special requirements. During his busy life Steiner had been in touch with almost all classes of people. He had lectured to socialistic workmen and to members of the aristocracy, to the clergy and to scientists; he had been the friend of many leading German and Austrian philosophers and scientists, and he had never lost contact with everyday life. But both his new knowledge and his increasing power had left him free from worldly ambition.

Yet few people had so many enemies as Rudolf Steiner, and this becomes comprehensible when one recalls the revolutionary character of his teaching. He claimed to have a deeper understanding of life, of the sciences and of religion than have other men. Though his knowledge was often either unknown or unintelligible to many representatives of the learned professions, most people who had troubled to study anthroposophy accepted Steiner's views. Those who fought against him had never bothered to study his message, and they simply repeated the distorted versions of it that they read in the newspapers.

Antagonism caused uneasiness to Steiner only in so far as the spreading of his doctrine was hindered thereby. His enemies accused him of spiritual fraud, or of being a Jesuit, or taunted him with being a converted Eastern Jew. His most private life, that of a very unselfish character, was defamed and, though he never spoke of it, he must have suffered deeply from so many malignant slanders.

V

To Steiner himself his unusual gifts were so much a part of his very nature that he no longer considered them in any way extraordinary, and his natural modesty was never affected by them. Once he foretold with uncanny precision an intimate detail in the private life of one of his friends, and when the prediction proved correct his friend exclaimed enthusiastically: 'It is really wonderful that you should see this.' 'Wonderful?' answered Steiner; 'you should not think of it like that, one may or may not see such things.'

One of the most reliable authorities to quote with regard to

Steiner's strange powers is Dr. Friedrich Rittelmeyer, one of the most distinguished pre-war preachers in Berlin and a man of profound scholarship and unquestioned moral integrity. When at a mature age he came into touch with Steiner's teaching, he possessed all the equipment necessary for a study of it. Nevertheless he spent ten years studying anthroposophy before finally accepting it. He confessed later that he was quite ignorant of all occult things and that he approached them with great scepticism.

Rittelmeyer noticed how much Steiner's ease in using his occult gifts had grown in the course of time. 'In earlier years,' says Rittelmeyer, 'it seemed to me that when Steiner was giving advice to people he liked to sit where he would not be obliged to face the light. When he began to use his faculties of spiritual sight one noticed a certain deliberate adjustment of his being, often accompanied by a lowering of the eyes. . . . As the years went on I noticed this less and less, and finally not at all. . . . It was as if both states of consciousness, that of sense perception and of spiritual perception, were for him, freely and naturally, one beside the other.'

In the opinion of experts clairvoyance is a natural gift like a talent for painting or a fine voice, and is therefore quite independent of all other characteristics. One may have the gift of seeing events hundreds of miles away, without being able to understand the most simple objects around one.

Humanity always believed in clairvoyance. One of the most characteristic examples of clairvoyance, or rather of one of its forms known as *mantics*, accepted and venerated as a divine gift, is to be found in the oracle of Delphi. The priestesses or rather pythonesses were women with clairvoyant gifts and, though even in the ancient days there were often cases of deliberate fraud, there were many examples of genuine visions and predictions of a clairvoyant kind. It was not only the masses who believed in the genuineness of the occult visions obtained by a Pythian. Even such thinkers as Pythagoras and Plato acknowledged the institution at Delphi, and considered the 'divine madness' (furor divinus) as the highest and most direct means of obtaining knowledge, and the logical and positive Aristotle admitted that there is a science of 'spiritual vision'.

Occultists believe in the existence of three different kinds of clairvoyance: hereditary, karmic and conscious. Hereditary clairvoyance is a gift inherited from our ancestors; karmic[1] clairvoyance

[1] See footnote, p. 38.

is transmitted from our own previous incarnation. Though they are both gifts handed down to the owner and not created by himself, karmic clairvoyance has been consciously developed in a previous incarnation. The most important form of clairvoyance is that which is trained in our present life and in full consciousness.

Rudolf Steiner claimed, from the very beginning, to possess karmic clairvoyance. Certain incidents in his later life point to the fact that he may also have suspected the remains of an hereditary clairvoyance which we sometimes possess without knowing it. The moment Steiner saw that the occult world was a scientific certainty to him, he strove towards the development of conscious clairvoyance. If he were to penetrate through material things into a spiritual Beyond merely because he possessed gifts he could not account for, he could not claim scientific justification for his results. Even the possibility of such a clairvoyance had to be eliminated.

Nothing destroys such a gift so thoroughly as indulgence in wine or other strong drink. Many stipulations made by religious sects in regard to wine are based partly on that fact. Wine leads man to a lower state of consciousness. Hence the drinking of wine was part of the ancient mysteries of which the aim was to disclose the next stage of human consciousness.

The consciousness of the Greeks was, according to others besides Steiner, of a dream-pictorial character. Life was 'seen' in pictures, of which Plato's 'ideas' are the most perfect expression. In the Christian era man's consciousness descended from the visionary to the intellectual. The Greeks could reach such a consciousness only in the mysteries. This difference of consciousness is best illustrated by the difference between Apollo and Dionysos. In the words of Edward Schuré 'Apollo knows everything, and when he speaks it is in the name of his Father (Zeus). Dionysos knows nothing, but is everything, and his actions speak for him'. In the mysteries the worshippers of Dionysos gave themselves up to the enjoyment of wine and they thus descended to an intellectual and therefore earthly perception of the world. Thus the identification with Dionysos disclosed the coming stage of their evolution.

The first Greek who consciously perceived and acted on this was Aristotle. Without losing himself in the orgy of the mysteries he found the means for an intellectual understanding of the world. He was able to represent the world not in visions and ideas but in thoughts. It was not surprising that the intensely intellectual scholarship of the Middle Ages considered Aristotle one of the greatest men, if not the greatest, of all times.

Steiner believed that Jesus Christ did for the whole of humanity what Moses did for the Jews and Aristotle for the Greeks: He gave it the new earthly, intellectual consciousness. 'The movement of humanity,' says Edward Schuré, 'to the Christian era offers us the double spectacle of recoil and progress. On one side, the gradual loss of vision and of direct communion with the forces of nature . . . on the other, the active development of intelligence and reason, resulting in man's material domination of the world. Vision continues to be cultivated by a chosen few. . . . But vision and the faculty of divination diminish in the human race as a whole. . . .' From now onwards such knowledge as hitherto could only be found in mysteries had become a reality through the existence and the teaching of Christ. Wine could be drunk by everyone Steiner said in one of his books: 'The true life of Jesus was the actual happening, historically, of what before Him had only happened in initiation. All that up till then had been shrouded in the secrecy of the temple, was through Him to be displayed to the world in poignant reality. The life of Jesus is thus a public confirmation of the mysteries.'

In the days before the coming of Christ wine was said to hinder all higher spiritual knowledge. When an orthodox Jew married a Jewess only water was drunk at the ceremony, but otherwise—wine. The occult gifts had to be preserved within the race, but in union with a stranger the key to higher truth had to be destroyed. When at the wedding at Cana Christ changed water into wine He meant to show, according to Steiner, that from now onwards everyone could receive the higher knowledge and enter the kingdom of heaven. No longer was it necessary to drink nothing but water and only to marry members of the same race. One might drink wine and one might marry an alien. In fact, Christ insisted that people should no longer marry representatives of the same blood. All men were brothers to Him. Steiner believed that the period in which men were permitted to drink wine without damaging their higher powers of perception lasted as long as the influence of Christ's earthly life was still felt directly in the world. From then onwards wine again destroyed in man the faculties essential to a clear vision of the spiritual world, as against vague, intuitive impressions.

Steiner indulged for a short time in an excessive consumption of wine, and at the end of this period any possibility of hereditary clairvoyance was destroyed. After that experiment he never touched alcohol again. When in later years he accepted private pupils the main condition he always laid down was that they were never to drink wine.

The most important form of clairvoyance is, as we have seen, the conscious. How can it be achieved?

Even conscious clairvoyance requires a natural disposition. In the arts, such as poetry and painting, strict adherence to rules will not compensate for lack of native talent. And so with occult powers. This applies not only to individuals but also to whole nations. Certain people and certain nations are more gifted in this respect than others. We find the gift particularly common among the members of very pure races, and of families who have frequently intermarried, and thus we find it among royal and very ancient families. The island character of Great Britain has been responsible for intermarriage through the centuries, and its damp climate is very propitious to a natural, inner vegetative power like clairvoyance. In such a climate inner faculties can grow more readily than in a drier climate. The climate enhances not only the gift of the British for second sight, it is also responsible for their faculty for *seeing* life in pictures rather than thinking of it. The Germans *think* of life—this is the reason for their love of theories and abstractions. The British, who 'see' life as a reality, hate theory and premeditation. Not thought but visual memory is their strength, and clairvoyance is seeing and not thinking.

VI

The main exercises for the development of clairvoyance have to be done when we go to sleep, and in the morning when we wake. The moment at which we go to sleep the physical body is left inanimate; the spiritual 'I' can now go into space. This has to be done consciously the moment before sleep actually descends upon us. At this moment man's spiritual forces, which can manifest themselves normally only through the physical body, are freed. Now they can loose themselves into the world outside, into the universe. Now is the moment for the human ego to identify itself with the world outside; to get into it; to learn about it; to see its working, its spiritual instead of its merely material realities. Now has the moment come when we can gather occult knowledge of the world outside ourselves. This process of getting 'outside' the body and entering into space has definite cosmic laws and limitations, and depends entirely upon the stage of our occult development. Self-deception is here particularly frequent, and people often assume that their spirit has reached far more distant spheres than it actually has. These spheres are based on astronomic distances.

According to occult knowledge, the first real attainment of the ego is a penetration into space up to the sphere of the Moon; the next stage is penetration up to Mercury, the next one reaches Venus; the one after that the Sun. As far as to the sphere of the Sun the ego penetrates space in its personal form; it still carries its memories. After the fourth sphere comes the penetration to Mars. Between the Sun and Mars the ego loses its self-ness, from now on it becomes impersonal. This fifth sphere is the one that Buddha called nirvana, and Buddha's teaching is experience gathered in the fifth sphere. It is bliss without personality.

For the occultist who is consciously trying to break down all barriers of spiritual knowledge, clairvoyant penetration does not end in the land of bliss. The ego can go farther than into nirvana. In nirvana it had lost its personality and has become pure spirit. From now on it can become creative and its powers become focused on its future reincarnation. The sixth stage brings it to Jupiter, and here the ego gathers the necessary creative faculties. In the next stage, of Saturn, it prepares its personality for its next earthly incarnation. In the last stage, that of the fixed stars, the ego has definitely formed the new personality. Only one who can penetrate to the stage of the fixed stars can 'see' the 'personality' of his future reincarnation.

The next exercises are done on waking up in the morning. Our ego is then returning into its bodily consciousness, and the moment when the exercise is done is the very last moment before the actual awakening. It is that at which the ego takes final possession of its body. Our ordinary daily consciousness is not awake yet, and our spirit is nearest to our microcosm. Now we are quite close to the many phenomena that work within ourselves. Now is the moment when we can perceive the inside of the shell: our physical organs, their functioning, their interconnections, the reasons for their existence, their powers and their weaknesses. Now we are in a state when we can identify ourselves with our organs and our bodily functions, when we can gather occult knowledge of ourselves. But now again this has to be done with the fullest consciousness and in the infinitesimally short space of time that exists between being asleep and being awake.

Both the morning and the evening exercises develop naturally out of certain meditations done regularly before going to sleep and after waking. Both forms of clairvoyant 'seeing' should be eventually possessed in such a way as to be available at any given moment and not only during the exercises of the morning and the evening.

Occultism is to a great extent a science which teaches us how to do these and similar exercises. It gives us their right order; it tells us of the gradual identification with the phenomena outside and inside ourselves; it teaches us in what order we have to concentrate on the different organs and functions experienced during our 'visions'. A great deal of Egyptian hieroglyphic inscriptions, as well as the *Book of the Dead*, consists of such laws.

Steiner also gave very detailed instructions for the development of clairvoyance through exercises done in normal waking state. These instructions are to be found in his book *Knowledge of the Higher Worlds and its Attainment*, and are intended to lead to the attainment of perceptions purely spiritual. We gain second sight into the mineral, plant and animal kingdoms, and eventually into ourselves and others. There is nothing of mysticism or magic in those exercises, performed as consciously as a scientific experiment. During the exercises we meditate on the specific qualities of the mineral, vegetable and animal. Steiner believed that such meditations permit the development of inner organs with which we can 'see' and 'hear' the spiritual reality of a thing as clearly as we see and hear its physical reality with our physical eyes and ears. He called them 'the organs of clairvoyance'.

VII

If we accept the foregoing statements, we must also accept the fact that a general medical practitioner who possesses conscious occult knowledge knows more than a specialist who possesses none. The following instance will show that Steiner, though not a physician, had a deep medical knowledge in certain cases. The child of one of his friends had suffered since birth from a strange disease: the difference between the lower temperature of the upper part of her body and the higher temperature of the lower part far exceeding the normal difference. Not one of the German, Swiss and Austrian doctors who had been consulted was able to diagnose the disease or to prescribe a remedy, and eventually Steiner himself was asked to see the child.

'The family of one of the parents', he said, 'has consisted for many generations of tall fathers and short mothers This has resulted in a "symmetrophobia of the formative powers of bodily heat". This state will continue till the child is seven, and one can only counterbalance the natural symmetrophobia by giving the child barium.' Steiner explained that at the age of seven a child loses the 'model body' given by its parents and begins to build its own body; it casts off certain inherited physical features; it loses the first 'given' set of teeth and forms the first set of its 'own' teeth.

As the mother of the child was of noble origin her genealogy was not unknown, and it was ascertained that there had indeed been a long line of tall fathers and short mothers in her family. The illness disappeared entirely after the child had reached its seventh year.

Very often clairvoyance of one particular kind is developed, as we have seen in the case of Baron V.'s second sight. Though they were diametrically opposed, both Egyptian and Northern clair-voyance were onesided. It was only very much later that an all-round clairvoyance, comprising the perceptions won both in the macrocosm and in the microcosm, could be achieved. Steiner based himself to a certain extent on the first known system which included both kinds. This was expounded in the book *The Chemical Marriage*, by Valentin Andreae, published in 1604. The mysterious hero of this book is one 'Christian Rosenkreuz', an exponent of the mysticism of the Fraternity known as Rosicrucians.

Other sides of clairvoyance are developed with the help of those who bring one particular form to perfection. Steiner spoke several times to his most intimate friends about the occult connections between a disciple and the masters, and Dr. Rittelmeyer records one of them: 'What impressed me most,' he says, 'was the way Steiner spoke of the great teachers who had crossed his path. Men of extraordinary spirituality, entirely unknown in public life, were there at the right moment, helping him in decisive years to under-stand and develop critical faculties. After long preparation the neces-sary helpers are sent at the right moment. . . . The outer world has not the slightest inkling of it. . . . It was wonderful to hear in such detail of the actual existence of such spiritual leaders who ruled concealed behind the veil of human history. . . . Those who recall the intervention of one called "The Unknown" by Jakob Boehme[1] can gain some idea of the things of which Steiner spoke. . . .' When Dr. Rittelmeyer asked him whether the masters that Steiner had come in contact with were still living, he only replied: 'There is no need'.

Steiner was always very careful that his clairvoyance should not interfere with his knowledge of the world gained by ordinary means. When Rittelmeyer asked him in 1916 whether one could know how the war was going to end, Steiner answered: 'Certainly it would be possible, but then one would have to retire from all participation in events. It would not do to investigate these things by occult means and then to allow the knowledge so gained to colour one's own actions'. Steiner treated all occult matters with the greatest reverence, and he hated to speak about them to any but the few people whom he knew he could trust.

Steiner naturally believed in ancient knowledge which had been hidden either in esoteric schools or in ancient mysteries. In several of his books and several of his lectures he referred to such a knowledge, and for a number of years there existed an esoteric group within the Anthroposophical Society. Steiner lectured to the members of the group about subjects which were too advanced for the uninitiated. Outsiders used to invent stories about mystical rites and ceremonies within the esoteric group, but this was pure invention. Steiner often insisted that knowledge of that kind should not be imparted to the public at large, since it might be treated without the necessary respect.

On the other hand he believed that the moment had come when such a knowledge should no longer be confined to a few initiates, and that humanity was able to approach hidden knowledge through conscious thought. There were, however, powerful bodies in strong opposition to his attitude. There have always been two main currents in occult schools: the one anxiously guarding all esoteric knowledge for a few privileged people; the other considering that that knowledge should become the property of a wider circle. Steiner belonged to the second group. To the former belong most of the Churches.

Steiner was never vague as to his own occult duties and powers. He saw his mission very clearly as one based on conscious occult perceptions. 'In my life mission', he said once, 'I must confine myself to the occult—otherwise I shall not succeed'.

[1] Jakob Boehme (1575–1624), great mystic and philosopher.

VIII

It was quite natural for the Churches to condemn a teaching that tried through conscious understanding to gain possession of their specialized and privileged knowledge. The Churches will part with that knowledge only if it is shrouded in their own symbolism and their own dogmas. That knowledge must be based on authority and not on the deliberation of the individual. The Churches consider such knowledge too dangerous to be divulged in the manner in which Steiner seemed to divulge it; but it would be wrong to imagine Steiner, by birth a Roman Catholic, as anti-christian. He was deeply religious, and his occult experiences had widened his religious understanding.

Experienced theologians were struck by the profoundity of Steiner's conception of Christ, and Rittelmeyer gives us an account of a lecture on Christ given by Steiner to a group of theologians. 'I realized then', Rittelmeyer narrates, 'how a man in the very presence of Christ speaks of Christ. There was something more than devotional reverence in his words. In freedom and reverence a man was looking up to Christ whose presence was quite near. . . . The many hundreds of sermons I had heard about Christ came up in the background of my mind. They faded into shadows . . .' Rittelmeyer himself was considered one of the greatest German preachers of the day. In later years the Gospels were to become one of the most important foundations of Steiner's teaching, and this even resulted in the establishment of a new Church.

In Steiner's opinion the life of Christ was the main event in the history of the world, and everything before Christ nothing but a spiritual preparation for the crowning event in His life. He saw the highest form of such a spiritual preparation in pre-Christian mysteries such as those of Ephesus and Eleusis, which imparted their esoteric teaching to those who had been admitted to them by virtue of their occult gifts. The pupil who had undergone the necessary training was in spirit completely transformed by the mysteries. From then onwards he was an initiate.

It would lead us too far even to summarize the whole of Steiner's Christology, but some of its main points may perhaps be usefully given here.

The death on the cross distinguishes, for Steiner, the Christian from all other religions. Christ not only taught but also died for

what He taught. Thus Christianity begins with a deed, while other
religions begin with a doctrine. In Steiner's opinion Christ's death
became a source of the most vital changes in human history and in
every individual, no matter of what race or religion. It changed not
only man but even the very earth on which man lives.

Steiner is not alone in considering that a great part of the Gospels
is full of esoteric knowledge and that they can be understood fully
only if this truth is acknowledged. The crucial point of Golgotha
lay for Steiner in the fact that Christ made His sacrifice with full
consciousness of what He did Thus the words of St. John become
for him of the greatest significance: 'Therefore doth my Father love
me, because I lay down my life, that I might take it again. No man
taketh it from me, but I lay it down of myself.' According to Steiner,
this self-imposed sacrifice gives every one of us the power to enter
into the mystery of the life and the death of Christ. Golgotha contains for Steiner the concentrated wisdom of the whole universe.
By penetrating into it man can attain to the understanding of both
the macrocosm around him, and its reproduction within himself,
the microcosm.

IX

Both ordinary and occult knowledge were for Steiner necessities,
designed to enrich each other, but also to be used only in their
proper places. When Dr. Rittelmeyer asked him one day: 'Why was
it that in spite of all you must have known, even in your early years,
you were so completely silent about occult matters until your
fortieth year?', Steiner replied: 'I had to make a certain position
for myself in the world first. People may say nowadays that my
writings are mad, but my earlier work is also there, and they cannot
wholly ignore it. And moreover, I had to bring things to a certain
clarity in myself, to a point where I could give them form, before it
was possible to talk about them. That was not so easy. And then—
I admit it frankly—it needed courage to speak openly about such
things. I had first to acquire that courage '

In later years, just before his death, Steiner explained why he
waited so long before he felt entitled to make occult pronouncements. Before he was thirty-six he had been thinking about physical
things in the ordinary scientific way, later on he began to 'see'
things around him in their whole physical reality; and they now
evoked in him the same spiritual pictures that revealed themselves

E   65

in his occult visions. This process could be compared to the in-
spirations of a man like Wordsworth, of which Dean Inge said:
'Wordsworth's inspiration was . . . something which came direct
to him; a revelation of the unseen through natural objects, whereby
he was granted the power to see into the life of things.' The 'life
of things' was the very goal of Steiner's labours.

Not even thoughts and feelings were to be experienced through
the faculties of physical perception only, such as, for example, the
intellect. Steiner was aiming at the development of 'spiritual eyes'
with a view to observing the world as what Dean Inge calls 'something higher and deeper than itself'. Anthroposophy is primarily a
descriptive science, and its relation with the spiritual world is the
same as the relation of natural sciences with the physical world.

Dr. Rittelmeyer was anxious to test the scientific knowledge which
Steiner had acquired by means of his occult experiences. Not being
himself a scientist he employed others for the making of this test.
These specialists were to put questions on their particular branch of
science. Dozens of scientists were dispatched to 'examine' Steiner
but had to admit that his knowledge of their particular science was
greater than their own.

It was therefore not surprising that Steiner's headquarters became
an all-round scientific institute. Steiner began to build it during the
war, but as the German authorities would not allow him to build in
Munich, he accepted a site on a hill in Dornach, near Basle, offered
him by admirers. It was called in Goethe's honour the 'Goetheanum'.
The work of constructing it was a solitary instance of truly international collaboration at a time when most European nations were
at war. Steiner's pupils from seventeen different countries assembled
at Dornach to help in the building of the Goetheanum, and many of
them had to overcome great difficulties before they could reach
Dornach.

The Goetheanum was designed by Steiner himself. It was built
of wood like a musical instrument, and, since it was intended for
lectures, music and recitations, its acoustic properties were carefully
considered. Steiner used for its construction the same seven different
kinds of wood which are used for the construction of a violin, and
the ceiling of the main hall was as buoyant as the walls of a violin.
The building was conceived mainly as a piece of inner architecture,
and contained, besides the lecture hall and theatre, studios and the
usual offices. Scientists, taught by Steiner after they had gone through

their professional studies in the ordinary universities, lectured every day. The aim of the teaching was to give anthroposophical aspects of such subjects as biology, medicine, astronomy, stagecraft, agriculture, religion and eurhythmy (*see* p. 242). The theatrical and choreographic activities were directed mainly by Frau Steiner, who had been her husband's close collaborator for many years. Steiner himself was a lover of the theatre, and wrote a number of plays for performances at the Goetheanum, while Frau Steiner directed the classes of eurhythmy—rhythmical movements, designed to become 'visible speech'.

Once you began to study anthroposophy you realized the great difference between it and other spiritual systems. Its lack of emotionalism and its scientific character enabled it to be studied from books and lectures. While Keyserling's philosophy, though clearly of an ethical kind, was, at its best, without a clear system, Steiner created a scientific system that like any other could be studied and applied. Stefan George, most decidedly a poet, appealed foremost to the emotional faculties that are stored up in our subconscious; and these cannot easily be applied through a conscious and systematic study. Steiner tried to give to anthroposophy the exactness of mathematics.

X

It was with some excitement that I went to hear Steiner himself for the first time. The hall was packed and filled with an atmosphere of expectation. I have seen more devoted, more sentimental or hysterical audiences but I cannot recollect having ever seen a more expectant one.

Steiner began his lecture without preliminaries or introductions: he was 'in medias res' a minute after the lecture had begun. It took me much longer to overcome my unexpected inner reaction to his appearance. To be quite candid, I was slightly terrified. There was something frightening in the deepset eyes, in the ascetic face, bleak as a landscape in the moon, in the strands of jet-black hair falling over the pale forehead. I do not remember ever having seen a man in whose presence I had such an eerie feeling.

When I got used to the singularity of Steiner's appearance I could discern how human and simple he was. The impassioned way in which he spoke, the expressiveness of the Austrian intonation in his voice, the theatrical effect of his black bow tie, contrasted oddly

67

with the simplicity of his whole manner. My first impressions were lost entirely after a few more lectures. I understood only later why his face had impressed me in such an uncommon way: it was as though the face were not big enough to hold the whole intensity of its spiritual expression. When I showed a photograph of Steiner to a friend, she exclaimed. 'That man must have suffered terribly.' Indeed, his face bore the marks of untold experiences and sufferings.

XI

At the time when I was attending the lectures Steiner's main activities were still centred upon a subject that had become of paramount importance in his life, the 'Threefold Commonwealth of the Social Structure'. It was the result of his attempts to find a solution to political and economic difficulties brought to a head by the war. The war had been an event of the greatest personal concern to him.

Though he hoped for an Austro-German victory, he had a very shrewd notion of the true situation. He never subscribed to the common belief in the supremacy of Germany as expressed in terms of armies, guns and battleships Steiner had declared his mistrust of the generals long before others began to understand that it was futile to expect very much from them. At a time when the whole German nation was looking upon men like Ludendorff as their saviours, and when the slightest criticism was considered almost high treason, the following conversation took place between Steiner and Dr. Rittelmeyer. It was in the middle of the war and the whole of Germany was rejoicing over the recent appointment of Hindenburg and Ludendorff. Rittelmeyer was as enthusiastic as the rest of Germany, and he said: 'It is really a piece of good luck that we now have Hindenburg and Ludendorff', to which Steiner answered: 'Well, Hindenburg is an old man . . . the main work is being done by the Chief of the General Staff.' And when Rittelmeyer, expressing only the current opinion of the German nation, said: 'So the bright spot for Germany is now Ludendorff?', Steiner replied with the greatest earnestness: 'It is not in the interest of Germany to have such generals.'

Steiner believed in a German mission in the world. But he did not share the view of most Germans that Germany's mission could be fulfilled by her armies, and that her final goal was the Kaiser's 'place in the sun'. His esteem for Germany was not confined to the

Hohenzollern Reich. It embraced all that he believed best in the Germanic spirit, no matter whether it came from achievements with which Steiner himself was not in sympathy, such as Kant's philosophy, conceived on the shores of the Baltic; or from things he loved, such as the musical art of Vienna and Salzburg; or even from the work of the poets and thinkers in the Czech capital of Prague. Germany was for him not so much a political and geographical as an ideological reality. Hence the German mission could only be of a spiritual kind. Steiner had no doubt that the German spirit was more valuable when expressing itself through music, philosophy and science than through the deeds of William II, Ludendorff and Tirpitz.

Steiner was anxious that some sound expression of the necessities of Central Europe should be brought forward as a convincing answer to the suggestions of President Wilson. In the middle of the war he said: 'A word of the spirit must now go forth from Middle Europe. If this does not happen we shall succumb to the Wilson programme. Middle Europe cannot exist under Wilson's Fourteen Points. But they must be answered from within a spiritual understanding of Middle Europe.' Later on he expressed a similar opinion when saying: 'Wilson will bring great misfortune to Middle Europe and achieve nothing he wishes to achieve. . . .' Steiner hoped that a 'spiritual' programme for the solution of Middle-European problems would impress the Allied statesmen, who would then 'realize the existence in Germany of a spiritual power not lightly to be brushed aside'.

Accordingly he prepared a programme that by its greater vision was to be stronger than Wilson's Fourteen Points based merely on political premises. His ideas were expressed in a manifesto, and in a programme of the 'Threefold Commonwealth'. The Manifesto appeared in 1919. Its main points, reproduced by most continental newspapers, were based on Steiner's ideas of the 'Threefold Commonwealth'.

Man was for Steiner a 'threefold' being, composed of will-power, emotions and mind. The life of a nation was for him likewise a Threefold Commonwealth, created by economical, political, and intellectual and artistic activities.

Economics include the production, distribution and consumption of commodities and the welfare of the people. Politics are the expression of the native psychology of a people, and in Steiner's programme included military as well as political matters. The intellectual life included the sciences, education, letters and social services. Economics must be capable of adapting themselves from day to day to the existing conditions; they must be run by experts and must not be hindered by political necessities. Political life and administration are by the very nature of a given national psychology conservative, and Steiner therefore wanted to allow them to preserve their nature. This could only be achieved if they were run by men with the greatest experience of life, by the 'elders' of the nation. While economics are opportunistic and politics conservative, the intellectual current tends towards individualism. It should be directed by the greatest men, the most outstanding personalities.

These three primary characteristics of the life of a nation should be considered by the State as of fundamental importance. Hence the three great currents of national life must be kept independent of one another. Each one should be represented by its own legislative assembly, and thus the various activities of the nation would be directed by experts only. The leaders of the three assemblies would meet in a sort of Senate where common problems would be considered and decided upon.

At the time I was attending Steiner's lectures the first session of the new Republican Parliament was being held at Weimar Even in the first months of its existence all the drawbacks of immature democratic methods as applied by a people without political education or tradition could be perceived. Indeed, the moment was not very distant when members of thirty or more distinct political parties were squabbling in the Reichstag.

Steiner's ideas seemed extremely radical, and contradicted most of the existing political systems. And yet German public life could be saved from dissolution only if the three main currents of life were divorced from party politics and from the amateurishness of the new democratic politics. Steiner hoped that such a rationalization of German life would destroy all previously prevailing causes of an unreasonable nationalism. He also hoped that by a deeper understanding of the real necessities, even the national ambitions of the various peoples within the Habsburg Monarchy could be outweighed. A more logically founded state of affairs would make their aims as unnecessary as Wilson's Fourteen Points.

Steiner's political ideas did not seem to take sufficiently into consideration the individuality and the stifled ambitions of the nations concerned with them. Moreover they were published at inopportune moments during the war and in the years immediately after it and before the peoples concerned had had a chance of studying and digesting them.

In economic life Steiner advocated the same fundamental rationalization that he demanded for the political life of a country. This rationalization was introduced later, though in distorted or purely industrial forms, by various governments and by business undertakings all over the world.

I was more impressed by Steiner's personality than by his political ideas. But though I was conscious of the advantage of association with him, I was honest enough, or it may be that I was merely inexperienced enough, to assume that at this stage I could gather all I needed from Steiner's written works, and that any effort to be nearer him would only be an unfair trespass upon his time.

XII

The attacks on Rudolf Steiner did not cease till his death. On New Year's Eve, 1922, the new Goetheanum was burnt down. There was no doubt that this was an act of incendiarism inspired, or even committed, by Steiner's enemies. It was only one of the many blatant results of the poisonous propaganda directed against him and of the methods employed by the Germans in ideological warfare. As every detail of the Goetheanum had been conceived by Steiner himself, as most of it had been built by his pupils as an original 'work by hand', and as the whole structure consisted merely of carvings in wood, the loss was quite irreparable.

Steiner and his pupils fought the flames all through the night; but when the morning of the New Year broke on the hills of the Jura, little was left of his magnificent 'instrument'. The blow must have been very heavy. One of his closest pupils found him weeping in one of the rooms that had escaped destruction. Nobody had ever seen tears in Steiner's eyes before.

'Herr Doktor,' he said, 'I have never seen you weep before. You have withstood much heavier blows.'

'I am not crying because the work of ten years', Steiner answered, 'the result of the greatest sacrifices, has been destroyed. I am weeping because the Western world will not see a monument which more than anything else would have converted it to my way of thinking.'

71

THE UNKNOWN CONTINENT

Steiner believed that the Western world, which he regarded as less intellectual than the Central European or the Eastern, accepts a new teaching only if it can see it in action. The West must see things to believe in them The Goetheanum was for the West the most visible and most striking crystallization of Steiner's teaching. 'Central Europe', he went on, 'did not require the visible form of the Goetheanum. It can perceive new things through thought alone. The Goetheanum might have convinced the Western world.'

But he did not allow sentiment to affect his own activities or those of the people who had come to learn from him. Each year during Christmas the pupils produced a mystery play written for the occasion by Steiner, who insisted that the play should be acted even though the walls were still smouldering and most of the properties were burnt.

A saddened audience assembled to listen to the message of Christmas. The first character to enter what once had been the stage was the Angel of the Annunciation. As he advanced and found himself face to face with Steiner and his friends and pupils, exhausted and pale, sitting among the debris of the former Goetheanum, he broke down. This was the signal for a general reaction. The courage kept up all through the night was gone at last, and many in the audience burst into tears. But Steiner would not allow momentary weakness to interfere with what he considered of deeper importance, and he therefore persuaded the actors to go on with the play and the audience to listen until the end, in forgetfulness of the ruins round about them.

The next day Steiner went on with the work as usual, and drew up plans for a new Goetheanum. As he disliked theoretical work of any kind, he modelled the plans for the new building.

The new Goetheanum was to be much bigger than the first, and it was to include laboratories, special lecture-rooms, studios and workshops. But its animating purpose was to be quite different. Steiner explained to one of his nearest friends: 'The first Goetheanum was a work of love, made with money of love and sacrifice. It had to be a living structure. That's why I built it as a musical instrument in which the human voice can live. The new Goetheanum will be built from the money that the Insurance Companies will pay. They will hate to pay us. It will no longer be money given with love, and I must use it accordingly. The new Goetheanum will be built not of wood but of dead material—of concrete'. It seemed significant that Steiner only finished the model of the exterior before he died.

Though endless worry, strain and labour told on Steiner's health, he continued his work with undiminished fervour His work grew instead of decreasing. It was as if Steiner were anxious to leave behind all the spiritual knowledge that he had discovered. He considered his knowledge indispensable for the improvement of a world sinking fast into the mire of international disunity, national autarchy and various forms of modern materialism.

Several of Steiner's pupils wondered why he did not employ some of his supernatural powers in curing himself. Had he not cured many other people by finding the precise diagnosis and by prescribing the only helpful method of healing? But Steiner was not to become unfaithful to lifelong principles now that the physical end was near. He had considered that his occult powers could only be used for spreading knowledge and helping others and that he had no right to use them for his own good.

In fact Steiner was also hoping that the people round him would spare him more. Though he believed that his ordinary medical knowledge would be sufficient to fight the illness, this could only be done if he were spared the exhaustion of too much work. He considered that he could go on giving lectures without aggravating his condition, but, unfortunately, his faith in people—perhaps the only fundamental mistake of Steiner's whole life—proved once again wrong. He had always valued people too highly, and once again he was to be defeated by them.

Neither the visitors who used to come to the Goetheanum from all over the world nor the many pupils realized the gravity of Steiner's condition. Once or twice he asked them to be more considerate. Notices were even posted requesting people to apply for personal interviews only in cases of the greatest urgency. It helped but little. There was a constant stream of people who came to ask Steiner purely personal questions. And yet the days when he was quite unable to take any food were becoming more and more frequent. The interviews came on top of his lectures and his private work, and finally his physical resistance broke down altogether.

Though Steiner had now almost lost the power of taking nourishment, he was determined to carry on with one last piece of work on which he had been engaged for a number of years. It was the carving of an immense statue, representing Christ reforming the powers of

73

the world after His victory over the Spirit of Darkness. It consisted of several figures, and Steiner, though untrained as a sculptor, had carved most of the large group unaided. Now, reduced to a skeleton, he was spending hour after hour on the scaffolding erected round the monument. When he was too weak to stand on the scaffolding he had to abandon the statue, and his bed was brought into the shed where he worked and placed under it. Though no longer able to sit up, he went on working. All he could do was to model the plans for the new Goetheanum. The model was resting on his blanket till almost the very last moment. He died at the feet of his Christ on 30 March 1925, and the burial service was read by Dr. Rittelmeyer in the hall in which Steiner had given his most important lectures.

In England the *Contemporary Review* published an article by Sir Kenneth Mackenzie in which the writer said: "The work Dr. Steiner has done is so immense that it is really very hard to grasp its extent; nobody could keep up with him. He was at least a hundred years ahead of his time . . . hence the isolation in which he lived. . . . That he was widely loved, as well as deeply respected, is shown by the fact that thousands came from all over the Continent and even from England, pouring into Dornach for the funeral service, and completely overcrowding the town and neighbourhood. . . ."

XIII

Steiner is the 'scientist' of truth among the modern seers, who try to find it through religion, philosophy, mystical revelation or artistic inspiration. He is not satisfied with one aspect of truth, but approaches it through a hundred different channels.

After Steiner other exploits may seem something of an anticlimax. Should not Steiner have been 'saved up' for the end of this book, one might ask. But Steiner's place in this account must necessarily correspond to his place in the author's life. Besides, Steiner's road towards God was of a distinctly scientific and occult character. 'And', to quote Dean Inge, 'since the diverse faculties, which in their several ways bear witness to God, are developed in very different proportions by different individuals, we should expect to find that there are many paths up God's holy hill, though all meet at the top.'

PART TWO

THE ENGLISH ADVENTURE

'In my Father's house are many mansions.'
ST. JOHN XIV. 2.

INTRODUCTION

THE ENGLISH SCENE

I

'. . . those years immediately after the war—the era in England of physical exhaustion and psycho-analysis. We only allowed two virtues then, courage and "intellectual honesty", which meant that it doesn't matter what you do as long as you know you are doing it. . . . War profiteers were subscribing to war memorials and exhibiting righteous indignation at the miners having pianos in their cottages. The Church was pointing out that it had said all along God was on our side; . . . and the proletariat was in a sort of convalescent daze.' This is how a member of that generation which was too young to fight in the war, yet old enough to be aware of its consequences, described conditions in England after 1919.[1]

A foreigner coming to England would have hardly seen the situation in the same light. He would have seen only the soundness, the order and the calm of life in England, as contrasted with the theatrical and restless atmosphere of the Continent. What he would have noticed as most striking would have been the great gulf between most people's intellectual and their emotional responses: the intellectual reactions were hesitant and not always convincing, the emotional definite and strong. He would have expected most of the newer spiritual movements in England to have been founded upon an emotional basis.

Though generalizations are dangerous, it is true to say that among one group of British people alone—the 'dissatisfied'—were spiritual movements of an unconventional nature to be found. Those people who could find no fault with the leading tendencies of the time,

[1] *New Country*, "Letter to a Young Revolutionary", by C. Day Lewis (Hogarth Press)

and who were 'unshaken in the faith they held', constituted the majority.

'It is interesting to see', says Mr. C. Day Lewis, 'how our generation, sick to death of Protestant democratic liberalism and the intolerable burden of the individual conscience, are turning to the old and the new champions of order and authority, the Roman Catholic Church or Communism '

II

What distinguished the young Communist enthusiasts in England from their continental brethren was that while for the latter Communism was mainly a political creed, for many of the English Communists it was an ethical problem, and indeed a definite faith. Communism played the same part in their lives that the movements of Stefan George and Rudolf Steiner played in the lives of young Germans. We used to find those Communist enthusiasts often in some of the English universities, but it is necessary to distinguish the sincere adherents of Communism from those who have been attracted to it in the way that they might previously have been attracted to the study of Negro art, the Russian ballet or psycho-analysis. Some of its more earnest adherents were undergraduates at Oxford and Cambridge with an impressive academic record. The effects of 'conversion' were so violent in some that they at once began to neglect their studies at the University—for which, together with the rest of their former activities, they felt the utmost contempt—and devoted themselves to an orgy of 'party work'. Others, less resolute, still retained some individualistic traits and, while organizing processions and drawing up questionnaires, continued to sip sherry in each other's rooms, though with a conscience uneasy at such a betrayal of party principles.

Those young men who identified themselves completely with Communism and the more radical forms of Socialism were exponents of the constructive side of the dissatisfied English minority. The preceding generation had had no faith to look for, and could only satisfy their need by a restless search for fresh experience. The more frivolous, who had spent their time in an endless round of amusements, have been immortalized in the works of such writers as Noel Coward and Evelyn Waugh. The more serious, though cynical and disillusioned, were aware of their plight, which was identical with that revealed in the earlier poetry of T. S. Eliot. In Communism the

76

succeeding generation had found a faith, and in finding it they had broken through the prevailing indifference.

The more immediate cause of the movement was moral indignation at the iniquities that were being perpetrated under the Capitalist system, and the belief that such a system had exhibited its effeteness in the financial world crisis. Under Capitalism, they argued, war was inevitable. They substantiated their arguments with references to the ruthless methods of certain big business ramps, and the vulgar behaviour of the 'idle rich', who, in spite of their comparatively small numbers, loomed so large on the horizon of those young intellectuals as to epitomize for them the ultimate product of the Capitalist system They flaunted the works of Karl Marx in the faces of the 'bourgeois' disbelievers, though one may doubt whether they had penetrated very far into *Das Kapital*.

Had this generation of politically-minded and dissatisfied youths gone through all the experiences of German youth—weighed down with the despair of a defeated people, unemployed, without money, without prospects of improvement, and yet eaten up by a thirst for power—then it might have evolved some spiritual creed more genuinely British and deeper than alien Communism.

III

There were many attempts of a spiritual nature in England after the war, but such self-expression as the youth of Germany found in Nazism was unknown.

Though not many British people may find complete spiritual satisfaction in their established Churches these have become so much a part of British tradition and synonymous with order and security that a denial of them would amount almost to a denial of the whole structure of British life. Nevertheless some of the spiritual movements outside the Churches evoke the widest interest.

Britons hate organization and uniformity; to go through all the external formalities of joining a new movement invariably alienates them. But such superficial indications are deceptive. That a Briton does not 'discuss his religion' does not necessarily mean that he takes no interest in spiritual subjects. When the B.B.C. arranged a series of talks on 'Inquiry into the Unknown', they received thousands of letters—more, in fact, than they had ever before received.

THE ENGLISH ADVENTURE

With one exception, the nature of all the movements I had been in touch with in England was entirely in keeping with what appeared to me characteristic of the British attitude towards spiritual investigations. Neither the sentimental and slightly snobbish amateurishness of the British Israelites nor the devotional simplicity of the Four-square Gospellers; neither Theosophy in its later guise as created by Krishnamurti, nor the happy-go-lucky religiosity of Dr. Buchman was surprising.

British excursions into the world of the spirit had their roots either in emotionalism or in the traditional reverence for 'scientific truth'. The results of the former are Theosophy, Revivalism and Buchmanism—of the latter, the Society for Psychical Research. While in Germany the most outstanding names in post-war attempts to find new truths—Steiner, George, Keyserling—had a distinctly intellectual flavour, in England the names of Dr. Buchman, Annie Besant, Krishnamurti testified to the emotional nature of the movements. The importance of the Society for Psychical Research and the high regard in which it is held, point to the possible direction of future spiritual discoveries in England. The spiritual conception of life as opposed to an intellectual one will probably be generally accepted by British people through some particularly subtle form of scientific method or even instrument.

IV

It is perhaps surprising to find unconventional manifestations of a mystical longing such as we find them in the British Israel movement in the 'satisfied' upper classes. This began in 1879, and has spread since then over most of the English-speaking countries. It circulates its own magazines and papers, it counts among its members eminent people and, though it has never had spiritual aims of any consequence, its beliefs show that even many of the most 'satisfied' English people suffer from a spiritual thirst that legitimate religion seems unable to quench. It may suffice to mention briefly the few main beliefs of the movement. The Royal House of Great Britain is sprung from David; the perpetuation of the dynasty of David through the female line is the direct fulfilment of prophecy; English-speaking people are descended from the House of Israel, and are in possession of special blessings promised in the Bible, and have a special mission to fulfil in the world. The British Israelite adherents believe in the prophecies supposed to be contained in the Egyptian

78

pyramids, and they have demonstrated that the interval between the birth of King David and that of David, the present Prince of Wales, is 'exactly a hundred generations, each of thirty years'.[1] This yearning for a religious and historical truth that would transcend the present religious and historical limits, went so far as to establish to their own satisfaction a direct link between the British Royal House and Jesus Christ Himself. We read that 'Anna, the cousin of the Virgin Mary, assigned as the ancestress of the Tudor princes, was the daughter of Joseph of Arimathea, reputed to be the founder of a British Dynasty'.

V

Of the distinctively post-war movements, those of Krishnamurti, Dr. Buchman and Principal Jeffreys are the largest. Buchmanism, which requires the minimum of intellectual effort, has become the creed of a section of the wealthier middle classes. Krishnamurti has appealed to those with independent minds who have no longer been able to find any satisfaction in the dogmatized forms of post-war Theosophy. His followers belong to many nations and to all classes. The revivalist George Jeffreys, though scoffed at by the intellectuals and the Churches, has brought spiritual happiness to thousands. The mysterious Gurdjieff and the Parsee Shri Meher Baba have both had many followers in England. Among all these movements the success of a system as intellectual as Ouspensky's was alone surprising.

Though hardly any of these movements are distinctively English they are treated together as one 'English Adventure', for they have all originated or acquired their importance in this country.

[1] All this of course was written several years before the accession to the throne and the abdication of Edward VIII.

CHAPTER I

THE THRONE THAT WAS CHRIST'S

Krishnamurti

I

One Sunday morning I sat in a small panelled room in one of those fine Queen Anne houses that are still to be found in certain parts of Westminster. The street outside the window was deserted. It was raining hard, and the lowering sky robbed the room of the few bright colours that some roses in a vase and an old chair covered with tapestry had introduced into it. The house belonged to the Dowager Lady De La Warr, and I was waiting to meet Mr. Jiddu Krishnamurti, who was staying there on a short visit.

This was to be my first meeting with Krishnamurti. The young Indian was supposed to be rather shy, and, in view of all the sensational reports about him in the newspapers, I did not find this in the least surprising. I had determined to come to this meeting with an open mind, but I must confess I found it hard to feel anything but the profoundest scepticism. I recalled several of the strange tales that I had read in the course of the last few days. One of them remained in my memory with particular vividness, though it described an event that had taken place almost twenty years earlier. It was an account of a convention at Benares, and its author was at the time private secretary to Krishnamurti, then aged fifteen. He had written: 'The line of members began to pass up the central passage . . . with a bow to the Head [Krishnamurti]. . . . The whole atmosphere . . . was thrown into powerful vibration. . . . All saw the young figure draw itself up and take on an air of dignified majesty. . . . The approaching member involuntarily dropped on his knees, bowing his head to the ground. . . . A great coronet of brilliant shimmering blue appeared a foot or two above the young head and from this descended funnel-wise bright streams of blue light. . . . The Lord Maitreya was there embodying Himself in His Chosen. Within the coronet blazed the crimson of the symbol of the Master Jesus, the rosy cross . . .' I am afraid I did not read on much farther after the 'rosy cross'; but I

80

was told that the writer of these impressive lines was not the only one who claimed to have seen this colourful performance.

There seemed some justification for an attitude of scepticism, and as I sat waiting I experienced a feeling of superciliousness which we are all occasionally apt to indulge in when we know a particularly weak spot in the life of the person we are going to meet. In me this feeling had been strengthened by the fact that I had read in a newspaper only the night before that Krishnamurti's followers in Holland had finally proclaimed him the 'World Teacher'. He himself had uttered these words: 'Krishnamurti has entered into that life, which is represented by some as the Christ, by others as Buddha, by others still as the Lord Maitreya. . . .' These words had put the conscience of Krishnamurti's followers at ease and had induced them to proclaim him once and for all 'The Vehicle of the Lord'. For ordinary people this was, to say the least, alarming news.

I was thinking of all these strange things while I was looking on the empty street half hidden by the heavy drizzle I had plenty of information about Krishnamurti's life to counterbalance my scepticism I knew that some of the people who stood behind him were serious-minded and intelligent.

I had come across the name Krishnamurti directly only a few weeks previously at the house of Lady De La Warr at Wimbledon, where I had met some of his most intimate friends—experienced elderly men and women who were not at all the sort of people to be bluffed. The centre of the group was Mrs. Annie Besant, then almost eighty years old and a most attractive person, very bright and untheosophical, full of political and intellectual interests, which she expressed in a most lively and amusing manner. Next to her was Mr. George Lansbury, the veteran labour leader. He too was preoccupied with Indian and other political problems. There was very little to suggest a religious fanaticism in his slow, deep-voiced pronouncements. Anything more solid, more natural, could hardly be imagined Even our hostess mentioned the subject of theosophy only casually. Then there was a member of Parliament who, I believe, was an Under Secretary of State; he was evidently a great authority on India. There was nothing exalted or mystical about the other people in the room. These were Krishnamurti's closest friends in England. It was difficult to imagine these people talking of the 'great coronet of brilliant blue' and 'the rosy cross of the Lord Jesus'. Annie Besant herself was obviously a very shrewd woman. Though at the time I knew little about her or her work, I could see that there was not much in life that had escaped her.

II

And then Krishnamurti entered the room. He walked towards me with an inviting smile, and we shook hands. I was immediately struck by his remarkably handsome face, and after a few minutes' conversation I was equally charmed by his attractive personality. These two impressions were very strong, and I suppose they determined in some ways my future attitude towards him. I heard later from other people that their first impressions of Krishnamurti were the same as mine.

My former superciliousness gave way to a feeling of pleasure. At first I thought that this feeling was due to the aesthetic delight caused by his appearance.

Indeed, he was much more handsome than his photographs made him appear. He seemed no older than twenty-two or twenty-three, and he had the slender grace of a shy young animal. His eyes were large and deep and his features finely cut. His head was crowned with thick silky black hair. But it cannot have been the aesthetic impression or the musical quality of the voice alone that had put me at ease so quickly. He was obliging, though reserved; but in spite of this after half an hour's conversation he made me believe that I had known him most of my life, and yet there was nothing particularly easygoing about him, though there was a pronounced feeling of balance and proportion in his manner. And there was an undercurrent of human warmth which was responsible for the atmosphere of spiritual intimacy between us.

These were my first impressions of Mr. Jiddu Krishnamurti of Adyar, Madras, India; Castle Eerde, Ommen, Holland; Arya Vihara, Ojai, California and the Amphitheatre, Sydney, Australia.

III

Jiddu Krishnamurti was born in 1897 at Madanapalle in Southern India. He was the eighth child of Brahmin parents. His father Narayaniah had a minor post in the civil service, and afterwards became an official at the headquarters of the Theosophical Society at Adyar, Madras. One day in 1900 when little Krishnaji was bathing in the river with his younger brother Nityananda, the Rev. Charles Leadbeater saw them. Mr. Leadbeater was Mrs. Besant's closest collaborator and one of the leaders of the Theosophical Society. He talked to the boys and invited them to his bungalow. And now something took place which was to affect not only the life of the two Jiddu brothers but equally that of many thousands of people all over the world. Mr. Leadbeater discovered that the older boy Krishna-murti was none other than the 'Vehicle of the new World Teacher, the Lord Maitreya' whose last incarnation on earth had apparently been in the person of Jesus Christ.

Now, this was a most extraordinary discovery for anyone to make, even for a theosophical leader of some fame. Charles Leadbeater, however, not only believed in his vision but even convinced Mrs. Besant of the truth of it; and then began a series of events, almost unparalleled in modern history. Krishnamurti was to be prepared for his mission, and both he and his brother Nitya were taken into Charles Leadbeater's charge—Nitya merely as a playmate for his more exalted brother.

As there had previously been some gossip about Mr. Leadbeater, the father Narayaniah demanded the return of his two boys. The former renommée of Mr. Leadbeater seemed to have outweighed in the father's estimation the possibility of the future fame of his own son. There followed long struggles outside and inside the lawcourts. Mrs. Besant was appointed guardian of the boys, and excitement upon excitement kept newspaper correspondents busy for a long time until eventually Charles Leadbeater had to leave India, and the boys were sent to England. They were to receive an education that would complete the beginnings made in India, and that would prepare young Krishnaji for his future activities in the Western world.

The cheap publicity caused by Krishnamurti's association with Mr. Leadbeater entirely over-shadowed all that had been favourable to the boy in that association. Krishnamurti himself admitted in later years that thanks to Mr Leadbeater he had enjoyed all the privileges of an all-round education, combining the best of Eastern and Western methods. Such an education is usually available for only a few Indians. Thanks to Mr. Leadbeater, he had been rescued from a life of poverty and from the unhealthy conditions in which he had been reared and brought up and removed to surroundings that were beneficial to both mind and body. Krishnamurti also admitted that Mr. Leadbeater was always the most considerate guardian, and that he was never anything but the teacher anxious for the spiritual and bodily happiness of his pupil. In view of the slander that followed Mr. Leadbeater for many years it is important to state these facts as they really were.

Meanwhile in India a new society, 'The Order of the Star in the East', had been formed Its aim was to provide the necessary platform for the message of Krishnamurti, 'to proclaim the coming of a World-Teacher and to prepare the world for that event'. Most of its members were theosophists With Mrs. Besant they believed deeply in the truth of Charles Leadbeater's visions and in the part that Krishnamurti was to play in the future history of mankind. Nevertheless certain small sections of the Theosophical Society found it impossible to subscribe to the new doctrine, and felt obliged to leave the movement. The German branch of the Theosophical Society not only disapproved of the Krishnamurti legend but broke away altogether under the leadership of Rudolf Steiner.

There is another version of the origin of Krishnamurti's 'divine mission'. Hardly anyone knows it, and I heard it for the first time from Ouspensky; yet, since its source is impeccable, I shall quote it, even though Krishnamurti himself does not seem to know it.

According to this version, Leadbeater's original 'vision' was pure invention. Together with Mrs Besant he is supposed to have believed that a young human being brought up as a 'messiah'—educated in an appropriate manner and supported by a world-wide wave of love and the implicit faith of great masses of people—ought to develop certain Christlike qualities; and it appears that Leadbeater and Annie Besant believed to the very end that Krishnamurti was thus developing naturally into the personality of the 'World Teacher'.

The difference between the generally known and the above version is not quite as large as it appears to be at first—for in both cases Leadbeater and Mrs. Besant did not claim that Krishnamurti *was* the messiah but that about twenty years' preparation would be necessary for him to develop into the 'perfect vehicle' for the messiah. In either case they seem to have had no doubts as to the successful result of their method.

From 1912 to 1922 Krishnamurti and his brother lived in England, being educated partly at private schools and partly by tutors. They used to spend their holidays with Lady De La Warr, who became a sort of guardian to them. Krishnamurti was intended for Cambridge, but when it appeared that the university authorities were loath to accept a youth of his unique fame, it was decided that he should go on studying under private tutors.

He was intelligent and keen, and seemed to absorb Western learning with much greater zest and with even better results than does the ordinary English boy. Though certain influences during his early youth at Adyar may have been detrimental to him, there is no doubt that the spiritual training that he had to undergo in those years and the feeling of grave responsibility that had been instilled into him had a good effect. In England Krishnamurti was as popular with everyone who came into touch with him as he had been in India. His personal charm, which had impressed me in the first minutes of our meeting, must have had the same effect on other people. The influence of a woman of Mrs. Besant's wisdom and experience was, no doubt, also beneficial. There are many people who felt rather hostile towards Mrs. Besant, and perhaps not without reason, yet few have doubted the sincerity of her intentions and the power of her intellect. Such a mentor was bound to leave strong impressions upon the mind of a sensitive youth.

After the year 1921 Krishnamurti began to lead a more independent life. He travelled extensively; he gave up more and more of his time to writing poetry, and also he wrote articles for the many international publications of the 'Order of the Star'. Those were the days when Krishnamurti began to make friends with people outside the auspices of the Theosophical Society and the shadow of his own renown. He laid the foundations of many valuable friendships with men of letters, artists and musicians, who were all attracted by the charm of his unusual personality

Perhaps the closest friendship—and the most interesting to us—was that with Bourdelle, the French sculptor. After the death of Robin, Antoine Bourdelle was considered the leading French sculptor, and his fame extended far beyond Europe. In the days when the friendship between the old artist and the Indian youth had fully matured, *L'Intransigeant* published a report of an interview with Bourdelle. Bourdelle had been greatly impressed by Krishnamurti at their first meeting, and had subsequently modelled a large bust of him. He always considered it one of his most important works, and I remember that, in a posthumous exhibition of Bourdelle's sculpture in London, the bust of Krishnamurti had the place of honour. 'When one hears Krishnamurti speak one is astounded', said Bourdelle to the representative of *L'Intransigeant*; 'so much wisdom in so young a man!' Evidently Krishnamurti was a personality even without the labels that had been attached to him by his ardent followers. 'There is no-one in existence', Bourdelle went on, 'who is more impersonal, whose life is more dedicated to others. . . . In the desert of life Krishnamurti is an oasis.'

Krishnamurti's greatest following was in England, but it was interesting to note the impression he made on the French, who are, as a race, usually hostile to spiritual manifestations that cannot be defined in terms of logic. Nowhere have there appeared so many valuable books and articles about Krishnamurti as in France Frenchmen of an artistic disposition were the first to whom his personality appealed, quite apart from his fame or his supposed mission in the world. The blend of a beautiful appearance and a sensitive personality was bound to impress people with the artistic and intellectual fastidiousness of the French. Krishnamurti's exotic personality was no doubt an added attraction in the eyes of his French admirers.

Equally typical as his popularity in France was the suspicion with which he was regarded in Germany. The very fact that Krishnamurti's message came in a foreign language limited the extent of its influence. In the first place it could only appeal to those Germans who understood English. These were mostly people of a higher education, and they expected to find some clear philosophical structure in a spiritual message. It was the class that had been interested in Steiner, in Keyserling, in Stefan George. For the intellectual appetite of these people there was not enough solid fare in Krishnamurti's gospel, and his aesthetic assets were here of little avail.

In 1925 the Theosophical Society considered that the moment had come for Krishnamurti to acknowledge his destiny in more formal fashion, and this official recognition accordingly took place during the celebration of the jubilee of the Society. Theodore Besterman, a biographer of Mrs. Besant, describes most effectively the central scene of the proceedings: ' . . . In the shadow of the great banyan tree in the grounds of the Adyar headquarters, Mr. Krishnamurti was addressing some three thousand assembled delegates. . . . A few of those present had been warned what to expect, and these communicated their excitement to those around them. The whole audience was in the sort of state in which the individual is merged in the mass —a revivalist psychology. . . . The words of the speaker became more and more urgent. "We are all expecting Him", he said; "He will be with us soon." A pause, and then, with a dramatic change from the third person to the first, the voice went on, "I come to those who want sympathy, who want happiness. . . . I come not to destroy but to build." . . . And afterwards Mrs. Besant said that "the voice not heard on earth for two thousand years had once again been heard".'

It was now decided that Krishnamurti should have something more than the merely spiritual sphere of influence which was provided by the 'Order of the Star', and various properties were purchased for the establishment of enormous camps in different continents. A suitable territory was bought in the Ojai Valley in California, where people from all over America could gather for yearly meetings at which Krishnamurti would deliver his message. California was particularly dear to Krishnamurti's heart, since it was here that his beloved younger brother Nityananda had died a few years ealier. For the Australian followers there was erected the Amphitheatre in Sydney; for the Indian friends a camp in the Rishi Valley A Dutch nobleman, Baron Philip Pallandt van Eerde, an enthusiastic admirer of Krishnamurti, put at his disposal his Castle Eerde at Ommen in Holland with its old gardens and extensive grounds. Eerde was to become Krishnamurti's European headquarters, and here his European followers were to assemble at a vast camp meeting which was to be held every summer.

In January 1927 Krishnamurti spoke at a meeting in California, and concluded his speech by reading one of his recent poems, which ended with these words:

> '*I am the Truth,*
> *I am the Law,*
> *I am the Refuge,*
> *I am the Guide,*
> *The Companion and the Beloved.*'

The imaginative reporter of the *Theosophist* added to this a poetic summing up of the situation: 'As the last words were uttered there was a sprinkle of light rain that seemed like a benediction and, spanning the valley, a perfect rainbow arch shone out.' Meanwhile Mrs. Besant was travelling from country to country, giving lectures to packed halls and speaking in her masterly way of the new World Teacher.

Many details of this extraordinary 'life story' flashed through my mind when Krishnamurti entered that room. But after half an hour's conversation with him I was willing to forget most of the reports I had heard. The picturesque story of his life seemed to me no longer of much importance. How right I was I could not foresee at the time.

We parted friends, and I accepted an invitation to come to stay with Krishnamurti at Eerde. There I should meet his friends from all over the world; and, besides listening to his public speeches, I should also have an opportunity of further personal conversation.

IV

I actually went twice to Eerde in the course of the summer. The first time I could only spend two or three days there, so I decided to visit Krishnamurti again in a month's time, when I should be able to stay at least ten days, and witness the huge gathering of theosophists and members of Krishnamurti's own movement. There would be many visitors from the United States, from India and even from Australia.

To a writer of fiction the atmosphere at Eerde would probably offer the most attractive material. I could imagine all sorts of books inspired by it—psychological, devotional, religious, romantic, hysterical, lyrical, satirical. How tempting it would have been for a novelist to describe the little castle, an elegant building of the early eighteenth century rising up from a moat and connected with the 'mainland' by a delightful semicircular terrace; the romantic canal spanned by a decorative stone bridge; the long low pavilions on each side of the castle, the formal circular garden in front of it. And what opportunities were offered by the ancient park around the castle, its dignified avenues, its magnificent trees, its fields, its river, its water roses on the pond.

And then the guests themselves, wandering reverently along the garden paths, discussing under old trees the deepest problems of life, and greeting one another with smiles of forgiveness and looks of understanding.

There were fair Scandinavian girls with transparent complexions, and voices so soft that they seemed incapable of saying any but the holiest of things. Some of them helped in the kitchen, others in the offices, and in the evenings they sat together and held one another's hands. Though I have not found out for certain, I imagine that they were 'disciples' who had been driven by faith to leave their comfortable homes in Oslo or Stockholm and to come to the castle to work for the common good. There were several Americans in whose mouths the masters, gurus and astral worlds used to lose all their ethereal qualities and become convincingly matter of fact. There was a very learned French lady with at least three daughters who looked as though they preferred the Côte d'Azur to the Dutch scenery, but had to content themselves with their mother's knowledge of all sorts of *devas*, Chinese saints and Tibetan *gomtchengs*. There was an Italian countess who was always telling me of yet another dream she had had about Krishnamurti; and there were several elderly English ladies, quiet, kind, helpful, and wearing a surprising amount of jewelry, though their jewels, even if less obvious, were in a way like the taboos and charms of African Negroes, made of lions' teeth or human bones, since although they were mostly of gold and often of precious stones, their triangular or circular shapes showed clearly that they were worn for their symbolical significance and not in order to satisfy a craving after beauty. Then there were several Indians of indeterminate age but obviously higher education, who at night would sometimes appear in their attractive native coats, with tight white trousers and coloured shoes, the envy of their American, Dutch, British and Scandinavian brethren, many of whom wore homely sandals and looked altogether less picturesque. Some charming Australians and Anglo-Indians and a Scottish couple completed the house-party

The writer of fiction would have found even better models and more vivid 'local colour' in the large camp, situated in the woods a couple of miles outside the castle. Such readers as have ever attended a theosophical or practically any sort of religious convention will know the type, and I shall refrain from describing it at length. They generally abhor the idea of meat as violently as that of wine or tobacco; they look deep into your eyes when they talk to you; they have a weakness for sandals, for clothes without any particular distinction of shape, for the rougher kind of texiles and such colours as mauve, bottle-green and purple. The men affect long hair, while the women keep theirs short. There were several workmen and farmers among them who had been saving up their money for several years in order to come here. Two German youths had walked for two or three weeks from a distant part of Germany. Indeed, the three thousand visitors would have been worthy of a much more gifted pen than mine.

The organization of the camp lay in the hands of a few Dutch followers of Krishnamurti, experienced business men, who had succeeded in turning out this model camp city in the midst of uninhabited

forests and fields. Tourists and journalists from many countries
arrived solely to visit the camp, and organizers of similar gatherings
would come from distant countries in order to learn from the organization at Ommen. There were rows upon rows of tents of all sizes; there
were shower baths, attractive huts with post office, bookshops, photo-
grapher, ambulance and information bureau. In huge dining-tents
excellent vegetarian meals were served; there was a lecture tent with
seats for three thousand people and there was even an open-air
theatre. Everywhere one found helpful guides and interpreters and a
fine spirit of fellowship.

As the Dutch summer was at times trying—with incessant rain and
icy winds—the nerves of the people must have been somewhat strained.
Harmony could be achieved only by self-discipline. Ignorance of the
language was, no doubt, a tiresome handicap for many people. Some
of them must have come merely for the sake of a new experience and
for human fellowship, for the Serbs and Russians, South Americans,
Rumanians, Turks and Greeks who hardly knew one word of English
could not understand much during the lectures. And yet most of them
remained happy till the very last day. This was undoubtedly due, to a
very great extent, to the efficiency of the organization.

As I did not live in camp, which I visited only for the lectures and
an occasional meal, I knew the routine of life at the castle much better.

V

Since the castle itself was not large enough to accommodate the
twenty or more personal guests of Krishnamurti, most of us were put
up in the long pavilion flanking the castle. Besides Krishnamurti
and his closest friend Rajagopal, the head of the whole organization,
only a few friends stayed within the castle itself. The dining-room,
library, reception rooms and offices were on the ground floor. In the
reception rooms there were several attractive pieces of Dutch furniture, and the main room, called the state room, contained, besides
some fine panelling, four handsome Flemish tapestries specially
made for the castle. An ingeniously constructed wooden Louis
XIV staircase led from the entrance hall to the first floor and to the
bedrooms.

The former owner of the castle, Baron van Pallandt, was a quiet
middle-aged gentleman, who had kept for himself only one or two of
the castle rooms. He went on administering the big estate, and all the

secretarial, clerical and household work, besides that of organizing the movement itself, was done voluntarily.

I stayed in one of the two pavilions, where all the rooms were alike —simple, attractive and comfortable. Every visitor had to look after his own room and make his own bed. When, however, after a day or two some kind spirit had discovered that my talent for manual domestic work was more original than effective, my services in this direction were no longer expected, and for the remainder of my stay there, whenever I returned to my room after breakfast, I found that my bed had already been made with enviable skill.

In the morning we assembled in the big state room. We took off our shoes—more experienced guests than myself would appear in bedroom slippers—and sat down on the floor to meditate. Perhaps it was my native cynicism that prevented my enjoying the morning meditations as much as I ought to have done. It always put me into the wrong frame of mind.

There were several problems connected with the morning meditations about which I wished to be enlightened. Of course I might have asked any of the other twelve or fifteen fellow guests attending this service, but I could never summon the courage to do this, for fear lest they might find out how ignorant I really was. I wanted to ask them whether they considered it necessary to meditate in a crowd. I sincerely believed in meditation, but I always found it much more successful in solitude or with a single companion. Just when I was getting into the right frame of mind, one of the meditators must needs sneeze or cough, and thereupon all my limited powers of concentration would be dissipated.

And I should have liked also to ask whether it was essential to sit on the floor without having been instructed previously how to do it. Most of us had been brought up in the Western world, and were not used to Eastern attitudes. I found that my attention had to be directed towards my aching spine and ankles, and a good deal of the energy that was wanted for a better purpose was thus wasted. Eastern postures for meditation are taught solely by the yoga of body control, and can be learnt successfully only in the Far East. Of the eighty-four different postures for the various meditations, only the first few have ever been mastered by any European. Even the elementary 'lotus posture' which is indispensable to meditation done in the pose adopted by my fellow meditators, can only be comfortably assumed after many patient and painful exercises. How, then, could I expect all these people, most of whom had never been to the East, or undergone the essential training, to have the necessary command over their bodies? I could see for myself that hardly one of them was sitting in the correct attitude—that of intertwined ankles and straight spine. Possibly the worst indication of my own immaturity was to be found in the fact that the sight of all these people sitting there in stockinged feet always evoked in me a schoolboy propensity for practical joking.

Had it not been for my shortcomings, the morning meditations would undoubtedly have provided me with a source of inspiration. Someone read aloud a few words—I believe it was always one of Krishnamurti's sayings—and after that we were meant to meditate upon it. The tightly shut eyes of the other guests made me feel very envious of the wonderful ten minutes they were spending on some blissful plane.

From the state room we moved into the dining-room for breakfast, which was always an enjoyable meal, with excellent honey and delectable nut pastes. Lunch, too, was a very attractive meal, not only by virtue of the quality of the vegetarian dishes but equally because hunger, and the pleasure of satisfying it, induced many of the guests to cast off their reserve and to show greater individuality of character than conversation at other times had led one to expect.

As a rule everyone attended to his own wants, but I was often permitted to wait on Annie Besant, and I several times had the privilege of sitting next to her at meals, and each time it was a joy to be near this exceptional woman. There was a childlike quality about her— not the childishness of old age, but rather the essential simplicity and happy disposition of childhood itself. You felt that she knew so much more than anybody else present; but her greater wisdom and experience never interfered with her manner of treating even the youngest members of the party as her equals.

The saintliness that hung over Eerde, like a pink cloud in a play, made me somewhat sceptical; and yet the first meeting between Annie Besant and Krishnamurti on her arrival at the castle had greatly impressed me.

Krishnamurti had been waiting for the car that was bringing his guest, in the circular garden in front of the castle. He was by himself and we, his other guests, kept in the background. One could see that he was nervous. When the car arrived, Krishnamurti walked up to it to open the door. Annie Besant appeared, dressed in white Indian robes with white shoes, and a white shawl over her snow-white hair.

THE THRONE THAT WAS CHRIST'S

Krishnamurti bowed his head and kissed the old lady's hand. She in her turn put both her hands on his black hair and whispered a few words to him. In her face there was the expression of the deepest tenderness, and I could see that she was crying. It was obvious that their welcome was an expression of their personal affection for each other and had nothing to do with their theosophical relationship. Krishnamurti took Annie Besant's arm and led her slowly towards the castle. We were introduced to her and shook hands. Her eyes were still moist and the loving smile was still lingering on her lips.

Krishnamurti hardly ever came down to breakfast. Generally he remained in his bedroom. It was a very simple bedroom, and must have been the smallest in the castle. Each morning after breakfast some of his most intimate fellow workers used to walk up the staircase and disappear into a room which connected with Krishnamurti's bedroom. My curiosity was pricked by these morning processions. I imagined mysterious happenings behind the doors: special initiations or mental exercises of a higher order, reserved only for the 'inner circle'. I never found out what went on behind the doors—probably household bills and questions of daily routine were discussed.

In the mornings and on most afternoons there were lectures in the big tent in the woods. Krishnamurti spoke almost every day, and then there followed speeches by Annie Besant, Mr. Jinarajadasa, the vice-president of the Theosophical Society, a Frenchman Prof. Marcault, a Dutch scholar Dr. van der Leeuw, and one or two other followers of Krishnamurti The main tenor of Krishnamurti's talks was that the kingdom of happiness lies within ourselves, and the other lecturers spoke on very much the same lines. Krishnamurti's principal talks were of an autobiographical kind, and he tried to explain in them how he himself had found truth by giving up all conventional conceptions of life one after another.

There were several meetings at the castle in the afternoon, and often at these there were visitors, both legitimate and also of a less legitimate but more intrusive kind. Many people from the camp would come to see the home in which their prophet lived. They were taken inside the castle and along the quiet garden paths, and they often hardly dared utter a word. There were also sightseers and tourists, who had heard of the new messiah from India and who would peep through the gates as though expecting strange miracles to occur at any moment. They looked at Krishnamurti's guests, apparently convinced that we were the disciples of a magician or of a yogi. Each time I left the castle or came back, I noticed the inquisitive glances of the occupants of some motor car, and I would hear their interested chatter. This embarrassed me and made me wish that I had the power to produce white rabbits from my coat pocket or flames from my mouth, since I always felt as though the people in the cars were not being treated with that consideration to which they believed themselves entitled.

In the hall of the castle there was a very large and very new gramophone, given to Krishnamurti by one of his admirers and placed here for the enjoyment of the guests. I knew that Krishnamurti was a great lover of music, and I caught him one evening sitting by himself in the corner of a little study off the main hall. It was after dinner and the room was quite dark. I can still remember the record: it was the slow movement of the G Minor Quartette by Debussy—that almost unreal piece of strangely coloured cascades and sudden melancholy halts. Whenever I hear that movement I see the night over the castle and Krishnamurti sitting by himself in the little room and listening joyfully to the violins.

Several members of our house-party were fond of music, and would spend the evening listening to the gramophone. The prevailing taste seemed to be *Parsifal*, *Götterdämmerung*, and *Siegfried*. The listeners would sit in just those attitudes in which you would have expected to find them, when revelling in the superior boredom of Kundry's endless laments or Siegfried's narratives. Their eyes were closed, their souls no doubt very wide open, in their faces was a mixture of happiness and reverence, and you could see all the silver and mauve ethereal pictures that the music painted for them. Perhaps I was too frivolous for them, and at times I would become genuinely alarmed by my cynicism, and would decide never again to make critical comments even to myself. And yet there was one thing which gave real cause for a certain irritation.

VI

My inability to find the true meaning of Krishnamurti's teaching led to the anxiety that my visit might be an utter failure. Krishnamurti's lectures were too vague to give me clear answers to any of my questions.

I had been hoping to find those answers among the people who stayed at the castle and who must have known exactly what was to be understood. They were only too willing to help me; but it seemed to me that they had all sacrificed their personalities in order to become members of the Order of the Star in the East. I talked to many of them in the course of the day, but they left too little impression to enable me to distinguish them in my mind later on. They all met me halfway; and they would talk of reincarnation and *karma* with an understanding smile on their lips and as though they were speaking of the next train from Ommen to the Hook of Holland. They did their very best to copy Krishnamurti, to be kind and sincere or to make jokes and show how jolly they were. But I was not among doctors, farmers, schoolmasters, politicians, housewives; I was just among theosophists and members of the Order of the Star. I had expected that their new spiritual experience would have made them more enlightened about their former problems; that they would talk with greater understanding about the world at large. There were political and economical congresses, religious disputes, naval conferences going on all over the world; new movements in art, in literature, music, the theatre, the cinema were being experimented with; the world talked of unemployment and reparations; there were thousands of things that had to be discussed, improved upon—but none of them seemed to have penetrated the woods of Eerde.

One day I was told that the moment had arrived when Krishnamurti's message would be heard by the outside world which had hitherto known it only through distorted newspaper reports. A new organ was to be founded. My opinion was sought, since I had had some experience and enjoyed press connections that might be helpful. The publications of the Order of the Star—periodicals, pamphlets and news-sheets—were run by amateurs. I knew that the outside world could only be reached if one were to use a language intelligible to it. Devotional poetry, accounts of personal visions were not likely to convince men and women used to a matter-of-fact world. Those lawyers, business men, theologians and scientists of the outside world would only grasp Krishnamurti's ideas if they could be presented in a clear and sober way. People must see that they were dealing not with dreamers but with men who knew the world and her needs better than others did, and who therefore might be able to solve some of the most pressing problems.

The few people with whom the plans were discussed listened patiently to my suggestions; they nodded obligingly, and assured me that this was the right way to proceed. In actual practice not one of these suggestions was adopted, and the events of the following

95

months showed that a metaphorical and semi-theosophical jargon was still being employed for enlightening the world at large about the 'World Teacher'.

VII

I am sure that none but myself was to blame for my intellectual disappointment. The general atmosphere of adoration had put me into a state of expectancy which simply could not be satisfied anyhow or by anyone. My intellectual upbringing had made me expect a clearer message than Krishnamurti was willing or able to offer. I had not yet found in his friends and followers that inner readjustment to life that would have allowed me to accept the new message in the form in which it was offered.

I had gathered enough to see that Krishnamurti's teaching was not Eastern—that it repudiated passivity. Everyone should find truth for himself; should listen to no-one but himself; should consider unification with happiness as the final goal. But when I asked how this could be achieved I received no clear answers. It is not enough to see the summit of Mont Blanc. If we want to reach the top, we must be informed as to the most advantageous season, the best route, and such details of equipment as the most suitable boots to wear. Most of Krishnamurti's answers would be dissipated in similes and metaphors. You asked him about your personal troubles, your religious beliefs, your intellectual doubts, your emotional difficulties, and he would talk to you about mountain peaks and streams running through fields. When asked about his own road and the road along which one might find happiness, he would answer: 'The direct path, which I have trodden, you will tread when you leave on one side the paths that lead to complications. That path alone gives you the understanding of life. . . . If you are walking along the straight path, you need no signposts ' But where, exactly, the direct path lay, or how we were to find it, he did not disclose. The very same day Krishnamurti might renounce all paths and say that no one path was better than any other.

I had several talks with him, and each time I eagerly looked forward to our meeting. We would talk as we walked through the woods and across the fields of Eerde. One afternoon we suddenly found ourselves in front of a charming little house, flat roofed and rather modern, surrounded by high trees but with a view on one side across the fields. It was Krishnamurti's retreat, a self-contained little home,

where he could get away from people, meditate and rest in solitude
He must have been very sensitive to solitude. He was not very strong
physically, and though he went in for all sorts of games and was a
great lover of lawn tennis, he remained rather delicate. The camp
with its thousands of people, with its daily lectures, interviews and
visitors, must have been a heavy strain on his health.

I found no further intellectual satisfaction either in Krishnamurti's
lectures or in his books, and I wondered whether this was not due
to his Eastern origin. On the other hand, I had experienced no similar
difficulties when reading the writings of Eastern sages. Even if one
did not grasp their full meaning, there still remained enough to provide intellectual contentment. Among the books by Krishnamurti
that I tried to read were *Temple Talks*, *The Kingdom of Happiness*
and *The Pool of Wisdom*. There were also a few volumes of poetry.
I admired their oriental beauty and their deep ring of sincerity, but
I was baffled by their vagueness It is certainly unfair to judge lyrical
poetry by the same rules as those by which we attempt to judge
scientific books. On the other hand Krishnamurti's poetry was
supposed to contain not only the lyrical confession of a sensitive
youth with the gift for poetry but also the account of a deep spiritual
experience. When I read.

> '*As the flower contains the scent,*
> *So I hold Thee,*
> *O world,*
> *In my heart.*
> *Keep me within the heart,*
> *For I am liberation*
> *And happiness.*
>
> *As the precious stone*
> *Lies deep in the earth,*
> *So I am hidden*
> *Deep in thy heart . . .*'

I enjoyed the beauty of the poem and I felt the truth in it. But this
poem, called 'I am with thee' and written in 1927, was considered by
Krishnamurti's followers and even his biographer Lily Heber as of
great importance. I seemed to remember having seen poems of that
kind in various anthologies containing Eastern poetry. At times you
would even find such poems in those slender volumes published by

young men who had come down from Oxford and Cambridge and had been greeted by some of the London critics with prophecies of a splendid literary future.

But we were not dealing with a talented young man whose earlier poems had been accepted by the Editor of the *Oxford Outlook*. We were dealing with a teacher who did not repudiate this title; who allowed thousands to come and listen to him and to expect guiding principles from him, and who must have been conscious of the immense responsibility that all this implied. I felt that I had a right not only to expect answers but even to expect them in a language that I could understand; in a language that was common to people of the Western world. I even felt entitled to expect perfection in everything he said or did. The unity between the content and the form was of great importance in a person like Krishnamurti When I read:

> *'Thou must cleanse thyself*
> *Of the conceit of little knowledge ;*
> *Thou must purify thyself*
> *Of thy heart and mind ;*
> *Thou must renounce all*
> *Thy companions,*
> *Thy friends, thy family,*
> *Thy father, thy mother,*
> *Thy sister and thy brother ;*
> *Yea,*
> *Thou must renounce all ;*
> *Thou must destroy*
> *Thy self utterly*
> *To find the beloved.'*

I could see a glimpse of Krishnamurti's philosophy, but I felt that the same truth might have been expressed less pretentiously: 'Thou must purify thyself of thy heart and mind. Thou must renounce all thy companions, thy friends, thy family, thy father, thy mother, thy sister and thy brother . . .' If we write these lines without the lineal demarcation of poetry we acknowledge at once the fine statement contained in them, but we do not maintain that they are poetry. And yet I wanted Krishnamurti to write poetry that would convince people, and such as I might show to my sceptical friends.

When after a certain time I was able to perceive the main idea of Krishnamurti's teaching I understood that it was complete liberation, which means complete happiness. It is achieved by love and it rests within our own inherent power. Krishnamurti defined it in later years when he said: 'The goal of human feeling is love which is complete in itself, utterly detached, knowing neither subject nor object, a love which gives equally to all without demanding anything whatever in return, a love which is its own eternity.'

As far as I understand, this is the teaching of Christ, the teaching of Buddha. We all heard these words when we were given our first religious instruction. I asked myself, therefore: If Krishnamurti's teaching is just a repetition of the teaching of Christ, or of Buddha, then why all this theosophical background, why the Star in the East, that huge organisation; why the talk of a new path; why the followers, camps and labels? Would it not have been wiser to remain in our old-established Churches which give us clearer words for all these messages? Is it all humbug?

I was very fond of Krishnamurti, otherwise I should have left Eerde after the first few days. But I wanted Krishnamurti to be able to help me in my own way, and to help the other three thousand people in their own way. I wanted to be able to convince the cynic within myself that Krishnamurti was right and capable of helping, and that he had fulfilled my highest expectations. Instead, I felt uncomfortable when the Saul within myself would say to the Paul after every talk I had with Krishnamurti: 'Wasn't I right? Did you grasp more to-day than yesterday? Didn't I tell you it would be a waste of time? Why don't you talk instead to the rivers and the trees? Their language will be more intelligible.'

And yet there were people, with less intellectual resistance, who perceived Krishnamurti's message quite clearly. Looking back on those days I am particularly struck by the impression Krishnamurti made on a man brought up in the rough school of English working-class life, a man matured in political battles. I mean George Lansbury. This is what the old labour leader wrote after one of the meetings at Ommen: 'I have seen the glorious march of the Socialists in Paris, in Brussels, in Stockholm and in our own country, and I have seen them sitting and standing round our platform. But I think that these gatherings round the camp fire . . . are somehow the most wonderful sight of all. . . . When we Socialists come together, we come together pledging ourselves to fight in order to raise the material conditions of ourselves and our fellows. Round this camp fire we were listening to one who is teaching us the hardest of all

99

truths . . . that if mankind is to be redeemed it must be redeemed through the individual action of each one of us. . . . There must be great hope for the future . . . whilst there are living in our midst those who are inspired by a great ideal—to work and toil for impersonal causes.'

I hoped that Mr. Lansbury was right, and that some of the characteristics that I seemed to have found among Krishnamurti's followers were only evident when they were all together. They may have talked and behaved in quite a different manner when left to themselves in their normal surroundings. Perhaps all these people were really leaders in their various professions, efficient and capable of reforming their individual worlds in a direction that had disclosed itself to them during their visit to Eerde. Perhaps it was only due to blindness on my own part that even when I saw them later in London at one or two gatherings and in several offices, I again had the impression they had given me at Ommen.

Though my intellect remained critical, I felt that I was indeed becoming happier every day through my contact with Krishnamurti, and that only intellectual barriers within myself prevented me from accepting him as wholeheartedly as I longed to do. But even this reaction irritated me. I knew that the three thousand people who had come here were as anxious to catch his smile and were almost in a fever every time Krishnaji, as they called him affectionately, addressed or approached them. I had imagined myself more critical than they.

VIII

Only the evenings round the camp fire were really impressive. After dinner we would drive out in cars belonging to members of our house-party to the camp fire in the woods. A large amphitheatre had been built there, with innumerable circular rows of seats; in their midst was Krishnamurti's own seat. This was made of large tree trunks and suggested some huge Niebelungen throne. Each time I saw this seat I imagined that Wotan and Hunding and the many substantial valkyries must have sat in such chairs when attending a family party in Valhalla. Krishnamurti, slender, dark, rather shy, looked strange and lost on his Wagnerian throne.

Most of the people who had come to the camp at Ommen looked upon the evening gatherings, quite rightly, as the climax of the day. Krishnamurti, stepping into the centre of the amphitheatre where a huge heap of wood for a beacon had been prepared, would kindle it and stand in front of it for a few minutes watching the fire grow higher and higher. Then he would walk back slowly to his seat. Smoke would begin to rise to the sky and the flames would suffuse thousands of eager faces with a red glow. Many members of the audience were sitting with their hands resting quietly in their laps and their eyes shut, and you could see how deeply they enjoyed the moment. In the evenings there was a festive feeling, there was an atmosphere of human fellowship and spiritual satisfaction. It was a real holiday to the three thousand people. On one or two occasions the light of the flames and the last pink of a sun that had disappeared more than an hour ago would merge into each other and would produce striking colour effects in which, I daresay, some of the people present discovered symbolical meanings.

I have never heard Krishnamurti speak so well as he did in the evenings round the camp fire. On the whole he was not a very effective speaker; he often repeated himself; he often halted; and many of his sentences were too long. His hold over the masses was not due to any forensic talents. In the evening his words seemed to come more easily to him, and his voice would carry melodiously across the silent crowd, the pictures evoked by his words becoming more clearly visible and the whole atmosphere more convincing.

Now and then he would begin an Indian chant at the end of the evening, and on such occasions he was even more impressive than during his speech. Though he spoke English with mastery, you could not help feeling that English was not his language. It was, I remember thinking at the time, the melodious quality of his voice that may have given that impression. In the evenings round the camp fire the contrast between his entire personality and the English language would become more striking. For he then wore Indian clothes, a simple brown coat reaching below the knees and buttoned up to the neck, tight white trousers and white shoes, and his appearance would only emphasize the emotion produced by his voice. During the Indian chants the precise meaning of his words seemed to matter little, and there was no longer a gulf between the man and his words. In the unintelligible Hindustani there was the magic sound that words assume in a strange tongue.

After his chants Krishnamurti would sit silently for a few minutes, with an expression of great serenity on his face. He would then leave his seat and walk away to the car that took him back to the castle.

THE ENGLISH ADVENTURE

IX

One or two experiences may help to show what a real influence Krishnamurti had on my life. It may be considered a mere coincidence that when I met Krishnamurti for the first time, on that rainy Sunday morning in Westminster, I gave up smoking. I had smoked since I was seventeen, usually thirty cigarettes a day, and I had become something of a slave to the habit. Nevertheless I had never tried to give up smoking, because I had never seen any convincing reason for so doing. Even to-day I cannot explain clearly why I should have given it up the day I met Krishnamurti. We did not discuss the subject; I did not know that he himself did not smoke. And yet to give up smoking at once seemed the most natural thing. Though I carried a cigarette case in my pocket for many days I never felt tempted to light another cigarette. Nor have I smoked since.

The other incident is more difficult to describe. I had been trying for a long time to meditate in the evenings on a particular subject. I used to do it in bed before going to sleep. For months on end I would reach a certain point in my meditation after which it would break up. Either my attention would falter or else I fell asleep before getting beyond the particular point. A few days after I had met Krishnamurti I succeeded for the first time. I experienced the feeling of sinking into a deep well. Though the well seemed bottomless I had simultaneously the two opposed sensations of going on sinking and yet of having reached the bottom. This was accompanied by a very vivid impression of light. The strongest impression, however, was of receiving at once an emotional shock and a mathematical revelation. It is difficult to describe this last sensation: no metaphor or comparison represents it correctly. Though I do not claim any mystical significance for my experience, I can best translate it into words by quoting an abler pen than my own. When Dean Inge once described mystical experiences he said: 'What can be described and handed on is not the vision itself but the inadequate symbols in which the seer tries to preserve it in his memory. . . . But such experiences, which rather possess a man than are possessed by him, are in their nature as transient as the glories of a sunset. . . Language, which was not made for such purposes, fails lamentably to reproduce even their pale reflection.' What, however, can be said is the fact that the culminating point of my experience made me unspeakably happy.

THE THRONE THAT WAS CHRIST'S

It was such an acute happiness that it was almost like a feeling of physical delight or physical pain. The division between delight and pain seemed lifted. How long the moment lasted I could not tell; but I imagine it to have been no more than the fraction of a second. When it was all over, I was awake and fully conscious, and I recorded my experience to myself with a feeling of deep gratitude.

The above experiences showed me that Krishnamurti's effect upon me was vital enough to act even against my intellectual resistance.

X

In the summer of 1929 I found in a newspaper a report which described at some length how Krishnamurti had suddenly dissolved the Order of the Star, broken deliberately all connections with the Theosophical Society and their teaching about himself, and renounced all the claims that had been made in his name. He had, then, at last summoned the courage to sever all the ties that had held back his own spiritual convictions through so many years, and that had forced him to act in the shadow of what looked like spiritual usurpation.

The recent rupture had taken place on 3 August 1929 at the yearly summer camp at Ommen. Krishnamurti decided to renounce all the authority that thousands of people had been using as comfortable crutches for their own spiritual incapacity. This is how Mr. Theodore Besterman described the critical meeting in his biography of Mrs. Besant: 'One morning Mr. Krishnamurti rose to deliver his address to the assembled campers. It could be seen at once that he was now speaking for himself and not merely as a mouthpiece; and his words confirmed the impression in no dubious manner. . . . He announced the dissolution of the Order of the Star and at one blow laid low the whole elaborate structure so painfully and painstakingly built up by Mrs. Besant during the past eighteen years. "I maintain", Krishnamurti said, "that Truth is a pathless land, and you cannot approach it by any path whatsoever, by any religion, by any sect. That is my point of view and I adhere to that absolutely and unconditionally. . . . A belief is purely an individual matter, and you cannot and must not organize it." He declared that he did not want followers . . . he made it unmistakably clear that his words were directed against those who had built up the elaborate structure for him during those eighteen years. Krishnamurti added: "You have been preparing for this event, for the coming of the World Teacher. For eighteen years you have organized, you have looked for someone who would give a new delight to your hearts . . . who would set you free. . . . In what matter has such a belief swept away all the unessential things in life? In what way are you freer, greater? . . ." Mr. Krishnamurti continued. "You can form other organizations and expect someone else. With that I am not concerned, nor with creating new cages. . . . My only concern is to set men absolutely, unconditionally free." After this Mr. Krishnamurti gave up all the possessions heaped upon him, and gradually severed his connection with all organizations.'

It was not difficult to perceive what enormous courage it needed to make such a far-reaching decision. To understand its magnitude one has to remember what Krishnamurti was renouncing. There existed an organization with many thousands of members; there were platforms from which to speak in the four most important corners of the globe; there was an independent commercial organization with its magazines, its books and various publications in a dozen different languages; there were helpers among all classes of society, willing to make practically any mental or material sacrifice, there was, in short, a working machine for the transmission of a spiritual message, as powerful as any institution had ever been. To understand what it must have meant to give it all up, one has to visualize the money, the worry, the energy, the time needed for the establishment of an organization for the disseminating of non-commercial ideals, no matter whether of a religious, social, political, intellectual or any other kind. To throw it overboard as though it meant nothing required personal courage, moral integrity and spiritual conviction

I was glad that I had doubted neither Krishnamurti's sincerity nor his intrinsic spiritual value. The events of August 1929 strengthened the impression I had received when the young Indian entered the dark panelled room in Westminster. Had I not suddenly seen that it mattered little what his life had been up till then? And had I not felt that his personality had nothing in common with the striking headlines in the newspapers?

CHAPTER II

PORTRAIT OF A "PERFECT MASTER"

Shri Meher Baba

I

When I arrived, a procession of his disciples filed out. First a bevy of beautiful young girls passed me, then several young Indians departed. Meher Baba was sitting on a sofa. He wore a dressing gown, and a soft blue silken scarf round his neck.

'He is a slender man of thirty-eight, but he looks ten years younger. He wears his dark brown hair very long. It flows down to his shoulders. He reminded me of the young Paderewski. . . . The chin is rather pointed and not powerful. . . . His eyes sparkle with happiness and serene joy. . . . He is ebulliently healthy. . . . His hands are eloquently artistic. They talk. They are hypnotic. He has immense magnetism. As I entered the room I felt a rush of personal fascination and force. . . As he grasped my hand I felt a strange thrill. . . . During our talk he perpetually caressed me, laying his hand on mine, or touching me on the back. A very magnetic personality. . . . I melted under his enchantment in spite of my caution. Meher Baba does not speak. . . . Our talk was conducted through a young Indian who rapidly interpreted the master's signs On his knees rested a small board with the letters of the Roman alphabet painted on it. His slim fingers flicked from letter to letter. . . . His interpreter reads the alphabet. . . . I had prepared a questionnaire with the help of Sir Denison Ross, the oriental scholar. It was designed to trap the teacher, but he smilingly threaded his way through it without stumbling. . . . "Do you know Gandhi?" I asked. "Yes, he is not as far advanced as I am. He asked me to help him. . . ." "Are you divine?" He smiled. "I am one with God. I live in Him like Buddha, like Christ, like Krishna. They knew Him as I know Him. . . ." "Is there any way out of the world crisis?" "Yes." "How long will it last?" "Only another year."'

II

The above prophecy was published early in 1932. It was contained in an interview which appeared on the front page of the London

Sunday Express, and was preceded by ten large headlines, two of which ran across the whole page. In the middle there was a large photograph of Shri Sadguru Meher Baba. The author of the interview was the popular British journalist, Mr. James Douglas, a well-known writer of religious and moral articles.

A few weeks after the publication of Mr. Douglas's article I had an interview with Shri Meher Baba. It had been arranged by one of his chief British disciples.

I arrived on a chilly spring morning at one of those large houses off Lancaster Gate, which might once in opulent Edwardian days have been attractive but had become gloomy and uncared for since they had been transformed into understaffed lodgings, boarding houses and residential hotels. I was received by a somewhat forbidding domestic who said that she would call 'one of them Arabs' for me; but after a few minutes a more presentable young woman appeared, only to assure me that nothing was known to her about an interview —if, however, I maintained that an interview had been arranged, it was probably so, and she would immediately inquire. A few minutes later a little Indian with a kind face appeared. He wore European clothes and had a black moustache. 'Oh yes, Mr Shri Meher Baba will be delighted to see you; he knows all about you, and it won't be a moment.' After he went, I counted for about twenty minutes the number of leaves in the pattern of the wallpaper in the narrow entrance hall. Eventually, however, another lady appeared and asked me to follow her upstairs.

I climbed five flights of stairs, and was received on the top landing by another little man with a black moustache. He, too, had an inviting smile, and he said: 'Please, do come in. Mr. Shri Meher Baba has been expecting you.' He opened the door, and I found myself in a small bedroom. The bed had not been made yet, and the furniture was simple and typical of the smaller residential hotels in the district.

Shri Meher Baba (whom I shall call for simplicity's sake Baba) was sitting in the middle of the room in an easy chair. He corresponded in his appearance exactly to the description by Mr. James Douglas, but I waited in vain for the 'rush of personal fascination and force'; I missed the 'strange thrill' when he grasped my hand, and though he 'caressed me, laying his hand on mine', I could not make myself 'melt away under his enchantment'. He was wearing a dressing-gown, bedroom slippers and a woollen

106

scarf round his neck. He was holding in his hands the little black-board with the white letters of the Roman alphabet written upon it. Two Indian interpreters were placed behind him, and they interpreted to me each of the many quick movements of Baba's flickering fingers.

Unfortunately my questions must have been badly prepared, or awkwardly presented, for the answer was almost invariably. 'This question requires a more elaborate answer and a longer discussion. I shall have to write this answer to you in a day or two.' After this had been going on for about three-quarters of an hour I decided that it would be unfair to trespass any longer on my host's time. I had been informed that Baba was leaving for America in a few days' time, and I was certain that he had a lot to do before his departure. But, after I had turned towards the door, Baba suddenly began making more signs on his board. One of his two interpreters stopped me: 'Baba says that he is going to help you in the future.' I was taken by surprise, and though I tried to express thanks for this unsought promise, I must have done so not without embarrassment.

III

A thick letter from Baba arrived a week after my interview, containing a number of sheets of paper, covered with the handwritten answers to my questions.

'The spiritual revival that you ask about', said the letter, 'is not very far off and I am going to bring it about in the near future, utilizing the tremendous amount of misapplied energy possessed by America for the purpose. Such a spiritual outburst as I visualize usually takes place every seven or eight hundred years, at the end or beginning of a cycle, and it is only the Perfect One, who has reached the Christ state of consciousness, that can appeal and work so very universally. My work will embrace everything; it will affect and control every phase of life. . . . In the general spiritual push that I shall impart to the world, problems such as politics, economics and sex . . . will all be automatically solved and adjusted. All collective movements and religions hinge round one personality who supplies the motive force—without this centrifugal force all movements are bound to fail. . . . Perfect masters impart spirituality by personal contact and influence, and the benefit that will accrue to different nations, when I bring about the spiritual upheaval, will largely depend upon the amount of energy each one possesses.' There followed several passages about the possibility of performing miracles, and on the last page I found the following sentences: 'I now take orders from no-one; it is all my supreme will. Everything is, because I will it to be. Nothing is beyond my knowledge; I am in everything. There is no time and space for me, it is I who give them their relative existence. I see the past and the future as clearly and vividly as you see material things about you.'

When I read these statements Baba was on his way to the country in which he was to utilize the 'tremendous amount of misapplied energy' for the bringing about of a spiritual revival A few weeks later I received a letter from the English disciple, through whose help I had been granted my interview, and who was now among those who accompanied Baba on his trip to America. He wrote from Hollywood: 'We arrived in Los Angeles two weeks ago to-day. Baba had a terrific amount of work there, and none of us had more than four hours' sleep a night, there was so much to be done. In addition to all the private interviews, he had one general reception given at the Knickerbocker Hotel, Hollywood, where over a thousand people came . . . another one given to him by Douglas Fairbanks and Mary Pickford. . . . He went several times to Paramount Studios and also to Universal and Metro-Goldwyn. I am so grateful to you for your letters of introduction to Sternberg and Lubitsch. They were both charming to us. We went to Paramount to meet Sternberg and Marlene Dietrich, and the next day we motored to Santa Monica to have tea with Lubitsch. . . . Baba liked them both very much, and is looking forward to seeing them again. He also saw Tallulah Bankhead several times, Marie Dressler, Gary Cooper, Tom Mix, Virginia Bruce, Maurice Chevalier and a good many others.'

IV

At the same time there appeared an article in *Everyman* in which the editor published a biographical sketch of Baba under the title 'More about the Perfect Master'. Its main facts were: 'Shri Sadguru Meher Baba is a Persian born in Poona, South India, on 25 February 1895. . . . His father is a Zoroastrian, and Meher Baba was brought up in that religion. He went to school and college in Poona. When he was seventeen he was met by Shri Hazrat Babajan, an ancient woman, as a result of which Meher Baba entered a superconscious state in which he remained for nine months entirely oblivious of earthly life. It took seven years before he regained normal human consciousness. During the whole of that time he had to be taken care of. His return to normal consciousness was brought about in 1921.'

The strange meeting with the 'ancient woman' consisted apparently of a kiss. But this kiss had the most far-reaching consequences. Baba himself described this incident in the following words: 'Until then I was worldly as other youths. Hazrat Babajan unlocked the door for me. Her kiss was the turning point. I felt as though the universe was receding into space, and I was left entirely alone. Yes—I was alone with God. For months I could not sleep. And yet I grew no weaker but remained as strong as before My father did not understand. . . . He called in one doctor and then another. They gave me medicines and tried injections, but they were all wrong. I had lost hold of normal existence and it took me a long time to get back.'

'He spent the first two years after that experience', continues the editor of *Everyman*, 'in writing an account of what happened to him. This book has not been seen by anyone. He never married, nor did he ever engage in any trade or occupation; for he was still at college when the experience I have mentioned came to him. His time has been spent during the past eleven years in travelling throughout India, alternating with periods of complete retirement. He visited the West for the first time last September (1931) when he spent about three weeks in England, and afterwards went to America for a few weeks. . . On his first visit to this country he saw a few people. . . . On the present occasion, however, the news of his coming was spread from India, and he was met on arrival with the full blast of British newspaper publicity. . . . He has not spoken for more than seven years. . . . This silence is not the result of a vow, but is undertaken for spiritual reasons. He says that he will break it soon in America.'

V

Baba's spiritual message can be summed up in the few words which he himself dictated to the press reporters who came to see him when he arrived in England. He said: 'My coming to the West is not with the object of establishing a new creed . . . but is intended to make people understand religion in its true sense. True religion consists of developing that attitude of mind which ultimately results in seeing one infinite existence prevailing throughout the universe, thus finding the same divinity in art and science and experiencing the highest consciousness and invisible bliss in everyday life. . . . Organized efforts such as the League of Nations are being made to solve world problems. . . . This is like groping in the dark I intend to bring together all religions and cults like beads on one string and to revitalize them for individual and collective needs. This is my mission to the West.'

During the following months I met several of Baba's disciples, and I was given many accounts of his powers and of his wisdom. A journalist, Mr Paul Brunton, decided to study Baba more closely, and even went to visit him in India. He recorded his many meetings with Baba in a very interesting book, *A Search in Secret India.* One of his first interviews finished in a similar manner to that of my own. Without having been asked for any help, Baba said to Mr. Brunton: 'You are very fortunate. I will help you to obtain advanced powers.' Though Mr. Brunton went out to India to stay with Baba at his *ashram*, he did not receive any of the answers he had been promised, and he left the Parsee in a state of disillusionment. 'I find', he says in his book, 'that Meher Baba is a fallible authority, a man subject to constantly changing moods, and an egotist who demands complete enslavement on the part of his brain-stupefied followers. And lastly I find that he is a prophet whose predictions are seldom verified. . . .' In spite of this Mr. Bruton continues: 'I candidly confess to myself . . . that Meher Baba possesses religious genius. Whatever success he may have will arise from that last quality.'

A few years after my meeting with Baba I was given an opportunity of verifying his utterances to Mr. James Douglas with regard to Gandhi. I was travelling to America in the same boat as Miss Madeleine Slade, Gandhi's English disciple and companion. I asked Miraben (as Miss Slade was called, since she had become a Hindu) about Baba's conversations with Gandhi. 'I know all the details about the connection between the two men,' she said; 'it was always Shri Meher Baba who went to see Gandhi, never otherwise. They first met when Gandhi travelled in the *Rajputana* to England to attend the Round Table Conference. Shri Meher Baba sent round a word, asking whether Gandhi would receive him. Gandhi, of course, consented. They had a talk, and after that Shri Meher Baba visited Gandhi again in London. But you may state quite emphatically that Gandhi never asked Meher Baba for help or for spiritual or other advice. He liked Meher Baba, and he talked to him, as he talks to everyone who wants to see him—that was all.'

For a certain time I wondered whether I should not give up all further study of Shri Meher Baba, and limit myself to classifying him as one of the many 'saints' who appear every now and then in the East, and who suffer from nothing so much as from self-delusion. Eventually, however, I decided that it would be premature to discard a man only because certain aspects of his teaching or his personality were not quite convincing. Every teacher has his own method, and what appears to us to be trickery or self-delusion may be, for all we know, part of a very wise system. I was therefore anxious to find out more about Baba's methods with regard to his followers, and, if possible, I wanted to hear about it from one of his most experienced and most intelligent pupils.

Another reason that made me go on studying Baba was that there had been several sound statements in his first letter to me. 'No general rule or process', Baba wrote in that letter, 'can be laid down for the attainment of the ultimate reality. . . . Every individual has got to work out his own salvation. . . . The panaceas the world knows of, the so-called religions for the guidance of humanity, do not go a long way towards solving the problem. As time goes on the founder is thrown into the background of time and obscurity, religion loses its glamour, and there takes place a mental revolt against the old order of things and a demand is created for something more sensibly substantial and practical. . . . I don't believe in external renunciation; for the West particularly it is impracticable and inadvisable. Renunciation should be mental. One should live in the world, perform all legitimate duties and yet feel mentally detached from everything; one should be in the world, but not of the world.'

VI

I continued questioning people about Baba, wrote letters to some of his pupils, and gathered any material I could lay hands on. But no source was so enlightening as the one I came across unexpectedly in the person of a very beautiful woman in New York. She possessed all the qualifications that I had been anxious to meet with in one of Baba's disciples and that I had almost given up hope of ever finding.

She had given up her former life in order to serve him; she had a thorough knowledge of Baba's methods, she took part in his daily life, every detail of which she knew as she knew her own, and above all, she was intelligent.

As a young girl she had married a distinguished German author; at an early age she had become a famous actress, and later a screen actress for a few years; she had then married a prince, and had left him in order to follow Baba. She had been celebrated for her beauty, and she still possessed one of the most striking appearances I had ever encountered. She had an infectious zest for life, but she also revealed a certain spiritual quality which helped to explain why she should have achieved her greatest stage success in a drama in which she had to play the Madonna. Her devotion to Baba suggested that as she was no longer able to play the Madonna she found happiness in playing in real life the part of Mary of Bethany, sitting at the feet of the Master.

When I met her in New York the passion of the great actress had not left her. It might have been the centre of a stage with thousands of spectators watching her and not an apartment off Fifth Avenue in which she received me. Even her eyes and her hands were vocal. A disciplined rhythm controlled the movements of her body; her black silk dress clung tight to her figure, and to relieve the sombreness of her dress there were ropes of pearls round her neck. Her head was enveloped in a white turban of a delicate silken fabric I had been told that she always wore that turban since she had become a disciple of Baba. Heavy odour of incense pervaded the rooms, the lighting was dim, and I noticed pictures of mediaeval saints and other works of art which, though originally conceived as documents of spiritual devotion, had become part of a modern luxurious existence.

My hostess was Italian by birth, but her English was perfect, and she always succeeded in using the right and not merely the obvious word. When she quoted German she betrayed no trace of a foreign accent; her French was equally good. Her intellectual perspicacity was able to balance her passionate convictions, and technique had taught her that a hidden flame is more effective than an open one. Carpets and rugs softened the ardent flow of her words. We drank tea from cups made of glass, and the whole room disclosed that peculiarly opulent taste that one finds so often in apartments near Fifth Avenue.

112

PORTRAIT OF A "PERFECT MASTER"

'How did you meet Shri Meher Baba?' I asked her.

'I doubt whether that experience can be expressed in words,' she replied, and opened her hands in a helpless gesture; 'I had heard about him, but I remained sceptical. I had followed teacher after teacher. And yet none of the teachers I met could ever reassure me. Eventually I consented to go with a friend to the place where Baba stayed in New York. I entered the room in which he was sitting, surrounded by followers and disciples. That very moment an experience began, full of wonder and beauty. Suddenly I had to run through the room, and I found myself on the floor at his feet, weeping, weeping, weeping. Oh, how I was weeping! But I also began to laugh, and the streams running down my cheeks and the outbursts of laughter were one. I was resting my head on Baba's hand, and my whole body was shaken with the terrific sobs of liberation. Eventually I quietened down Baba then took my face between his hands and looked for a long time first into one of my eyes, then into the other, and then back into the first eye. And then he spoke to me or rather made signs on his spelling board '

'What were his first words to you?' I interrupted.

My hostess raised her head, fixed me with her eyes as though testing whether I would comprehend the whole weight of her words, and said slowly: 'His first words were. "I am man and woman and child. I am sexless." He then paused for a while, brought his face nearer to mine, and said: "Have no fear." An incredible joy went through me. I went into the next room and lay down on a sofa, weeping still with joy Suddenly the door opened and Shri Meher Baba came in. I knew by now that my whole life had no meaning if it was not dedicated to the Perfect Master, and so I said to him "Baba, please take me with you." But his only answer was: "It is yet too soon." I could have died with grief when he said these words ' The beautiful woman spread dramatically the fingers of one hand over her heart as though indicating that her heart had almost stopped when she had heard Baba's refusal.

'I had to try three times before he finally accepted me,' she then continued; 'I followed him to Europe, but he sent me back to America, whence I had come. You see, it was not a fit of hasty enthusiasm that made me renounce my whole previous existence, divorce my husband whom I loved and who loved me, and sacrifice my whole life and everything I possess to the Perfect Master. But I know that I was right. To-day I live to serve a higher purpose instead of living to satisfy my own little ego, my own little envies and greeds. To-day I live in conformity with a higher plan and for higher good.'

I wondered what the fruits of the higher plan and the higher good were, but I only asked: 'How do you know?'

'How can I doubt it?' came the quick answer. 'Since Baba is the Perfect Master he knows everything that is good; he directs everything in the universe. If I submit to his will I can only do what I, as a spiritual being, am meant to do, and not what my selfish little self always tempts me to do.'

'But does this not imply your complete submission to somebody else's will?'

'Not at all—because Baba, who knows my spiritual path, makes me only do things that come from within my nature. He does not force his will upon me, but induces me to act according to the demands of my personality.' My hostess stopped and remained silent as though indicating that there was nothing to doubt and that all the facts mentioned by her were beyond dispute.

'How does Baba instruct his other pupils, and how does he act when, in your words, he "directs the universe"?' I asked after a while.

'He acts upon physical things as they actually are. He directs *maya*.'

'What do you mean by *maya*? *Maya* as the physical world, which the East believes to be nothing but an illusion?'

'Exactly, *maya* in its orthodox sense. Baba employs those illusions to destroy other illusions of our worldly life.'

'Can you illustrate this?'

'Of course I can. Let's assume that a friend of Baba's is in danger of being drowned in a lake. Baba, though hundreds of miles away, knows of the imminent danger. He will ask his pupils to bring a basin of water; he will put his hands into it, and by doing it he will influence the water of the lake, thus producing there certain conditions that will save his friend. He always employs equal elements for his actions.'

'And you really believe all that?' I interrupted.

'Of course I do', she answered with such determination that I no longer felt like opposing her with my intellectual criticism.

My hostess was, in a way, nothing but Baba's mouthpiece, almost more explicit than Baba himself. I could not have wished for a more perfect source of information, and it was not for me to decide whether she was suffering from self-delusion or to what extent the admiration of such a fascinating woman had turned Baba's oriental head. Though some of the facts I was presented with were fantastic, many of the details were too revealing not to be recorded.

'Please tell me,' 1 asked, 'how does Baba spend his days?' In the opinion of my hostess Baba was what she called a Perfect Master, and had therefore a place at the very top of some mysterious hierarchy. It was interesting to know how such an exalted being spends his days.

'He gets up very early,' was the answer, 'hours before the rest of the household. He takes a very hot bath, and his hair is attended to with the greatest care He is, as you must have noticed, extremely tidy in his appearance, and no-one can imagine the amount of time spent over the washing, combing and brushing of his beautiful hair. He then goes from room to room, stops for a while in front of every bed, looks at the sleeping person, and, no doubt, directs in his own way the life of the disciple for the rest of the day. Many activities follow: newspapers, a huge correspondence, interviews.'

'Does he read much?'

'He never reads books, but he knows everything.'

'But he reads newspapers, doesn't he?'

'Yes, he reads them, or rather they serve him as a medium for directing the daily destinies of the world.'

'Destinies of the world?' I whispered.

'Yes, you see, Baba does not read a paper. He just goes over the headlines. But while doing this he places his hands and fingers on the printed lines'—she illustrated Baba's movements with her own expressive hands—'and through such a contact with the print he affects the results of events described in the article.'

'He does that?'

'Of course he does', she answered, and went on demonstrating the way in which a 'perfect master' directs the events of our world. 'Perfect Masters work in many different ways,' she went on; 'and Baba uses many things in life as transmitting stations for directing events. He also uses us, his disciples, for his work. He spiritualizes the world by creating certain spiritual centres in various parts of the world: they serve as transmitting stations for Baba's spiritual radiation. Generally he has groups of twelve in every one of these centres.'

I now remember that Baba himself had once made a statement about the external organization of his work. Mr. Brunton reports

115

this statement in his book· 'Others will continue my work. My circle of twelve selected disciples, of whom one will become a Master in the appointed time. They have all been with me in past births, and I am bound to help them. There will be also an outer circle with forty-four members. They will be men and women of a lower spiritual grade; their duty will be to assist the twelve chief disciples, after the latter have attained perfection.'

'What other methods does Baba employ?' I asked.

'He works in many different ways, for example in the cinema. We go very often to a cinema, at times even twice or three times a day. Of course the actual film does not interest Baba. But when the audience is so absorbed by the film that it has given up its inner resistance, he can work upon it in his own way.'

'Is he fond of music?'

'Indeed he is. And of the theatre too. We often have to play for him special plays written and produced by ourselves. And we have to make music for him. Sometimes we have only a gramophone, but he does not mind it, as long as it is folk music Spanish, Eastern, Negro or Russian music. He has little use for what he calls classical music.'

I felt I knew enough about the life of a 'perfect master'. I had come to the end of my investigations. There was only one other point on which I wished to be enlightened. 'Do you know Baba's attitude', I asked, 'towards other teachers, towards men like Krishnamurti, Steiner, Ouspensky or Keyserling?'

'Oh, he does not mind them. He knows them all, he knows their exact position in the spiritual world and the whole of their teaching without bothering to study it. I remember his actually making a statement with regard to Krishnamurti. He said that Krishnamurti possessed great possibilities within himself and that he is on the right path, but he won't fulfil himself or become truly great as long as he does not come to visit Baba. You see,' she concluded in an almost apologetic tone, 'everyone, even a person like Krishnamurti, needs the personal contact with a Supreme Master. Otherwise he cannot fulfil himself.'

VII

When I got home I opened once again the book in which Mr. Brunton recorded his experiences with Baba. He had spent a whole month in Baba's Indian *ashram*, he had seen Baba daily, had mixed constantly with his disciples and had become saturated in the atmosphere of Baba's life. And this is what he has to say at the end of his investigations· 'I discovered that he is really an irresolute man, influenced by others and by circumstances. His small pointed chin is eloquent on this point. . . .' Mr. Brunton turns then to Baba's followers: 'His followers will never admit that Meher Baba can commit blunders. Always they naively assume that mysterious esoteric purpose lies behind everything he says or does. They are content to follow blindly, as indeed they must, for reason soon rebels at what they have to swallow.' Mr. Brunton then proceeds to express his hypothesis of the reasons for Baba's strange personality: 'My own theory', he says, 'is that the old woman *faqueer*,[1] Hazrat Babajan, did really create an upheaval in Meher Baba's character that upset his equilibrium. . . . The kiss which she gave him was nothing in itself, but became important as the symbolic conveyance of her psychic inner grace. . . . He was quite clearly unprepared for it. He had gone through no training and no discipline to fit himself for what might be tantamount to a yogic initiation. . . . I believe that the youthful Meher became quite unbalanced as a result of this unexpected experience. This was obvious enough when he fell into a condition of semi-idiocy and behaved like a human robot. . . . I believe that Meher Baba had not yet recovered from the first intoxication of his exalted mood. . . .' Mr. Brunton ends with a shrewd analysis of Baba's character: 'He shows, on the one hand, all the qualities of a mystic—love, gentleness, religious intuition, and so on, but on the other hand he shows signs of the mental disease of paranoia. . . . He fails to illustrate in himself the high message which he proposes to convey—to others. I realize that I need not deny that many high and sublime sayings have been communicated through the lithe fingers of Meher Baba. . . . Nevertheless, one is compelled to condemn the theatrical methods which he has used. No great religious teacher worthy of the name has ever used them. . . .'

VIII

Though I have not quite succeeded in perceiving the significance of Shri Meher Baba, some people believe in his mission and the power of his saintliness. This book would be incomplete without the portrait of a man who believes himself to be a 'perfect master', and who shows how easy it is to impose an imaginary picture upon others. My

[1] Mr Brunton's form of the word, more commonly spelt 'fakir'

personal contact with Baba may be considered of little importance; yet as an example of the many queer ways and means by which spiritual thirst tries to find satisfaction, Baba himself makes it imperative that he be included in an account which deals with more than one aspect of modern spiritual pursuits. In a world in which there is a Steiner there must also be room for a Shri Meher Baba—for the world of spiritual research contains as many kinds and degrees as any other world.

CHAPTER III

MIRACLE AT THE ALBERT HALL

Principal George Jeffreys

I

Every year early in the spring the same large poster appears in the streets of London. It portrays the head of a youngish man with curly hair, and it invites you to the Albert Hall on Easter Monday to attend three separate meetings: a healing service in the morning, baptism in the afternoon, and holy communion in the evening. The organizers are the Elim Foursquare Revivalists.

I often used to pass these huge posters, and they vaguely suggested to me Negro revivalist services, as I had seen them in Harlem in New York· services full of ecstasy, the remembrance of which always makes me feel uncomfortable. They also suggested Sunday, huge crowds and a popular entertainment. But a religious movement powerful enough for its supporters to hire the Albert Hall year after year eventually excited my curiosity. Most of the spiritual researches with which I had hitherto come into direct contact had rested upon an intellectual basis. They had appealed more particularly to the educated classes, from whom it was reasonable to expect a certain amount of discrimination. The posters in the streets, on the other hand, advertised a movement that seemed organized for people with very little critical faculty. My knowledge of revivalist movements was rather limited, and in 1934 I decided to attend the meetings at the Albert Hall.

I went to buy my ticket a week beforehand. I was anxious to be close enough to the waters of the baptismal tank to hear the splash, and close enough to see clearly the miracles of healing. The obliging young man at the box office informed me that the seats in the stalls were free, and that I could secure any of them by arriving early enough on Easter Monday, or preferably on Sunday night. The seats in the tiers encircling the stalls were sold out with the exception of one or two in the back rows. Even so, I was only half disappointed. I had already been wondering whether the huge posters were just a stunt, and whether I should find myself on Easter Monday in an empty hall. I remembered vividly a meeting at the Albert Hall, advertised some years before with equal publicity. The organizer of the meeting called himself, as far as I remember, the Negro Emperor, and his London meeting was intended to prepare the way for a revolution among the Negroes all over the world. Unfortunately London produced only some two-score Negroes who looked as though they had had no success in Shaftesbury Avenue, and had been lured to the Albert Hall in the hope of meeting some manager who wanted 'local colour' for his next show There were also about a hundred of those middle-aged, nondescript women who are always ready to pay the price of a cinema ticket for the promise of spiritual salvation, and a handful of younger men and women whose clothes and behaviour betrayed their Chelsea origin. The emptiness of the vast hall had contrasted painfully with the vigour of the black speaker. When the young man at the box office assured me once more that no better seats were available, the uncomfortable memory of the sweating black Emperor gave way to a pleasant feeling of anticipation.

II

The meeting was to begin at 10.30, and I arrived at the Albert Hall soon after 10, on a brilliant Easter Monday morning, to find a jumble of taxis, bath-chairs and even ambulances in the street outside. In the crowd there were people on crutches, men and women with deformed limbs or with bandaged heads or eyes, mothers with sick children in their arms.

The long circular passages inside the building were full. Many of the congregation carried little suitcases or parcels. Most people wore their Sunday clothes, and many had arrived with their entire family. They seemed well provided with sandwiches, chocolate and oranges. The crowd in the passages was getting denser, yet there was none of the nervous intolerance so often manifested by continental crowds on such occasions. The prevailing spirit was festive and good-natured, and the crowds took the heat and the pushing laughingly as a part of their holiday pleasure

The hall was already more than half full, and just as I was trying to find my seat, the organ began and the four or five thousand people broke into a hymn. The tune was not at all what you would have expected at a religious service, and as for the words, they ran:

120

MIRACLE AT THE ALBERT HALL

'There never was a sweeter melody,
It's a melody of love.
In my heart there rings a melody.
There rings a melody. . . .'

The hall was filling quickly, and long before 10.30 there was not a seat left. Middle-aged women predominated. The stalls and the rows round the platform were filled with young Foursquare Gospellers. The boys in dark suits and the girls in white dresses wore round their shoulders a striped sash of silk, bearing the words 'Elim Crusader'. The audience consisted mainly of working-class people. Many of them had come from Wales, from Yorkshire, from the Midlands, and much less Cockney was heard than is usual on popular occasions at the Albert Hall. Food, and bottles containing tea or coffee, were stowed under the seats.

Lilies, daffodils and red azaleas formed a decorative frame in front of the platform and the organ. I wondered idly whether the flowers had been chosen haphazard or with a psychological purpose. The choice of white lilies was alone obvious. The yellow daffodils may have been chosen for reasons which would give proof of the subtle knowledge of human nature on the part of the organizers. They created not only a feeling of spring time but suggested, too, the little gardens adjoining so many provincial and suburban houses which at this moment were full of them. The masses of yellow flowers must have created a familiar atmosphere for many in this audience, bringing a feeling of intimacy even into the vast Albert Hall. The vivid red azaleas might have been chosen to create a festive atmosphere, and to stir the emotions. It is more than likely, however, that the flowers had been chosen simply because they were pretty and because they happened to be in season

Men only were sitting on the platform. Some wore clerical collars, and all of them were dressed in dark suits. The hymns were now conducted by a man standing in the front row on the platform. Nearly all the ten thousand people joined in and sang:

'There'll be music at the fountain—
Will you, will you meet me there?
Yes, I'll meet you at the fountain,
At the fountain, bright and fair. . .'

When the leader at the microphone began to sing, with a smiling face,

THE ENGLISH ADVENTURE

'Faithful I'll be to-day,
Glad day, glad day!'

his last few words, carried across by the loudspeakers, were drowned by the joyous response from ten thousand throats,

'And I will freely tell
Why I should love Him so well,
For He is my all to-day.'

I could not foresee that, though the literary quality of the hymns was not always of the highest order, 'He' would indeed be theirs all through this Easter Monday.

III

The man whom ten thousand people from all over the British Isles had come to see and to listen to had mounted the platform quite unobserved. Though my eyes had rarely left the platform I did not see the entry of George Jeffreys, the founder and leader of the Elim Evangelists, and I only discovered later that he had been sitting for some time among his friends in the front row. He was wearing a dark suit as were all the other men around him, and there was no mark to distinguish him from the others. I saw through my opera glasses a strong face with rather a soft mouth, dark curly hair and a fine presence in which there was nothing calculated to play upon the emotions. He possessed none of the characteristics that I had expected to find in the leader of a revivalist movement. Had I not seen Mrs. Aimée McPherson from Los Angeles preaching in this very hall, and equipped with all the tricks of an ingenious stage technique? Smiles, golden curls, searchlights and trumpets crowded my recollections while I watched the group on the platform.

The moment Jeffreys began to speak the impression of impersonality disappeared. He came up to the microphone to say a prayer, and at the sound of his very first words there came into my mind the same thought that I had had some time earlier when I met Kerenski for the first time. The voice of Jeffreys was strong, but not so aggressive as Kerenski's; it was a baritone, and full of the melody which we are accustomed to find in a Welsh voice. Kerenski's voice had the dramatic quality of the typically Russian bass, but it lacked the humanity of the voice at the microphone. I have been told by people who

122

heard Kerenski when he harangued the masses during the Russian revolution that his main asset was the deep ringing sound of his voice. Had his vocal cords been unable to produce this far-reaching sound, the history of Russia might have taken a different course. I did not doubt that the strong and sincere tone of the voice of Jeffreys was responsible for much of the veneration in which his followers held him. There was in it the reassuring note of fatherly advice and the attraction which we are told has its roots in the subconscious re-actions of sex. A George Jeffreys with a high-pitched tenor might never have become known.

After praying, Jeffreys addressed the audience for the first time. He held a sheet of paper in his hands and said: 'We have just received an answer to our telegram to H M. the King I will read it: "George Jeffreys, Albert Hall, Kensington. The King sincerely thanks you for your loyal message on the occasion of the ninth annual meeting of the Elim Foursquare Gospellers. Private Secretary." ' The audience applauded.

When Jeffreys came up to the microphone to say another prayer I began to understand why ten thousand people had come to listen to him. He was not a high priest but simply one of the people. Between them and their God there stood no altar of mystery, there was no priest in sacramental vestments; there was no complicated ceremony. They communicated with God without the help of symbols that had no meaning for many. The man who spoke to God in their name did not address Him in Latin or in the archaic words of a centuries-old Church. God approached in that way did not seem very distant. Jeffreys displayed none of the unctuousness of the average preacher. His prayers were almost colloquial.

In the intervals of praying the platform assumed the character of a committee room Telegrams arrived, were read and others dispatched, letters were opened, messengers sent out. Yet the whole procedure suggested rather a big family gathering than an office.

The hall became silent when Jeffreys stepped forward once again to deliver his sermon or—in the words of his Church—his message. The contents of his message were not new. At times their crude fundamentalism was irritating. So was the somewhat childish emphasis on the necessity of real baptism instead of 'the pagan Catholic sprinkling of children', as Jeffreys called it. But I was struck by the way in which he spoke. There was a quality in his delivery which I

123

can only describe as biblical. The Bible was obviously the source from which he had derived his knowledge and his powers as a speaker. But the main feature of his style was not merely the right adaptation of biblical knowledge: there was in his words a natural persuasiveness which can be derived only from full identification with the Bible. The whole philosophy of Jeffreys was neither emotional nor intellectual—it was just biblical. The man who has identified himself with the spirit of the Gospels speaks as though from another level. His reasoning does not come from his intellect but from a 'higher order of reality', and thus he becomes in a way above argument. It seemed that the Scriptures had become the very life-blood of George Jeffreys.

After his message Jeffreys called people who wished to be baptized. In moments when his emotions were roused he would raise his hands, as though to invoke his listeners. Though the gestures of his hands were not particularly marked, they seemed almost to pull people down from their distant seats high under the roof of the hall Many responded to his ringing voice and to the pleading of his hands. At first one or two voices sounded in the general silence, and in the vast auditorium they were like the voices of children. But they 'broke the ice'. More and more people—five, ten, twenty, fifty—cried out that they wanted to be baptized Jeffreys listened attentively to each one of them, and to each he exclaimed, 'God bless you'. The baptism was to take place in the afternoon.

IV

In the meantime the stalls were cleared in preparation for the healing service. The sick people descended into the stalls from all parts of the hall. They came down slowly one by one, many with the aid of relatives or nurses, others unassisted. Those of them who could kneel, knelt down on the floor; others remained in their seats, and a few in their bath-chairs.

The climax of the morning had arrived. I was feeling excited: I had never seen any miraculous healing before. In none of the spiritual movements which I had investigated had this form of religious activity been practised. I had the scepticism we all have when confronted with something we have never experienced. And yet I had read these words of Martin Luther only a few days before: 'How often has it happened, and still does, that devils have been driven out in the name of Christ; also, by calling on His name and prayer, that the sick have been healed.'

Jeffreys came down from the platform towards the sick, of whom there must have been some four or five hundred. He was followed by one of his helpers bearing a little receptacle containing oil, and by a few women who were there to assist the sick. Jeffreys approached them one after another, anointed their foreheads or merely put his hands on their heads, leant over them and uttered a few words. Though their eyes were shut they did not exhibit any signs of exalta-tion, and many of them had a faint smile on their lips. Others were sitting or kneeling, giving themselves up to the moment with such devotion that they had forgotten even to pray. Their inanimate arms hung down, their hands rested motionless in their laps. Some of them had raised their heads and had opened their hands as though waiting for God's healing power to flow into them. Many remained in the same position after Jeffreys had laid hands on them, but some began to sway to and fro for a while, and had to be helped by the attendant women. A few fell down on the floor as if in a dead faint, sometimes at the very moment Jeffreys touched them—sometimes after he had left them.

While the organ played softly, the vast audience looked down on the stalls. There was none of the morbid curiosity that crowds general manifest when confronted with something outside their usual ex-perience. They were sitting quietly, many of them with tears running down their cheeks; some prayed to themselves with numb lips, others prayed aloud with clasped hands. The atmosphere of faith that per-vaded the hall was beginning to overpower one's critical faculty. After all, Jeffreys would not be the first to give proofs of bodily healing through faith and grace. When I got home I found a passage in John Wesley in which he records a case of his own illness: 'I called on Jesus aloud to increase my faith. . . . While I was speaking my pain vanished away, my fever left me, and my bodily strength returned, and for many weeks I felt neither weariness nor pain.'

The playing of the organ had become so soft that the steps of Jeffreys and his helpers walking from row to row could be heard quite distinctly. Only when someone fell to the floor was there any commotion.

In one of the farthest rows of the stalls there was a woman in a bathchair, with a nurse at her side. I had already noticed the woman once or twice· her whole appearance suggested a class which was rather the exception here. All through the morning she had been sitting motionless in her bathchair, but now I noticed some excitement around her. Supported by her nurse she was half standing in her chair, her face bright red and covered with beads of sweat. She was raising her arms in slow, backward movements, performed with great difficulty, which suggested some odd gymnastic exercise. She exclaimed time after time, loud enough to be heard all round: 'I can move them now, I can move them'. She went on moving her arms in slow circles; and in her face there was such an expression of terrifying excitement that I had to force myself to go on watching it. This expression suggested neither hysteria nor joy, but rather an awfully intense curiosity and surprise.

My head was beginning to ache. It must have been the heat and the novelty of the experience. I left the Albert Hall and went home for lunch.

V

When I came back in the afternoon I found the scene within the building the same as before except that in front of the platform there was a large water tank of green canvas. George Jeffreys was sitting on the platform in a black gown, the organ was playing and hymn after hymn was sung. Jeffreys got up and asked people to testify to their healings in the years gone by, and voice after voice cried back from different corners of the hall, stating its individual case. I spoke to several of these people afterwards. They were workmen, artisans and small tradesmen, and it was difficult to doubt the honesty of their testimony. As I discovered later, hundreds of the most striking cases had been collected in book form, together with the original reports, and photographs of the subjects. In the course of half an hour the following healings of the last nine years were testified to:

33 cripples,
17 people who had been blind in one or both eyes,
77 people who had suffered from tumour, growth or cancer,
40 consumptives.

Some of these could not be prevented from coming down all the way to the platform to state their case. One middle-aged man with a

126

dark moustache climbed up on to the platform, anxious to give an account of some dreadful disease he had been cured of by Jeffreys only a year earlier. He was beaming with self-contentment, and spared no detail of his illness, revelling in the horrors of his previous sufferings with such obvious delight that I almost suspected he was sorry to have been healed. At the end of the gruesome tale he cried out, 'Hallelujah, praise the Lord', and stepped down from the platform with the expression of a tenor who has just acknowledged the applause of an enthusiastic audience after his big aria.

VI

I saw the details of the baptismal service as clearly as I wished, only a few months later at a meeting at the Crystal Palace. The summer meetings there had become as much yearly occasions for the Elim Gospellers as the Easter meeting at the Albert Hall. The vast grounds in front of the Crystal Palace were gay with their red flowers and green lawns. This time there were over twenty thousand people. Inside the huge glass structure there were no ecclesiastical banners, garlands, or carpets to suggest a religious ceremony and to hide the dreariness of the place. The huge glass shell with its exhibition stalls and cases and its cafés looked just as it did during any other of its shows I arrived during the interval between two meetings, and many people were wandering through the halls. It looked just as though some big fair were taking place. The stall in the middle of the main hall, reserved for the exhibits of the various branches of the Elim Movement, was symbolic of the movement itself. It showed that Elim revivalism satisfied other needs of its followers besides the religious. A large part of the stall was reserved for the books by Jeffreys and various of his pastors; next to it the weekly magazine of the movement was on sale; large posters showed the various branches of the Foursquare Gospel Church: one of them said 'Elim Holiday Homes', another 'Elim Bible College', a third 'Crusader and Cadet Movement', a fourth 'Foreign Missionary Branch'. In one part of the stall a gramophone played hymns, and young girls were selling gramophone records of choruses, organ solos, and orchestral music.

The programme for the day was fuller than any programme I had seen at any Congress. The meetings had begun at ten in the morning, and they were going on till nine at night. There were prayer meetings,

127

choir meetings, lectures, healing, baptism, holy communion. At times there were two meetings simultaneously. The refreshment rooms were crowded and on the grass slopes just in front of the building many people were having their meal sitting between their food baskets and bottles just as if they were on holiday at the seaside One would have looked in vain for signs of that irrational disposition which one generally associates with religious revivalism. The whole meeting was extremely 'British' and in the intervals the people clung together in groups as English crowds always do on holiday.

The British character of the whole meeting was as evident in the intervals as it was during the singing. I had arrived this time as the guest of the organizers, and had received a ticket which entitled me to a seat on the platform among the helpers of Principal Jeffreys in a letter which ended with the words: 'With greetings, Yours sincerely in Him.' Before making use of this privilege I preferred to stroll for some time among the people and to attend one or two meetings as an unprivileged member of the big audience. Singing was an outstanding feature of all the meetings, and I do not remember having seen a man or a woman who did not take part in it or who sang only out of habit. Nothing seemed to make them so happy as singing. They sang the glory of God and they no doubt believed every word of their hymns; but they also shouted at the top of their voices, revelling in the physical enjoyment of 'letting themselves go'. This primitive form of self-realization is an important factor in mass movements. An old gentleman with a withered face, snow-white hair and a pair of old-fashioned steel-rimmed spectacles no doubt felt entitled to express himself as loudly as he could, whether he was asked to or not, and each time Jeffreys put, during the delivery of his message, an obviously rhetorical question the old gentleman would shout his reply across hundreds of listeners. 'Who died for us on the Cross?' came the speaker's words from the platform. 'Jesus Christ, our Lord!' was the answer flung back to the platform by the white-haired gentleman. 'What can the Lord do for us? . . .' Jeffreys continued . . . 'Save us' came an answering shout from the shrivelled lips.

For all the obvious enthusiasm of the crowd it seemed surprising that they could stand the strain of a full day of such concentrated religion. Later I asked one of the pastors present about it. 'Meetings like this", he replied, 'are the greatest impulses in the life of these people. They are like an electric current that charges the batteries for months to come. When the batteries have run down a bit, another meeting will charge them. People simply live for months in the memory of these days. They are the greatest joys of their lives. Would not all people be much more religious if they could only find the proper stimulus? It is not religious feeling that they are lacking, but impulses to make their religious motors run. 'Most of these people', the pastor went on, 'will feed on the fare given them to-day when they return to their dreary surroundings in some London slum, to their work in factories, in the black towns of the Midlands. . . . During all those months at work they will have something to look forward to—next Easter at the Albert Hall.'

VII

The event I was awaiting with the greatest eagerness was the baptismal service, and I decided to make use of my special ticket, and to witness the baptisms from the platform. I had been promised a meeting with George Jeffreys, and this would probably be the most suitable meeting ground. The platform for the baptismal ceremony was erected in the bandstand in the middle of the grounds and fronting the Crystal Palace. When I arrived at the bandstand a young man with the innocent pink face of a cherub was playing hymns on a little organ, the sounds of which were amplified by loudspeakers all over the grounds. I was feeling self-conscious when I mounted the steps to the bandstand, and found myself scrutinized by two dozen men, with sunburned faces and clerical collars. Fortunately their curiosity gave way within a few seconds to an attitude of helpfulness, and after a few minutes I felt quite at ease. The cherub at the organ was none other than George Jeffreys' secretary, with whom I had been corresponding for some months.

A small canvas water tank had been erected in the middle of the bandstand. Jeffreys, with five or six young men dressed like himself at his heels, arrived for the service in grey flannel trousers and a cricket shirt. About fifteen or twenty young women in mackintoshes were grouped just outside the bandstand. In front of it were assembled over twenty thousand people. The first two rows were occupied by some sixty men and women who during one of the morning services had expressed their wish to be baptized.

I   129

They looked like a local cricket team that had somehow got mixed up with the members of a ladies' swimming club. The women wore white rubber bathing caps, long white garments and white shoes; the men wore grey or white flannels, cricket shirts and white shoes.

The converts were led one by one into the tank, where Jeffreys and his helpers, standing in the water up to their waists, awaited them. One or two of the white figures shivered when they stepped into the water. Among the first to enter were a number of families. Jeffreys would put one of his hands on their backs and duck them with his other hand. While doing this he would say loudly, 'On the confession of thy faith I baptize thee in the name of the Father and the Son and the Holy Ghost, Amen.' Some of the converts walked out of the tank briskly and smilingly, as though saying 'how jolly'. Most of them were serious, a few let themselves be led out of the tank with their eyes shut tight and their hands folded in prayer. A few collapsed, and had to be carried by the girls in mackintoshes. Most of them shivered, and it was most gratifying to see that the girls in mackintoshes provided them with wraps or overcoats before leading them into the building, where they were presumably warmed and dried.

VIII

After the baptismal service I was at last allowed to meet George Jeffreys. 'I am afraid it was very hard to persuade the Principal to see you,' said one of his helpers coming up to me; 'he never sees anyone unconnected with his work. He does not even receive gentlemen who write for the press. I don't think he will be able to give you more than five minutes."

When I shook hands with Jeffreys I saw for myself that his friend had not exaggerated The man who had such power over the largest masses seemed painfully shy. He was feeling nervous, and he obviously hated himself for having promised to receive me. He looked very tired. His day had been filled up till now with one healing service and two baptismal services, besides sermons, prayers and the constant guidance of over twenty thousand people. Another healing service, one or two other services including holy communion were still to come. Jeffreys looked slightly older than he had seemed from a distance. In the corners of his mouth there was a trace of sadness that reminded me of a similar expression in the mouths of Rudolf Steiner and of Krishnamurti. Was it a result of the inner experiences that precede a spiritual attainment?

I disliked interviewing Jeffreys as much as he disliked being interviewed, and I did not know how to begin. Nor did the surroundings help me much. The vast and bare room was modestly called 'the ambassadors' room', and we sat at a table long enough to accommodate all the foreign Ambassadors and Ministers accredited to the Court of St. James.

After we had eventually exchanged a few preliminary remarks, I began to feel a little less embarrassed and I asked Jeffreys: 'How did it come about that you knew the possibility of divine healing?'

'Through personal experience. I was healed myself as a boy. The impression was terrific.'

'Do you mean the mental or the physical impression?'

'The physical impression. It was like an electric current that struck my head.' The words 'terrific' and 'current' and 'struck' were said with the emphasis that had been so convincing when Jeffreys spoke from the platform.

'Are you quite conscious of what you are doing when you lay your hands on people's heads? Is it you who heal them or do you consider yourself just an instrument?'

Jeffreys looked at me for a second as though surprised at the question, and then he said: 'Of course it is the power of God that only works through me. I claim no powers of any sort. It is the Lord who manifests Himself through me. I am nothing but His work. I can only say with the Master, "I can of mine own self do nothing. . . . I seek not mine own will, but the will of the Father which hath sent me." '

'So you don't think your healing has anything to do with the mind of the sick themselves?'

'The one teacher I believe in is the Lord. I believe in the Gospels from cover to cover and in all the fundamentals of the Christian faith. Intellectual interpretations of individual parts of the Bible are outside me. I accept the Bible in its entirety as the word of God. The sick must have faith, must pray, must hope that they will be healed. But it is not the effect of mind over matter that manifests itself in healing. It is solely and only the power of Christ over disease.'

131

'Is it true that you believe in the second coming of Christ?'

'I do with all my faith, and I see the signs of His second coming. I see them in the last war, in the unrest of the world, in crisis coming after crisis.'

When we shook hands to say good-bye, he was looking much more at his ease than he did before our conversation. After he had gone I was left in the room by myself for a few moments, and I could not help wondering how many educated Englishmen know anything about George Jeffreys, the man who has made thousands of their fellow citizens happy and has restored their faith? I myself knew nothing further about him than that which I had seen with my own eyes. It was only later and through prolonged efforts that I learned more about his life.

IX

George Jeffreys never talked to anyone about himself, outside his work he led the life of a recluse, and was extremely shy in his private life. I began to make friends with people who had come to his meetings for several years, I talked to one or two of his pastors. Each one of them told me a little, but none of them knew more than the most obvious events in the life of the 'Principal' as they all called him. Eventually I asked his secretary to lunch and begged him to talk. In young and enthusiastic people there is no premeditation, and no distortion of fact from motives of propaganda.

My guest had been with Jeffreys for the last six years; he was his secretary, his leading musician and one of the three members of the revivalist party which, headed by Jeffreys himself, conducted the large revivalist campaigns. 'When you are with the Principal you always feel the presence of God', my guest said. 'You feel it in the Principal's modesty, his simplicity, his humility. We four all live together, we travel together. Yet there is always that feeling of divine presence when the Principal is with us. He has probably healed more people than anyone alive; few people in the world get such huge crowds for their meetings as he does; the largest halls in the towns we are visiting are too small to accommodate all the people who want to come and listen to him. People worship him because they feel the divine presence in him; and yet he is as simple as though he were no-one in particular.'

132

MIRACLE AT THE ALBERT HALL

'You have revivalist campaigns only in the British Isles?'

'No—though the Principal is concentrating at present on Great Britain. Yet there is hardly a day without letters arriving from India, South Africa, Canada, America, and from practically every country in Europe, asking the Principal to come. They guarantee his expenses, and they promise a lot of money; but he only listens to God, from whom he gets direction, where to go and what places to visit. The Principal never accepts money as the price of his coming. We went to Switzerland this summer because a friend of the Principal at Bienne had been asking him for many years to come. We spent three weeks in Switzerland. We might have been there twice as many months. We held our meetings in the biggest churches or halls of the chief towns, and they were not only packed, but people stood outside for hours waiting for the Principal to come out after the meeting was over. And often we had three meetings a day. This happened at Bienne, at Geneva, Basle, Berne, Zurich.'

I remember having read in continental papers of the enormous success of the Foursquare Revivalists in Switzerland.

'In which country did Principal Jeffreys begin his movement?'

'In Northern Ireland in 1915. He did not come to England till after the war.'

The family of George Jeffreys lived at Llynvi Valley in Wales. They were religious people, and it had always been the young boy's great ambition to become a clergyman. He was coached for a ministry in the Welsh Congregational Church, but paralysis threatened to cut short both his work and his life. Speaking of those days Jeffreys says: 'My weak state began to manifest itself in facial paralysis down one whole side. . . . I knew that unless a miracle was wrought in me, life was to be very short. When my mouth began to be affected, the one thing that distressed me greatly was the possibility of my not realizing the one call and ambition of my life— the Christian ministry. From the earliest days of childhood there was the consciousness borne within me that I was called to preach the Gospel. When this affliction came it seemed as if the end of all that was worth living for had come—there was no other purpose for me in life if I could not preach.' The doctors predicted that the boy could not live more than a few years.

But he had always believed in bodily healing through faith. The

133

words of the Bible, 'I am the Lord that healeth thee', cast an almost mystical spell over him. Jeffreys considers that the course of his life was changed by a miracle, which happened one Sunday morning. The family were kneeling in prayer in their sitting-room, and the boy offered up a special prayer for health. He had never doubted the truth of God's words with regard to healing, and when I asked Jeffreys what he had prayed for, he answered: 'I reminded God of His promise in Exodus.' Suddenly he felt the shock which he had described to me during our first conversation. 'I can only liken the experience', he stated on another occasion, 'to being charged with electricity. It seemed as if my head were connected to a most powerful electric battery. My whole body from head to foot was quickened.' The face and body were suddenly restored to a normal state. To-day Jeffreys shows no trace of any facial or other ailment.

The wave of strength and joy that flowed through the boy was followed instantly by a feeling of compassion. Great inner joys often produce such a reaction. In Jeffreys the experience was based on deep faith and a clear aim in life. He believed that in the act of healing God revealed Himself to him and showed him the right direction. The healing provided him with a 'witness within to the faithfulness of God's word'. His aim was now to go into the world and to preach the word of God—no longer as an ordinary preacher, but as the teacher whose office had been described in the Gospels by the words: 'They shall lay hands on the sick, and they shall recover', and this passage in St. Mark became henceforth the young man's crucial doctrine.

Once his faith had been proved and his decision made, the establishing of the most suitable external forms became merely a matter of time. The Elim Foursquare revivalism had spiritually come into existence on that Sunday morning at Llynvi Valley in Wales. Jeffreys chose the name of his movement from the Bible. 'It signifies the four-sided aspect of the Gospel of Christ . . . the cardinal truths of the doctrine held by the movement, namely: Jesus the Saviour, Healer, Baptizer and Coming King.' The name Elim, too, was taken from the Bible: 'And they came to Elim, where were twelve wells of water, and threescore and ten palm trees: and they encamped there by the waters.'

In 1915 the new movement had not extended beyond Northern Ireland. Jeffreys did not bring it over to England till after the war.

MIRACLE AT THE ALBERT HALL

At first it consisted merely of revivalist campaigns in different parts of England. Each campaign brought new members. Later on as many as ten thousand people were converted in one town during a single campaign. The growth of the new movement can be gathered from the fact that between 1919 and 1934 Jeffreys had opened about two hundred churches under his own supervision in the British Isles. He has his own theological college; he has ordained over a hundred and fifty ministers for his own churches; and he supports thirteen missionaries in foreign countries. The most important activity of the movement is, however, the series of campaigns in the different towns, where even the largest halls are always filled. Crowds, like those I had seen at the Albert Hall and the Crystal Palace, queued up hours beforehand in order to get into the Queen's Hall and the Alexandra Palace in London, the City Temple in Glasgow, the Royal Dome in Brighton, the Ulster Hall in Belfast, the Usher Hall in Edinburgh, the Bingley Exhibition Hall and the Caird Hall in Dundee. They are the biggest halls in the British Isles, and each has on these occasions proved to be too small, though only a few of the seats were free—most of them costing between one and three shillings each.

'Has Principal Jeffreys got any money of his own?' I further asked my guest. 'Is your movement self-supporting or has it got rich patrons?'

'We are entirely self-supporting, and we have enough money to run our churches and all the movements connected with Elim revivalism. But don't imagine that we are rich. Most of our congregations belong to the poorer classes. The Principal himself hasn't got a penny of his own. He does not even get paid for his strenuous work. Our pastors naturally get their salaries like any other minister in England. The Principal just gets his expenses paid; that's all. As he has no hobbies of any kind, does not smoke or drink, does not travel except on our campaigns, his expenses amount to very little indeed. We three members of his revivalist party don't get any wages either, but the Elim movement pays for our expenses. That's all. I personally should not know what to do with money. None of us would.'

'Does Principal Jeffreys go to the theatre, to concerts? Does he read?'

'Not what you would call "read". He only reads books on religious subjects. Practically only the Bible, which he studies con-

135

stantly. He is not interested in the theatre, art, politics. At least I have never heard him talk about them in the six years that I have been with him. His spiritual mission occupies all his attention, all his thoughts.'

'Doesn't he ever take a rest?'

'Rarely. In most years there are meetings every day. We visit town after town. In the bigger ones we may spend a whole month and there may be several services a day. Nevertheless none of us seems to get tired. After all, we, his three revivalists, also work day after day, often conducting meeting after meeting. Ten or more hours' concentrated work are the rule rather than the exception. We are supposed to have one day a week, Friday, to ourselves. But often there are meetings even on a Friday. And yet people remark how healthy we all look.' Indeed, my guest looked as though he had just returned from a holiday. Yet actually he was in the midst of a large campaign in the London suburbs, that would take three weeks, and there were meetings every night. He had to play the organ and the piano, to sing, to conduct some of the services. I remembered that the other helpers of Jeffreys whom I had met at the Crystal Palace had looked equally healthy. 'I suppose it is the joy of our work', my guest went on, 'that keeps us so well. It is a constant invigoration. Once a year we force the Principal to take a rest. On such occasions, which last several days, he likes going slowly through the countryside by car. He likes nothing better than motoring in leisurely fashion through England.'

'How is it that your music during the services is so gay? Who writes it and who writes your hymns?'

My guest blushed. 'We use certain old hymns, but most are written by our own pastors Some of the music I have written myself. Somebody has to. . . . Parts of our music are taken from tunes of the moment. We believe in letting people sing music that is in their ears and has a nice familiar sound. We don't go in of course for any wild jazzy stuff, but anything pleasant that happens to be in the air might be adopted for a hymn. After all, there is no reason why God should prefer gloomy or solemn tunes to jolly ones.'

My guest drank no wine at lunch and after the meal he did not smoke. 'Doesn't your movement allow drinking or smoking?'

'We have no definite rules. We ourselves do not drink or smoke, but if any members of the Elim Church want to do either they may.

MIRACLE AT THE ALBERT HALL

The Principal, though such a strict follower of the Bible, does not believe in compulsion. You may have noticed how easygoing he is even during the services. We believe that the Lord can be present among us no matter what rules we have and how we dress up. Like the ministers in the old Scottish Church, our pastors wear no special vestments at church, and only rarely a clerical collar. The Principal himself is hardly conscious of such things as clothes and outward ceremonies. The word of the Lord is the one thing he is conscious of. Constantly. You have probably noticed that he came for the baptismal service in a black gown. He is supposed to wear it in the water all through the service. But almost every time the same thing happens. He suddenly remembers that the gown hinders him in the water. and so he discards it, and walks into the tank in grey flannels and shirt. Some people would probably say that an important service should be treated with greater reverence. But for the Principal the thing that matters is the power of the baptism and of Christ's words.'

X

I remembered this informality in Jeffreys and thought how strongly it contrasted with his seriousness of speech which had proved particularly striking at the Crystal Palace after my interview with him. Later in the afternoon I had gone to attend the healing service. Though I had seen one at the Albert Hall, I wanted to watch Jeffreys more closely this time, to see whether he used a special formula when he laid hands on the sick. By the movements of his hands it might be possible to discern whether it was conscious healing or whether he really was just an 'instrument'.

The healing service took place in a hall which must have held some two or three thousand people. Jeffreys was walking from row to row of several hundred people who were sitting or kneeling in the front of the hall, waiting for his approach. Though he was as concentrated as ever, he would often laugh aloud when exclaiming 'Hallelujah'. This time I was standing quite close to the sufferers, and I could see Jeffreys very clearly when he put his hands on their heads. I doubted no longer that he had no deeper knowledge of his own performance, and that he was merely a 'medium'. I could hear every word he said, and he never repeated the same words twice running, though some of them occurred with greater frequency

137

than others. His most frequent invocations were: 'Pray to the Lord' or just 'Glory' or 'In the name of the Lord'. But he also spoke to the sick when stooping down to them: 'You are shut in with God', or 'Concentrate on Jesus Christ', or 'The power of God is within us', or 'The power of God is here to heal'.

People collapsed more often than at the Albert Hall, the moment the hand of the healer had touched their head. I spoke to several of them, and this is what one of them told me: 'The moment the Principal had approached me and had laid hands upon me, I was struck by such a powerful shock that though I was perfectly conscious I could not help falling down as if dead.' I had watched them from quite close and with the greatest attention, and I had noticed that they had indeed fallen, like felled trees, as though their bodies had lost all strength. They remained stiff and motionless on the floor for many minutes. I might have known even without asking that it could not have been a fit of faintness. I had observed for myself that when they were able to get up, they did not seem at all giddy; there was none of that slow return to reality, accompanied by the usual question, 'Where am I?' The moment the people here had opened their eyes, they got up with a smile or even a grin on their faces, they seemed perfectly conscious of their surroundings. In most cases they exclaimed 'Hallelujah' or 'Glory'. And yet two or three men had remained on the floor in the stiff attitude of a corpse for over ten minutes.

One could not judge how real or how lasting the effect of the healings was. Yet for most of the people concerned these moments were the highest of their lives. It was all very well to criticize the primitiveness of this religion—its crudeness, its lack of discrimination—and to feel superior to people who believed in miracles; but in reality it mattered little whether the basis of the healings was the power of the healer, the faith or even the hysteria of the followers. We are—as yet—unable to offer clear rational explanations for miraculous healings—a purely intellectual criticism cannot therefore do them justice. The words of St. John came to my mind: 'And a great multitude followed him, because they saw his miracles which he did on them that were diseased.' The decisive factor, in an estimation of Jeffreys, seemed to me the support of thousands of people who had found proofs of their faith through him, and that those who had knelt down on the floor with frightened and anxious

138

faces, full of expectation, had got up and walked out with faces that radiated joy.

When the healing ceremony was over George Jeffreys stepped into the middle of the hall and began to sing a hymn. The congregation was sitting and standing about him, and now he was literally a member of it. He was singing very quietly and very slowly and the assembled people took up the song with equal softness. After each verse Jeffreys stopped to say a few words, addressed directly to the people around him: 'Do you all feel now the presence of our Lord? Do you feel how He is now with us, here in this very hall?' His voice sounded even more earnest than before. He seemed deeply conscious of what he was saying He went on with the hymn and stopped again after the next verse. Now he spoke to the people in the remoter corners of the hall. 'Don't try to come more forward. The Lord is in your corner of the hall as much as in mine. He is with us everywhere. He is in each one of us Shut your eyes Concentrate on the Lord. Open yourself so that He may enter into you.' He went on singing and the people sang with him. The man at the piano on the platform forgot to play: he was sitting on his stool with his eyes shut, quietly singing the hymn. Jeffreys stopped again: 'Do you feel how wonderful the presence of the Lord is? Do you now feel the joy, O the happiness of having the Lord with us? O Jesus Christ our Lord, we thank Thee for Thy presence and for Thy help, and we rejoice in it with all our hearts. In the name of Jesus Christ our Lord.'

The people who an hour or two ago had been scrambling to get tea, who had been making jokes during their picnic, were standing with closed eyes, with faces that were happy but tense.

It seemed as though the presence of God really filled the hall. And there was nothing miraculous in it. The people who were assembled round their leader had always known that God is everywhere and in everyone, but it had been a problem for them how to find Him. It had been difficult for them to hear His voice, to become conscious of Him. What Jeffreys did was to compress their consciousness of God, to vitalize it, to force it into a concentration that was more powerful than any state they were able to achieve by themselves. Jeffreys forced their God to emerge from the shadows of their longings, and to manifest Himself in their conscious feelings. He made Him their living God. And after he had revealed Him to them the two or three thousand people had probably felt Him in the glowing stream of joy that ran through them, and that made them much more alive, much richer. The faces of these people suggested that they were living at this moment with God and in God. The one great miracle of all religions seemed to have happened: God had descended into man and had become a part of his consciousness.

CHAPTER IV

THE MAN WHOSE GOD IS A MILLIONAIRE

Dr. Frank Buchman

I

We were supposed to meet at luncheon. I was very much looking forward to a conversation with the man who had succeeded in winning over so many English people to an American revivalism and who seemed to wipe out racial, religious and social differences wherever he went.

Dr. Buchman was sitting not far from our table, lunching with two elderly ladies. He was short, stoutish and benevolent-looking, with a smile on his thin but firm lips and with a pair of extremely bright, keen eyes that were always watching something from behind gold-rimmed spectacles. The only thing he did not suggest was religion. He might have been a bank manager or a successful American impresario. This discrepancy between his looks and his vocation only increased my desire to meet him.

No hosts could have been more charming or more obliging than the six or seven leading Buchmanites who put me at my ease immediately and treated me as an old acquaintance. There were a Scotsman, a South African, an Englishman and three Americans among them; one of them was an engineer, one a university lecturer and one a clergyman. They were a cheerful lot and rather more affectionate with one another than is usual among British or American men. They called one another by their Christian names, and referred to Dr. Buchman as Frank. There was something boyish and rather engaging about them, and it was only towards the end of luncheon, when I began to put inquisitive questions, that they became more reserved. But no-one cares to be cross-examined by a stranger, and intellectual conversation is, I suppose, rather out of place at luncheon.

I had attended a meeting of the Buchmanites the evening before, and another that very morning. I had seen hundreds of enthusiastic people fill the huge reception hall of the Hotel Metropole in London and enjoy wholeheartedly their latest religious experience, so I was no longer quite ignorant of what the new movement stood for.

141

THE ENGLISH ADVENTURE

Before we finished luncheon one member of our party crossed over to Dr. Buchman's table and conversed with him for a minute or two. I imagined that Dr. Buchman was to join us after lunch, but he passed our table and, giving me first a somewhat inquisitive look and then a kind smile, walked on. Afterwards I saw him in the lounge having coffee with a lady whom I recognized as the wife of a well-known peer.

I do not remember what excuse was given to me, but unfortunately I did not meet Dr. Buchman, and I was promised my talk another time.

II

Dr. Frank Buchman claims to be the descendant of a certain Bibliander who was the successor of Zwingli in the chair of Theology at Zurich. He was born in 1878 at Pennsburg, Pennsylvania, took his degree at Muhlenberg College, and became Lutheran minister at a church in Philadelphia. He started later a settlement house for poor boys, but had to leave it after some differences with the trustees. During a visit to England in 1908 he had a 'vision of the Cross', which determined the whole of his future career. It did not take place at Oxford, as most people believe, but at Keswick. 'He wandered one day', related Mr. J. M. Roots in his *An Apostle to Youth*, 'into a little country church where a woman was speaking on some aspect of the cross. He does not know her name, but something in what she said stirred him to the depths, and he saw himself for what he truly was ... for the first time in his life he felt the power of Christ as an inward reality.'

Soon after that incident Dr. Buchman believed he had discovered within himself a new power. One evening during a visit at Cambridge while walking with an undergraduate he found he had 'changed the life' of his young friend. This episode may well have given him the first glimpse of his future mission.

For the next few years he was the secretary of the Y.M.C.A. at an American State College, and it was during that period that he began to evolve the principles of the Oxford Group Movement, or, as he sometimes called it, 'A First Century Christian Fellowship'. In the words of the American author, Alva Johnston, he then 'perfected himself in the great art of extracting confessions from adolescents'. In 1916 he became extension lecturer at an American Seminary, and from 1917 till 1919 he stayed in the Far East. In 1921 he went to

142

THE MAN WHOSE GOD IS A MILLIONAIRE

Cambridge and, in fulfilment of the request of two friends in China, visited their undergraduate sons. Three undergraduates whose lives he 'changed' went with him on his first crusade to Oxford. In rooms at Christ Church he spoke of the lives he had changed from 'selfishness and lust to purity and service'. In August of the same year the first European 'house-party' took place at Cambridge.

Thenceforward the movement grew rapidly both within and without the Universities. 'Houseparty' succeeded 'houseparty' and the name of Dr. Buchman became renowned.

He chose the English Universities for his movement because, in the words of his followers, 'they are the most neglected and ill-handled field of spiritual endeavour'. Though the University authorities hardly encouraged the new movement, it grew steadily under Buchman's most efficient leadership. In organizing his movement he proved to be almost a genius. He had a shrewd notion both of publicity methods and of English psychology. He was tactful, quiet, discreet, industrious and never lacking in new ideas. He was clever enough to keep in the background without, however, allowing the reins to pass from his own into other hands. His financial talent enabled him to put his movement on the sort of basis of which other movements have dreamt for years in vain. Dr. Buchman countenanced the luxurious mode of living among the groups, though this was held by many to be incompatible with a movement which claimed to be purely spiritual. Buchman did not share that opinion, and when asked one day why the groupers always stayed at such 'posh' hotels only answered: 'Why shouldn't we stay in posh hotels? Isn't God a millionaire?'

In his quiet manner he approached everywhere the right sort of people whose names, means or connections were of use to his movement. This method was extended to the right choice of undergraduates, and, according to Alva Johnston, 'even in the College the Buchmanites concentrate on apple-cheeked boys of wealth and family. . . . But it is a sound principle that has caused the Buchmanites to show less concern for the shaggy oafs than for presentable youngsters with influence in the college communities'.

In 1926 Buchman entertained Queen Marie of Rumania in a house owned by John D. Rockefeller, jr., in New York. He knew, no doubt, that certain women love being scolded by men, especially if they are not dependent upon them, for when the Queen asked him what her main sins were, Buchman answered with a tactful smile:

'Pride and self-satisfaction.' The Queen was most impressed by his shrewd observation, and allowed him to hang yet another royal scalp round his waist—the scalps of ex-King George of Greece and King Prajadhipok of Siam were hanging there already. Buchman realized that it paid to satisfy the snobbishness of his followers even in their religious pursuits. The list of his titled patrons and followers was bound to impress the average sinner who found himself all of a sudden by virtue of his new religion sharing sins side by side with bishops, members of the Upper House, and foreign women of title.

On the other hand certain serious-minded people who failed to see the necessity of marrying religion to society were shocked. Their opinions were summarized in a letter from the Bishop of Durham to *The Times*, published in 1933. The Bishop stated that many people had written to him about Buchmanism, expressing 'disgust at the toadying to rich and prominent individuals, at the unscrupulous and even unwarranted use made of well-known names'. This, however, could not deter Dr. Buchman from unswervingly following his own road, and helping his movement to grow in what Mr. Ken Twitchell, his charming American right-hand man, called in a conversation with me 'geometrical and no longer arithmetical proportions'.

'Houseparties' and campaigns in foreign countries were the main channels through which Buchmanism sought to conquer the world. 'Houseparties', one of those inventions of Dr. Buchman in which society and religion can be blended together, are large semi-religious gatherings, 'guests are treated as guests . . . gloom is conspicuous by its absence, and there is more laughter . . . than at many ordinary social gatherings'. 'Groups are held in the living-room, and people are free to go or not as they choose. Informality is the order of the day. . . . The object of the houseparty is frankly to relate modern individuals to Jesus Christ. . . . Bible study usually takes up an important part of each day. Separate groups for men and women . . . provide an opportunity for discussion of various problems connected with sex or money . . .' (J. M. Roots). Besides a big yearly houseparty in the summer at Oxford, there were others in various parts of Great Britain, in the United States, South Africa, Canada and in most continental countries. 'Houseparties' took place in University colleges rented for that'purpose, in big hotels at popular spas, and even in the private country houses of rich members. Games, motor drives and dinner parties formed an important part of these

gatherings. Miss Marjorie Harrison, a serious student of Buchmanism, sums up these houseparties amusingly, though somewhat
bitingly, in her entertaining book *Saints Run Mad*: 'When they are
not eating,' she says, 'they are meeting, and when they are not
meeting they are confessing their sins. . . .'

To-day there must be Buchman groups in some fifty countries,
and the number of 'changed lives' must go into many thousands.
When I asked Mr. Ken Twitchell about the approximate size and
growth of Buchmanism, he only gave me a faint smile and made
a nonchalant gesture with one hand, as though saying that the
movement was beyond counting the number of its converts. There
are Anglican bishops, American millionaires, Scandinavian mag-
nates, colonial dignitaries, sport celebrities, elderly hostesses, movie
stars, Christians, Jews, Mohammedans in the Oxford group, which
is probably one of the largest modern religious movements. In real
influence or popularity it cannot be compared with the Salvation
Army or the Y.M.C.A., but its methods of self-advertising are
much more effective, and the names of some of its members render
it much better 'news' in the press.

There are few living men of whom I heard more praise or more
criticism than of Dr. Buchman, and I was really anxious to meet him
personally. His young friends kept promising that I should see him
'as soon as Frank has finished the present house-party'. But as these
parties seemed to be following one after another, no meeting could
be arranged, and the cheerful young men comforted me meanwhile
with their latest publications and with impressive stories of recent
conversions, described in their phraseology as 'changed lives'. In the
summer of 1934 they even asked me to join them on their Scandinavian campaign in the autumn, during which I should be able
to study those aspects of their movement that might have escaped
my attention in England, and I was genuinely sorry that lack of time
prevented me from joining them.

III

'The Oxford group has no membership list, subscriptions, rules.
It is a name for a group of people who . . . have surrendered their
lives to God and who are endeavouring to lead a spiritual quality of
life under the guidance of the Holy Spirit.' The main methods by
which the groupers believe that we can achieve such a life are:

'1. The sharing of our sins and temptations with another Christian life given to God, and to help others, still unchanged, to recognize and acknowledge their sins.

'2. Surrender of our life, past, present and future, into God's keeping and direction.

'3. Restitution to all whom we have wronged directly or indirectly.

'4. Listening to, accepting, relying on God's guidance.'

IV

There are various principles in Buchmanism which are valuable and for the rediscovery of which Dr. Buchman deserves gratitude. On the other hand much will have to be changed before those friendly sections of the public, who agree with its most important principles but find it impossible to subscribe to certain distortions of an otherwise sound doctrine, will accept Buchmanism. Paradoxically enough, movements that pride themselves on their rapid growth are apt to forget that in reality their following is much smaller than it might be. A cheerful, simple and unintellectual revivalism such as Buchmanism should appeal not merely to twenty or thirty thousand British people but to a hundred times as many.

Unfortunately the groups believe that they must cut themselves off from all criticism and they forget that not all criticism is antagonistic. This superiority or fear suggests an inner weakness. It seems that even within the movement criticism is not tolerated. Miss Harrison, who knows the groups intimately, states that 'Criticism from outside is combated not by a defence—for criticism is desperately feared—within the group criticism is absolutely forbidden.' If this is true, then the groups almost deliberately cut themselves off from the thinking section of their sympathetic observers.

One of the first things that alienate many friends of Buchmanism is its assumption that there is only one road to truth, happiness and Christian life, and that this is the one prescribed by Dr. Buchman. 'Truth is not the exclusive possession of any group or society', says Mr. R. H. S. Crossman, one of the most serious students of Buchmanism.[1] 'The chief accusation levelled against the critic of the groups is spiritual pride, but is exclusiveness so very different a sin?' he asks, not without justification. Time and again former sinners

[1] *Oxford and the Groups.*

have found their way to God, without feeling the urge to confess their sins in public, without trying to convert others, without pretending that their most trivial decisions have been dictated directly by God.

V

Let us examine some of the principles of Buchmanism.

Strangely enough, sin is its entire basis. It has even led to a somewhat schoolboyish explanation of the word 'sin'. We are told that 'in the "I" in the word sin lies the secret of sin's power. The I or the ego is more important to sinners than spiritual health . . . If we can surrender that I to God, sin goes with it; when we live without that I in our lives we are without sin.' Such a formula probably helps people along who like being guided by a cheap symbolism, or by a knowledge gained through tempting slogans.

Though the 'I' in sin is considered by the groups as man's greatest enemy, in practice it plays the predominant part in Buchmanism. All the confessions of the groupers are built round the former wickedness and the present salvation of the I. Every confession can be reduced to the formula: 'Formerly I did that, and then I did something else, and eventually I surrendered, and now I do only this.'

Should a religious revival ever be based on the idea of sin? Constant preoccupation with certain ideas makes them real to us. The majority of serious teachers tell us that one way of eliminating the evil within us is by neglecting it and by concentrating instead on what is good. When in certain parts of Burma a man approaches his hour of death, people assemble in his room and remind him one by one of all the good deeds he has ever performed. Should not modern revivalism be based on a similar attitude?

VI

'Surrender', or the conversion of a sinner, is the first commandment of Buchmanism. In the terminology of the groups, 'Surrender to God is our actual passing from a life of sin to a life God-guided and Christ-conscious . . . it is the giving up of our old ineffective spiritual lives and taking on of a life of spiritual activity in everything we think, do or say. . . .'

The groups are right in demanding that we should listen more to God and less to ourselves, and they deserve our grateful acknowledgement for having brought home that truth to thousands of people. On the other hand, have not millions of people surrendered their lives to God even before the coming of Buchmanism?

There are various anomalies in the movement which weaken the principle of surrender. Thus we are asked to effect our surrender through the hands of young boys and girls whose knowledge of life is practically nil. We are expected to surrender in all the glare of a public ceremony. A hilarious public performance is surely not the perfect background for such a mysterious act as man's surrender to God. Surveying surrender as practised by the groups, Mr. Crossman notices 'the appalling danger of giving such specialized pastoral work to young people of no experience', and 'the risk of the release, when achieved, being of short duration'. 'In their recent American tour,' he continues, 'the groups on at least three occasions . . . found the work of conversion far harder in towns where they had previously worked: still more significantly at Louisville, where two years previously hundreds had made their surrender, they had found only eleven who had remained in any sense active members ' Miss Harrison thinks that 'it is a healthy sign that so many of the Buchman converts fall away quickly'. It seems sad that it should be so, though it must be admitted that through 'the irresistible temptation to collect conversions, and to magnify past sins for the sake of the effect they create . . . truth is bound to be sacrificed to effect.'[1]

VII

Most important after surrender is sharing, the 'telling of, or talking over, our sins with another whose life has already been surrendered'. Sharing, which plays the paramount role in Buchmanism, offers us the main key to its understanding

Sharing of sins is certainly very helpful to some people. By adopting and systematizing the practice of confession, the Roman Catholic Church has dealt more effectively than any other religious body with that problem, and the discussion of such personal matters as 'sin' forms an important part of the educational system of various esoteric schools. But this is done after the most careful preparation and in the most restrained language. Both in the Roman Catholic

[1] *Oxford and the Groups.*

THE MAN WHOSE GOD IS A MILLIONAIRE

Church and in esoteric schools confession is always treated with the utmost discretion and discrimination.

My first experiences of sharing as practised by the Buchmanites surprised me greatly. I was sitting in the packed hall of the Hotel Metropole, asking myself constantly whether I hadn't come to the wrong place. The flavour of the whole performance was one of amateur theatricals, and other serious-minded people with whom I discussed my experience told me that they had carried away exactly the same impression. There were one or two hesitant and genuine confessions—but on account of their triviality even they failed to be impressive. What was one to say when a girl of about seventeen got up and confessed that she had 'made a broad survey of religion', had realized that no religion 'was any good', and that Buchmanism was the only true faith that could give 'spiritual happiness' . . . and when a thousand grown-up people clapped their approval? Most of the confessions had all the signs of a carefully prepared performance. Though the production was clever, the utter lack of reverence made it singularly ineffective. Jokes were made with the regularity of those in a vaudeville theatre.

My original suspicion proved justified when I went to other meetings and discovered that the same young men and women confessed the same sins, repeating the same jokes, forcing the same laughter and the same interruptions from a *claque* distributed cleverly in the hall. But that was not all. The young men and women who were supposed to have adopted a 'Christlike quality' of life—absolute honesty and truthfulness—were often not honest. There were distinct variations in the same confessions made by the same people. Those variations were so small that the inexperienced listener would hardly have discovered them. In one instance, the sum involved in a particular confession was £5, next time it became £10; likewise the character or extent of certain confessed sins such as minor frauds, lies, motoring offences, was rarely exactly the same at different meetings.

There was no doubt about it—either the whole confession was an invention, or an original little misdeed was twisted round, exaggerated and treated with little respect for truth. And yet those confessions were supposed to be the genuine and spontaneous expressions of a sinner who had at last recognized God and felt bound to share the joy of a newfound happiness with others.

There were, of course, confessions that appeared to be honest. They mostly dealt with such trivial matters or were expressed in

149

such a way that it was impossible to take them seriously. A few examples may suffice.

1. 'Sharing' in rooms at one of the Universities. A youth of about twenty, with a very serious expression on his face, got up and confessed· 'My trouble was the weather.' Long pause. 'Formerly I used to be worried by the weather, wondering whether it would rain or not. I used to go constantly to the window, looking at the sky. Since I have surrendered, and listen-in to God every morning, I no longer worry about the weather.' He sat down, and remained serious for the rest of the meeting.

2. Another undergraduate: 'My sin was self-abuse. Formerly I always had a bad conscience, because when I indulged in self-abuse I accompanied it by wicked thoughts Since my surrender I no longer need to have these thoughts.' No-one blushed; no-one even smiled.

3. A young girl confessed a trivial sin which she overcame by what she modestly explained as, 'I put Christ to the test, and Christ gave the victory.'

4. During a visit to New York the story of the following instance of 'sharing' was making the round. A famous young hostess and her butler had been 'changed' and became ardent Buchmanites. During one of the largest group meetings in New York the lady got up to confess intimate details of her matrimonial life and her differences with her husband. After her the butler got up, confessing former sinful thoughts about his mistress, speaking of his former spying upon her and elaborating matrimonial details previously divulged by the lady. The lady was the mother of several children who were at school, and her husband, as yet 'unchanged', occupied an important and most respectable position in New York.

Nothing upset me so much as the hilarity that accompanied most of the confessions. Dr. Buchman always instructs converts preparing for their first public confessions in the way they should speak, and he then stresses the paramount importance of being hilarious. At first I refused to believe this to be true, but later these instructions were confirmed by his own fellow workers and published by Miss Harrison in her book. Once you comprehended that schoolboyish lightheartedness, naïveté and goodfellowship were responsible for much of the success of Buchmanism, you perceived why hilarity was indispensable.

Hilarity was no doubt a natural expression of Dr. Buchman's own character; but his followers exaggerated it in the same way in which they exaggerate when they speak of his character. They use such phrases as 'Merriment bursts through the shaving soap', 'Astir with the birds', 'Crows with joy'. Mr. A. J. Russell, author of *For Sinners Only*, and the leading historian of the movement, says of Buchman that 'whatever he does he feels is right'. After such a statement one feels inclined to agree with the *New Yorker*, that brilliant American periodical, which says: 'The picture of radiant, soapy and laughing Buchman is, of course, elaborated in order to offset the suspicion that there is something unhealthy and lugubrious about the movement.'

Dr. Buchman's friends constantly speak of those 'bouncing' and even 'crackling' qualities of 'Frank', and thus simply force us to look out for these features in their leader. His praises are sung and printed in all the books of the movement. 'The extent of his (Buchman's) tireless devotion to work for Christ', we are told by the author of *What is the Oxford Group?* 'will never be fully reckoned by any man.' One can only hope that such exaggeration will not induce Dr. Buchman to forget that thousands of men before him have suffered, sacrificed themselves and died in the service of Christ.

But let us go back to 'sharing'. The usual procedure of a 'sharing' meeting is described most amusingly by Alva Johnston. 'The washing out,' he says, 'to use the Buchmanites' technical term of confession, starts on a seemingly accidental note with mild or slapstick confessions; talking back to a traffic cop, overspending the weekly allowance. . . . The confessing is then stepped up a little, to the smuggling through the customs of ear-rings in a jar of cold cream. . . . At about this time a *claqueur* breaks down, pleads guilty to an error in a parked car and tells how buoyant he feels because he has confessed it. If the ice is well broken some lad may now turn State's evidence against a governess or upstairs maid. . . . If the party grows warm, it may seem almost discourteous to the hosts not to contribute a few scarlet reminiscences. . . . The backward ones are exhorted to brace up, be men, play the game, and pull their weight in the boat by furnishing the company with their fair share of purple memoirs.'

I could never make myself leave a sharing meeting without feeling ashamed that one of the holiest things should have become the subject of playacting.

'Many persons, of whom I must admit that I am one,' says Dr. L. P. Jacks, the author of an important paper on Buchmanism, 'have a strong feeling which is probably instinctive that our sins,

whether great or small, are not a proper subject for publicity. . . .
It is a sense of decency. . . . There is something in many of us that
shrinks from spiritual nudism.'

VIII

This brings us to the very important subject of silence. Dr. Buchman's oldest fellow worker, Mr. Loudon Hamilton, expresses the
demands of his movement in the following words: 'We must learn
the secret of living and working together. We must be willing to
share not only our time, our homes, our money, but to take down
the mask and reveal our moral and spiritual struggles.'

Buchmanites are never left to themselves, never work by themselves, are supposed never to keep anything to themselves.

Can it possibly be the aim of a religion to destroy all privacy, so
essential for serious work, for real thought? Is it not one of the distinctions between man and animal that the latter prefers living in
families or herds whilst man likes to withdraw into himself every
now and again, to listen to the voices of what Dean Inge expressively
calls 'higher reality'? The social ideals of the Buchmanites seem to be
beehives and ants' nests

Silence is an important element in all religions. Not only does
natural modesty and shyness make us keep a great many things to
ourselves, but there is also that inborn fear of speaking before
thought and feeling have taken final shape. Eliphas Levi, the
French occultist, says in his *Le Grand Secret*: 'Silence is one of the
great laws of occultism', and 'To come to the realization of the
deepest secret we must . . . keep silence with determination.'

The silence of the mystics of the Scriptures, of Buddha is the
very opposite of the endless flood of words which accompany sharing, confessing and changing other people's lives.

The only form of silence advocated by Buchmanism is that
obtained during 'guidance'. This is 'direct communication from
God', and 'the Holy Spirit taking a normal intelligence and directing
it in the fullest harmony with His will for the good of the individual
and of his neighbours'.

The Gospel of God's direct guidance is accepted by most religions.
It is closely connected with the idea of submission under God's will,
called by the Buchmanites 'surrender'. 'Each morning', we are told,
'opens with a time of quiet, during which thought is directed towards

God in full conviction that . . . He can make known His will.' To achieve this the groupers sit and 'listen in' to God with a pad and pencil ready to write down His instructions.

All through human history man has tried to get into touch with God. We know from the Bible what effect God's voice had upon Moses, and we know how Jesus Christ prepared himself before he went to speak to God and hear His voice. As far as we know, only a limited number of men in possession of higher knowledge, mystics and saints, can claim to have been constantly or at will in direct communication with God.

The practice of 'quiet' is very sound, and one wishes that more people would adopt the habit of spending a certain time each day in absolute quietness. Where, however, the groups err is in their mistaken belief that such 'quiet time' establishes a direct contact with God. God has given us our mind and our will so that we may use them in daily life and make our decisions according to their commands. To sacrifice our mind and our will in order to let God decide whether we should have another piece of cake or put on the new green tie strikes ordinary people as blasphemous. This is, however, the way Buchmanites treat guidance. Not even the most trivial decision is taken without asking God for guidance. We are told (in *For Sinners Only*) that Dr. Buchman 'asks guidance for expenditure on postage'. When Dr. Buchman enquired at a big hotel in Canada about rooms for a houseparty and was informed that the price would be 12 dollars a day per head, he answered that 'God had told' him to pay no more than 3.50 a day. We are told by Miss Harrison that at a houseparty which she attended the members were instructed to 'ask God's guidance as to the amount' they 'should tip the hotel servants'.

The whole subject of group guidance was most admirably summed up in the following sentence in a leading article in *The Times*: 'Most of what is put forward as guidance received in these periods of relaxed attention is so trivial that it would be impious to ascribe it to the promptings of God.'

IX

It is not difficult to find the reasons for Dr. Buchman's success, especially in Great Britain. Public confession is not new in British religious life. Emotional, self-contented people delight in confessing their sins. Public confession is a form of exhibitionism common among people with little self-control. Many British people love to hear someone at a Salvation Army meeting confessing former drunkenness and debauchery. They love to hear from the Park orator of his religious, political or moral faith; they love the confession of a former agnostic at a revivalist meeting who now spends his days singing hymns and praising the Lord. There are many people who love speaking of their former wickedness and present holiness in front of elegantly dressed ladies and gentlemen.

Intellectual simplicity is another reason for the success of Buchmanism. Most people do not like religion to be complicated. The simple, hearty character of Buchmanism appeals to the rugger player, the hardened business man, the more 'sporting' kind of clergyman. To be able to combine religion with slapping one's neighbours on the back, telling them stories—even though under the guise of public confession—and getting into direct communication with God without racking one's brains must be very tempting to most sinners.

Dr. Buchman showed great tactical talent when he decided to remain within the Church. Many a priest has been worried in the years following the war about the dwindling attendance of young people at church In Buchmanism the clergy are confronted with a movement that by its heartiness, playacting and emotionalism makes religion attractive to many young people. It is not at all surprising that several Anglican bishops have joined the ranks of Dr. Buchman, and that many English clergymen see in him a powerful supporter, to whose doctrine they subscribe willingly.

This rather uncritical support on the part of some clerics may be one among the reasons for the groups' unwillingness to accept any criticism, and for their belief that they are above it. Why was I never allowed to make a definite appointment with Dr. Buchman? I was still in touch with some of his assistants who must have known that my sympathy with their movement was not uncritical. They continued to assure me that a meeting would be arranged without further delay, but a pressing question was generally met with such answers as 'Frank has just gone off to Switzerland', or 'Frank is taking a cure at Baden-Baden', or 'Frank has only just come back from a houseparty in Norway'. I began to suspect that 'Frank' was not only busy visiting and arranging houseparties and journeying all over Europe, but that he was avoiding me. When, however, the obliging young men assured me that I would see him before Christmas I thought I was being unfair to him, and I continued to look forward to the pleasure of a conversation with 'Frank'.

X

The groups assert that their methods can solve most problems of modern life. One of them is sex, and the groups boast of many sex cases, especially in England, in which their method was more successful than any other. Young men, particularly undergraduates, testify over and over again that Buchmanism has solved this problem for them. It is never stated quite clearly in what way this has been achieved, and we can only go by the statements made by the official representatives of the movement. 'The sex instinct', we read in Mr. Roots' pamphlet, 'is at bottom a God-given one; and while the groups do not condone any perversion of thought or word or deed, they know that the real problem is not one of suppression but one of control and sublimation. . . . The cure lies ultimately not in mere human force of will, but in the cleansing stream of spiritual life that follows upon a genuine conversion.'

No-one could argue that the sex problem is fundamentally a spiritual one, or that it can be solved spiritually. On the other hand it is doubtful whether the 'cleansing stream that follows upon a genuine conversion' has really the power to eliminate all the sexual difficulties of youth once and for all.

We can understand the attitude of the Buchmanites towards sex only in its connection with the corresponding attitude of the Englishman at large. Sex is not as important a problem in the life of an Englishman as it is in the life of most foreigners, and sublimation of sex thus comes more easily to him. Suppression of sex through sport and other methods taught by English education and the conventions of English life has been practised for generations and has led eventually to an inner fortitude, the result of which is the comparative sexual indifference of most Englishmen. Many an Englishman suppresses or, as the Buchmanites call it, sublimates his sex instinct and leads it into other channels without subscribing to the methods advocated by them. The successes of sex sublimation in the Oxford group would have been more impressive if they had been achieved among members of those nations in whose lives sex *really* plays a predominant part. Five 'sublimated' Arabs, Italians or

Frenchmen would prove the efficacy of Buchman's sex methods more convincingly than five hundred English undergraduates. But we look for them in vain, and can merely acknowledge that the sex salvation of Buchmanism is being achieved merely by the under-sexed.

XI

The groups are said to have been instrumental in the bringing about of a racial understanding between certain sections of the South African population. A less doubtful achievement of the Oxford group is the fellowship that has been created by and within the movement. People who formerly were left to themselves, or who were unable to kindle within themselves a feeling of friendship and altruism, began to develop these virtues, which struck me as the most attractive characteristic of the groups. The qualities of unselfish collaboration and understanding will probably remain as the important contribution of Buchmanism to modern life, long after most of its principles have been forgotten.

As to the elimination of racial prejudice I can only judge from personal experience. During one of the meetings I attended, a titled German woman spoke of the wonderful results Buchman had produced in her country: peasants and landowners, soldiers and storm troopers, workmen and students were gathering together to exchange their spiritual experiences and to establish a common basis of a Christlike life. 'What about the common basis and fellowship between the Nazis and the Jews?' someone in the audience shouted out. 'What about the understanding and lack of class distinction between Nazi Buchmanites and former intellectuals, and socialists, and liberals, between Nazi Buchmanites and non-Nazis?' The poor lady blushed violently and did not reply, but the inquisitive gentleman was more or less shouted down. When sceptical listeners made a similar enquiry at other meetings the result was the same—except that in most cases they were no longer allowed to finish their question.

This is where the movement seems to be failing: it claims too much and it advertises its successes too widely without ever admitting its failures. I was rather shocked when I picked up one day a book of famous murder cases and found in it a detailed report of a notorious trial in which the accused was a Buchmanite. The unfortunate case only showed that one can be a grouper who has 'surrendered, changed, shared and restituted' and even converted the sinful lives of other people and yet remain, to say the least, a crook. The famous Buchman crusade that went out in 1929 to 'change' South Africa included a certain young Englishman, D. M. This grouper remained in South Africa, eloped with a young girl, and was charged in the autumn of 1931 at Maritzburg with the murder and robbery of a native taxi-driver. After a long trial he was acquitted of the murder, but was found guilty of 'a number of lesser offences, including fraud and forgery. He had not long stepped from the dock when he was rearrested on these charges. . . . He pleaded guilty to charges of forgery and fraud. . . . At the close of the trial D. M. was recommitted to gaol on a warrant from Johannesburg which alleged additional charges of fraud against him.'

It would be absurd to forge a link between D. M.'s felonies and his being a Buchmanite, but the groups claim that it is sufficient for a man to be 'changed' to ensure in that man's life thenceforward all the Christlike qualities. The South African case shows us the most natural truth that no-one has the right to make such monstrous claims, for we are entitled to ask: Did D.M. commit his various frauds in accordance with 'guidance' obtained in his 'quiet time' or was the life-changing power of the groups so weak that it did not prevent him on such important occasions from acting on his own? It is dangerous to put the idea of divine guidance into the minds of inexperienced youths who have no education or discipline to enable them to distinguish between the voice of their conscience and that of their deeper desires. 'I can only say', writes Mr. Reginald Lennard. fellow and tutor of an Oxford college, in the *Nineteenth Century*, 'that I have known Oxford for three years as an undergraduate, and have worked in Oxford as a college tutor for some twenty-two years, and it seems to me that of all the movements . . . almost, if not quite the most depraving in its ultimate tendency, and the most insidiously inimical to the formation of fine character, is the group movement which Dr. Buchman has brought us from America.'

XII

The groups believe that they can solve social and economic problems as easily as religious and sexual ones. We are told a lot about the happiness that Buchmanism has brought into the lives of thousands of people; of the fellowship that exists within the groups among Communists, Fascists, Socialists and others; of the greater understanding between the employees and employers where the latter have become groupers. There is no doubt that the groups have indeed helped in thousands of individual cases. But can they solve as they claim any of the burning problems that involve not a few thousand individuals but humanity at large?

J. B. Priestley, who has never left any doubt as to the sincerity of his preoccupation with social conditions, expressed in 1934 his opinion of the methods of the groups for the solution of social problems. 'I do not think', he wrote, referring to a Buchmanite publication, 'I should have considered this pamphlet worth writing about—if it had not contained a paragraph headed "A Message to the Unemployed". In this paragraph the writer suggests that the movement is capable of doing more for the unemployed than can be done by anything else in the world. Not only can it bring them a spiritual comfort . . . it will bring them jobs again. This seems to me mischievous doctrine. If young men from Oxford and Cambridge like to confess their sins to one another, to listen-in to Heaven and go charging round Canada and South Africa in a state of hearty priggish self-complacency, that is their affair and not ours. . . . But when such people begin to talk nonsense of this kind to the unemployed it is time to protest. All new religious movements . . . are soon able to acquire funds. But it is quite another thing to assert that the business of the nation . . . can be put in order by the same easy-going methods. This is where the mischief begins. . . . There is no divine plan for keeping children in poverty and misery . . . until the hour when all undergraduates confess their sins and stop casting lustful glances upon barmaids.'

Mr. C. R. Morris, another student of the groups, says that 'All the appearances are that the group leaves its members at most vaguely interested in these things (social problems). It will stand as a hindrance to simple but necessary improvements in the common affairs of life. . . .' (*Oxford and the Groups*).

It seems as though Dr. Buchman's preoccupation with the financial and social side of his movement has made him forget the urgency of many social and economic problems. Two friends of mine visited him one day to discuss a business matter. When he told them that he had just come back from a group meeting in the East End, one of my friends expressed surprise at the quarter. 'Oh, I suppose we must have the poor with us', was Dr. Buchman's reply.

THE MAN WHOSE GOD IS A MILLIONAIRE

The groups acknowledge that the problem of money is connected with the problem of social injustice. 'Money and possessions are treated as belonging to the whole category of material things which are not in themselves either evil or good' (Roots). This is a very sound statement, and equally right is the conclusion drawn from it that 'to a man trying sincerely to do God's will rather than his own, and seeking daily guidance towards this end, there is no problem either of pride in receiving for his own needs or of miserliness in giving to supply the needs of others'. Optimistic detachment from money matters is no doubt a good attitude—but it is not enough to solve the economic problems of a nation. It is difficult to judge whether such an attitude—no matter how right in itself—would have been kept up by the groups had Dr. Buchman been a less ingenious organizer. 'Without him,' says R. H. S. Crossman in *Oxford and the Groups*, 'the movement would certainly not have the money to spend that it now has. There are at least thirty wholetime workers, living, and living comfortably, on contributions. It has been calculated that the last American tour must have cost more than £25,000. It is this money, and Dr. Buchman's organizing powers, which support these professional evangelists. . . . The remark made by one young evangelist, "I always wanted this kind of life: big hotels, comfort, powerful cars, and the best people—and as soon as I get changed, God gives them all to me!" is not mythical, and it is a warning.'

Dr. Buchman's private income does not exceed, in his own words, £50 a year.

XIII

Most of the failings that must needs shock many serious observers could easily be cured if the attitude of the Buchmanites were less superior, if they listened to well-meant criticism and if they admitted that, in a revivalism catering rather for the 'better classes', emotions must be blended with intellect. The contempt of the groupers for intellectual or merely serious conversation surprised me each time I came in touch with any of them. A movement that has adopted the name of one of the most distinguished Universities of the world and yet expresses contempt for all intellectual methods or discussions, becomes, to say the least of it, incomprehensible.

Undoubtedly the simpleton finds his way to heaven more easily than the 'brainy fellow'. Millions keep away from church—not because they are irreligious, but because they experience genuine difficulties in accepting uncritically the message of the Churches. Buchmanism preaches that we ought to give up all intellectual preoccupation with spiritual matters and base our lives solely on faith, when Buchman's message of happiness will become an actual life force in our existence. This may be true, but unfortunately most people find it difficult to accept blindly a new primitive gospel. The acceptance of a religious belief is not like that of a toothpaste or a brand of tobacco. Our religious needs are not easy to locate or to define and cannot be fed with a formula. The desire to doubt and to investigate new tracks is an inborn and divine instinct.

The intellectual needs of most of the groupers I met seemed so limited as not to worry them at all. Theirs was not the kind of intellect that loves probing to the root of a question They were perfectly happy to accept one thing as sin, another as God's voice, and a third as something equally clear cut and undeniable. If I questioned the truth of their assumptions they only answered: 'You'll see that it is so the moment you are changed Surrender will open your eyes.' It was rather like the answer of the Nazis in Germany who would always stop any argument by saying, 'Hitler says it, and so it must be right.' The groupers boasted about Dr Buchman 'persisting in his custom of refusing to argue about intellectual difficulties' (*For Sinners Only*).

None of the Buchmanites I came in touch with seemed to know much about other religions, philosophies or spiritual systems. People of their kind could easily be converted to almost any creed. As there are few people with exacting minds and independent spiritual ambitions—and millions without either of these—it can be assumed that Buchmanism will go on offering a spiritual haven to many more sinners.

Conversation with groupers invariably turned to stories of changed lives, to some 'topping' confession or restitution. Literature, art, music, politics, economics, might not have existed. I was reminded of conversation in Hollywood where every subject is viewed solely from its cinematographic aspects. When after the murder of the French President Doumer a visitor at a dinner party in Hollywood turned to his neighbour and said, 'How terrible about the murder of the President!' the answer came, 'Oh, who produced it?' Life outside the movie camera did not exist.

THE MAN WHOSE GOD IS A MILLIONAIRE

For the Buchmanites life outside Buchmanism did not exist. Each time I tried to introduce a topic unconnected with group activities, they listened politely for a few minutes, but after that their faces became blank, and their former cordiality gave place to that cool reserve that I had noticed at the end of my first luncheon at the Metropole.

The intellectual attitude of the groupers is best illustrated by their schoolboyish love of certain word concoctions. Dr. Buchman himself is the main inspirer of such a representation of spiritual truth. Thus he explains the word Pray as:

> Powerful
> Radiograms
> Always
> Yours

The letters of the name of Jesus are used by him to form the sentence Just Exactly Suits Us Sinners.

The Times summed up the intellectual attitude of the groupers in a leading article. 'It must be the most serious charge against the groups,' said the distinguished paper, 'that they encourage their members to shirk the discipline of thought in favour of impulses received from they know not where.'

XIV

Even a year after Dr. Buchman gave me that encouraging smile his young friends were still assuring me that I should meet him soon. I heard from one of his lieutenants that he had 'stressed the urgency of the matter' in a letter to Buchman's right-hand man Ken Twitchell. Though Dr. Buchman was at the time in London and though he was receiving in those weeks the visits of several titled ladies, I waited in vain for the urgency of the matter to take effect.

No-one could have a grudge against Dr. Buchman for preferring the visits of titled ladies to those of inquisitive authors. Nevertheless I am sorry I was never given the opportunity to talk with him, for I should have liked to tell him that much as I admired many of his principles, I hoped he would consent to make his movement less frivolous. I would have told him that since he has stirred the imagination of thousands of people and has brought home religion to them, he ought to change his revivalism in a manner which would allow it to develop from a philosophy for undergraduates and elderly titled ladies, into one for more serious people as well. I should have told him that shutting himself away from all criticism would prove the wrong policy in the end. And I should have told him how delighted I was to have met the most successful and shrewdest publicity agent of our time.

CHAPTER V

WAR AGAINST SLEEP

P. D. Ouspensky

I

Two years after the war Claude Bragdon, the distinguished American author, received the following telegram from Washington at his home in Rochester: '*Tertium Organum* interests me passionately. Desire very much to meet you if possible. Leaving for England end of month. Viscountess Rothermere.' Though Mr. Bragdon found it impossible to go and see the lady in Washington, he wrote in reply that he would be delighted to receive her at his home. She accepted his invitation.

The cause of the lady's excitement was a book which she had picked up on the bookstall of some railway station on her way to Washington. Since she had read it she could hardly wait to know more about the ideas expounded in it and about the personality of the author. His name was foreign and offered no key to his whereabouts; but as Claude Bragdon's name appeared on the title page as that of the translator, she chose what seemed the most direct way.

She arrived duly at Rochester and her first question was: 'Where is Ouspensky?' Mr. Bragdon answered that Ouspensky was at the moment in Constantinople. 'Why doesn't he come over to Europe, to England?' asked the impatient lady. Claude Bragdon had to explain that the times were not very propitious for Russian émigré authors who wrote bulky volumes on metaphysics, who had a family to support, and who would certainly find it difficult to make the long journey to England, no matter how much they might welcome such a change. The lady suggested that a certain sum of money might be sent immediately to Constantinople to enable Ouspensky to visit England. Claude Bragdon happened to know that Ouspensky had friends in this country and that he very much wanted to visit it. He sent the money to Constantinople and soon afterwards the author of *Tertium Organum* landed in England.

163

THE ENGLISH ADVENTURE

Claude Bragdon himself told me this story in his impressively slow sad way.[1]

Though *Tertium Organum* was a metaphysical book, it had the success of a popular novel, and exercised a strong influence on a great many people, especially in England and the United States.

'What made you translate *Tertium Organum*?' I asked Claude Bragdon.

II

'In the spring of 1918,' he answered, 'there appeared at my door a young Russian, Nicholas Bessaraboff. He had brought with him a Russian book for which he thought no praise could be too high. I had to read it, and I too became very enthusiastic. We decided to translate it together into English. He wrote down the translation word by word, and I had to make sense of it and to put it into intelligible English. We worked together for a very long time, and eventually I published the book myself. It had a very great success immediately, and sold for almost a year at the rate of a hundred and fifty copies a week, though it dealt with metaphysics and cost five dollars a copy.

'It took me a long time to find out where the author lived and where to send him his royalties and a copy of our translation. I gathered from his letters that he was enthusiastic about the publication of his book and its success, and that he wanted to come over to the States. He had lost everything in the Russian revolution, and in those days every foreigner visiting America for the first time had to find an American who would undertake a financial guarantee for him. I was unable to do this, but I wrote to Ouspensky and told him that, as his book was such a success, something was bound to turn up. Before my letter had reached him Viscountess Rothermere arrived, and we were able to send him money for his journey to England.'

III

Tertium Organum, which introduced the name of a hitherto unknown Russian author to Western readers, was called by its

[1] Claude Bragdon gives a detailed and most interesting account of this incident in the chapter 'The Romance and Mystery of *Tertium Organum*', in his book *Merely Players*, published by Alfred Knopf, New York, 1929.

164

P. D. OUSPENSKY

author 'A key to the enigmas of the world'. It was one of the very few books which, though introducing glimpses of the occult world into our conception of life, nevertheless was based on scientific investigations. It dealt with such subjects as 'Mathematics of the Infinite' or 'The Mystery of Time and Space', but it was not theoretical, and most of its astounding discoveries were based on personal observation. This personal element in a mainly scientific book was rather new at the time, and may account for part of its success.

Tertium Organum (which is the 'third canon of thought') was written before the war. Even more startling was Ouspensky's next book *A New Model of the Universe*. This volume of almost a quarter of a million words presented an entirely new conception of the world, in which purely spiritual discoveries were placed side by side with purely materialistic-scientific ones. The *New Model* cannot possibly be analysed here; and Ouspensky, moreover, had himself developed beyond some of its ideas which were conceived mostly before the war. The book dealt with subjects ranging from yoga to Einstein's relativity; with the Gospels, the study of dreams and a new theory of a six-dimensional universe. It was too scientific to follow *Tertium Organum* as a best seller, and too unorthodox in its whole conception to be accepted immediately by the necessarily slow and conservative machinery of official science. Ouspensky's positive attitude towards 'hidden' knowledge was convincingly balanced by his intellectual perspicacity and his scientific training. Here was a book that could be compared with Rudolf Steiner's best: the author displayed at once the same spirit of scientific detachment and the same open-mindedness with regard to spiritual knowledge which is not yet accepted by science, and though many of the purely scientific and mathematical parts were a closed book to me, I was told by experts that they were as new and as convincing as the less scientific sections. By the time I had reached the last page of the book, over which I spent an entire month's holiday, I understood the impatience of Lady Rothermere, who had been 'passionately interested' in *Tertium Organum*.

IV

After prolonged enquiries I succeeded in finding out that Ouspensky was living in England and holding classes in London. He seemed anxious that those classes should be attended only by those who felt a genuine need for such knowledge as is suggested in his two books. I was eventually asked to come to one of his lectures. It was to be the beginning of a new cycle; I should be able to study his method from the very beginning.

The meeting took place in a private house in Kensington. A lady with radiant eyes and the high cheekbones of a Russian was sitting in the front passage at a little table. She asked me my name, and wrote it down on a sheet of paper under a number of others. The lecture was to take place in a big room on the ground floor. About forty people were sitting facing a little table and the chair of the lecturer. The room had plain striped curtains and walls painted in a sober mauve-grey. Except for a vase with a few branches of cherry blossom made of mother of pearl and two modern brass trays on the mantelpiece, the room was undecorated. Next to the lecturer's table there was a blackboard, on which were the words 'Psychology as a Study of Objective Consciousness'.

The room filled up within five minutes, and altogether there must have been about seventy people present. They suggested a continental rather than a London audience: there were more men than women; most faces were rather intellectual; there was none of the elegance which one meets at occasional intellectual gatherings in Mayfair; neither were there any of the dark-coloured shirts and affected voices of Bloomsbury. I knew three of the men by sight: two of them were well-known professional men and the third was a peer, a fervent patron of the arts. There were a number of men and women in the early twenties, but middle-aged people prevailed.

V

Ouspensky entered the room almost unnoticed. He was white-haired, clean shaven, above the middle age, stout, bespectacled, and he walked up to the table, sat down, pulled a bundle of manuscripts out of his pocket and then began to speak without any introductory remarks. A more prosaic start to a lecture which aimed at revealing some of the deepest secrets of human existence could hardly be imagined.

I had some difficulty in understanding the first few sentences. The lecturer spoke English; but it was an English with soft melting vowels and with distinct and brisk consonants, the diction consisting of a mixture of soft cadences and sudden abrupt stops. It sounded as though he were really speaking Russian, though using English words. Once I became accustomed to his Russian accent I recognized that he had a fair command of English. When on the other hand he could not find the right word he simply said: 'or something else' or 'or anything you want' or 'how to say', and left it at that, without any sign of self-consciousness or embarrassment. You had to take it or leave it. This was impressive.

Though Ouspensky hardly ever took his eyes off the manuscript in front of him, he did not read it. It seemed to serve as a focus for his eyes, and he referred to it only occasionally, and when he did so a long pause ensued Ouspensky would take off his spectacles, and hold the manuscript close to his eyes. He would then read a sentence or two. This would be done not without an expression of strain on his face, as though he were reading something he had never seen before. There were none of the usual mannerisms which one so often meets with in professional lecturers. Ouspensky's movements were brisk but not hasty; the pauses and sudden halts seemed either the result of a natural reserve or merely lack of forensic gifts. There was nothing affected about them.

Though the speaker's manner of speech, with its clipped sentences and words that were left in the air, was at times bewildering, the lecture itself was extremely clear. The speaker's approach to his subject was very direct; the basis of his arguments painstakingly scientific, and altogether one felt that a searching mind of great independence was here revealed.

VI

One of the speaker's first sentences was: 'None of you here is awake. What you all do is—sleep.' After he had made this remark he stopped abruptly, as though withdrawing from the world of words into his own more comfortable world. His appearance suddenly suggested to me some modern version of Buddha. The audience waited for almost a minute. The lecturer then went on: 'The difference between your present state of consciousness and your consciousness at night while you sleep is very small. It is not a fundamental difference; merely a difference of degree.' After saying this, Buddha withdrew into his own world again. Ten seconds passed. Then he continued: 'I cannot give you definitions of the subjects I shall talk to you about, because the

167

meanings you attach to most words are wrong. Anyhow, as I give the words a different meaning, we should not understand each other. Therefore I can only try to develop my ideas to you, and you'll have to make an effort to grasp the meaning I attach to certain words as we go on.'

After this preface, Ouspensky tried to explain that he himself considered that modern psychology had taken over practically the whole range of interests that formerly belonged to philosophy, and that for him psychology was merely the knowledge of man not as a final being but as something unfinished and constantly changing. It was not hard to see that his psychological system would have very little in common with any other system.

'I personally consider', the lecturer continued, 'that subconsciousness or unconsciousness, of which modern psychologists speak so much, does not exist at all. There can only exist many different levels of consciousness, and in all of them the element of time plays an important part. Man can be selfconscious—conscious of himself—only for a fraction of a second. He thinks he can be conscious, but he never is. There are four states of consciousness: sleeping, waking, self-consciousness and objective consciousness. In objective consciousness man can know truth; in self-consciousness he can know truth about himself only; in waking he can know relative truth, and in sleep—no truth at all '

The lecturer stopped for a minute or so as though wanting his audience to think it all over. 'The highest consciousness, which is objective consciousness,' he went on, 'can only be obtained after we have become self-conscious. But what happens between these two states we do not know. The intermediate state is full of mystery. We acquire objective consciousness only in mystical or occult experiences and through certain inner illuminations.' Ouspensky pulled out his watch and said: 'We can intensify our present state of what I call "the sleeping state of consciousness" for no more than two minutes at most. Look at the hand of your watch; try to think at the same time of yourself watching the hand of the watch, which means try to be conscious of yourself and your actions at the same time. You cannot do it in an unbroken spell of time for more than two minutes; and even when you do it, you are not self-conscious yet. Your whole life is a state of automatic, mechanical actions, performed in a state of sleep.' He stopped again and smiled apologetically. I had noticed that smile several times before: it seemed to be

an apology for the statement he had made or was going to make
or perhaps for the inferiority of the listeners, implied in the statement. The smile disappeared with the same suddenness with which
it had lit up the face a moment earlier, and Ouspensky sank back
into his Buddha-like state, in which he remained for a minute or
two.

Then he went on: 'Your "I" does not exist. What you really have
is a thousand different "I's", but not one of them is your real "I"'.
He then went on to explain that man has got five minds, not just one,
and that he is composed of five different functions which are controlled by their respective minds. The five functions are: the intellectual, the emotional, the moving, the instinctive and the sex functions.
The sex functions can be studied only after all the other functions
are known; for they are the last ones to appear in man's life and they
always depend on the other functions. The five functions should be
working with the entire required independence or the required
collaboration, but generally they work in a muddled way and without
the necessary control of their respective minds Only through right
self-observation given by the right psychological system can we locate,
co-ordinate or detach them.

The lecture lasted exactly forty-five minutes. At its very end the
speaker turned to the audience —slowly lifting his eyes from the table
in front of him—and asked them to put questions to him. 'The
subject is very vast,' he said; 'I have only been able to suggest each
point. Each one of them requires many explanations and answers.'
Nobody uttered a word.

The silence was growing denser and denser, and eventually it
became like a threatening cloud. It was not the usual nervousness
that withholds inexperienced people from speaking in the presence
of utter strangers, and I suspected that no-one dared to formulate
a question in front of such a cruelly logical and matter-of-fact
lecturer. Most members of the audience were looking in the direction of the floor This almost unbearable state lasted for about
five minutes, though they seemed like as many hours. The very
silence must have robbed the listeners of their courage. Suddenly
the man at the table said: 'Ask me about anything that was not
clear.'

The ice had been broken at last. Now a voice sounded through
the room. Someone wanted to know whether the act of artistic
creation puts the creator on a higher level of consciousness. 'Not

in the least,' came the answer from the table; 'as a composer, poet or painter you are not different from any other man. Your work is as mechanical as the shoemaker's or that of a bricklayer. It is not you who does your work, but "it" does it. You are just the machine who follows the commands of the "it". You are a machine fitted out with certain wheels and screws and gadgets which shoemaker and bricklayer don't happen to possess. But don't imagine that being an artist makes you conscious. You compose your sonatas in the same state in which the bricklayer performs his functions.' Ouspensky finished his sentence, fell back into the chair and looked into the air. There was something irritating and at the same time impressive in those sudden impersonal endings to his answers.

A few more questions were asked; they were the questions of an educated and well-prepared audience. An hour after the questions had begun, Ouspensky said: 'You'll be informed in due time when there is to be another lecture.' He got up and walked out without looking at anyone or talking to any of the listeners. The audience rose and dispersed.

I waited for a while and then I asked the lady who had taken down my name at the entrance, when there would be another lecture. She smiled charmingly and said in her melodious Russian accent: 'We never can tell. There can be a lecture next Monday, or Monday after that. I will ring you up when there is to be another lecture.' I gave her my telephone number and departed.

Not for a long time have I felt intellectually so stimulated as I did on my way home through the unstimulating surroundings of High Street, Kensington. I had little doubt that I had been in touch with a system of a distinctly esoteric significance.

VII

I must warn the reader that this account of Ouspensky is anything but complete. Much more could certainly be said about him, though such an account does not yet exist. More important than any portrait of Ouspensky the man is a picture of his teaching or rather of the teaching which he represents—for there was little doubt in my mind that Ouspensky represented one of those systems of hidden knowledge that hardly ever exist in print and are only transmitted by word of mouth. It discloses itself only through constant work, through personal discoveries step by step. It can only be absorbed through a long process of questions and answers, through a constant collaboration between the lecturer and his listeners.

I spoke to Ouspensky on many occasions; I spoke to his listeners; I visited the classes in which he delivered his lectures; I compared his ideas with those of other teachers; I tried to translate them into my very actions and to adapt my life to them. In spite of all this, my picture of Ouspensky can only be partial.

Ouspensky had been popular for a number of years among a certain section of people in London and Paris. Since most of his listeners were not driven by curiosity or fashion but were trying year by year to follow his ideas, there could be no doubt that he had transformed the conceptions of a number of thinking folk.

The lady through whose kindness I had been admitted to Ouspensky's lectures was an old friend of his, and I begged her to arrange for me to meet him. She did not seem particularly pleased, and said that he might not want to receive me. 'He is rather elusive,' she remarked; 'and he does not care to meet people unless he knows that either he or his guest may derive some mental profit from the meeting He is sometimes even shy about too many people attending his classes.' Nevertheless she asked Ouspensky to receive me, and it was arranged that I should visit him at a house in Kent.

VIII

I expected to find what I imagined would be typically Russian 'atmosphere'. I visualized innumerable glasses of tea with lemon, cigarettes and in general a disorderly milieu worthy of an English drama about Russian émigrés abroad. The place which I reached after an hour's railway journey was, of course, entirely different. It was an attractive house in a large garden, and the modern drawing-room was furnished in an unobtrusive manner. The house belonged to some friends of Ouspensky.

When Ouspensky entered I noticed the same reserve that I had discerned during his lectures, and I did not realize until later on that this reserve was the outcome of an inner command not to talk and, in fact, not to do more than was essential. It was a self-discipline not to indulge in all those superfluous little activities that, being neither necessary nor sincere, compel us to substitute them for non-existent thoughts and feelings. Whatever Ouspensky had to say was said in the shortest possible way, and was followed by silence. Those sudden endings that had struck and even irritated me during his lecture were nothing but the logical end of a sentence in which everything had been said. Of course, it was difficult at first to carry on a conversation with a man who made no concessions to our habitual shortcomings or to social conventions. After a while I got used to it, and even began to feel the salutary effect of such a self-discipline.

In spite of Ouspensky's ascetic form of conversation I learned the main outline of his life. He was born in Moscow in 1878. His grandfather was a painter of religious pictures; both his parents were very cultured people. The father was an officer in the army, but his main hobbies were the arts and mathematics, especially the study of the fourth dimension. Thanks to an uncanny memory, Ouspensky still remembers himself at the age of two. Certain characteristics in him were determined at the age of six through reading two of the classics of Russian literature: Lermontoff's *Hero of Our Time* and Turgenyeff's *A Sportsman's Sketches*. Soon afterwards he began to develop a strong taste for poetry and painting which he considers even to-day the highest forms of art. At twelve he developed an interest in natural sciences. New discoveries and new interests seemed to come to him earlier than they do to most boys—a characteristic which he had in common with Steiner. When at the age of thirteen Ouspensky became interested in dreams, he turned immediately to the study of psychology; at sixteen he discovered for himself Nietzsche; at eighteen he began to travel and to write; and before he was twenty he had undertaken a serious study of science, soon coming, through his preoccupation with the natural sciences, to believe in the existence of hidden knowledge.

O.: 'I am only interested in a scientific approach to the problems surrounding us. Mysticism, occultism and the other supernatural movements interest me little. But I have felt that there must exist some deeper knowledge of our world than the one we are taught at our universities. I studied science after science; biology, mathematics and psychology, and I gathered as much of existing scientific knowledge as I could. I studied at a number of universities both in Russia and abroad, but after having acquainted myself with each science in turn I realized that I was always brought against a blank

172

wall, and that I could go no further. This limitation in the exact sciences filled me eventually with a deep mistrust of all academical knowledge. Though I had absorbed a great deal of this knowledge I could value it only up to a point. In fact I hated official academical science to such an extent that I made up my mind never to pass an examination or to take a degree.'

R. L.: 'But your books show that most of your investigations are based on a wide scientific knowledge. As a matter of fact, I was assured by friends who are scientists themselves that some of your mathematical and neo-physical discoveries are of paramount importance.'

O.: 'But they were not the outcome of the knowledge gained a universities. That knowledge formed only a part of the necessary material, but it did not bring me nearer truth. It always remained within its own special circle. True knowledge should never be limited to itself but should allow you to establish a connection with any other branch of knowledge. Though I was sceptical of scientific knowledge of the academical kind, I thought at the same time that there could be no new science in the world, and that everything must have been fixed somewhere, sometime.'

R. L : 'What exactly gave you the impulse to search for truth in those regions of human thought that official science does not take quite seriously?'

O.: 'In a way it was theosophy. In 1907 I came across theosophy, or rather the earlier theosophical books which were prohibited in Russia. The theosophists had not begun yet to repeat themselves, and they were still in contact with hidden truth. I am referring to books written before the beginning of this century.'

R. L.: 'Did you meet the theosophical leaders?'

O.: 'Yes, I went to Adyar in India, to the headquarters of the Theosophical Society, and spent some six weeks there, in contact with Annie Besant and several other leaders. Most theosophical books since then are nothing but a rehash of truths established by Mme. Blavatsky, Col. Olcott and the early writings of Annie Besant and Leadbeater. Later on I found out for myself that most esoteric knowledge is transmitted from century to century by word of mouth. I went to the Near East, I studied occult literature, I made all kinds of psychological experiments. I published several books, I lectured. In 1913 I went to Egypt, Ceylon and India, and did not return till after the beginning of the war, though I soon realized that to find

173

what I was seeking I should have had to stay in the East much longer. Eventually in 1915 and, so to speak, under my very nose, I met a system which contained more essential knowledge than any I had yet encountered. Everything that I had been hunting for in the East, in occult literature, in secret doctrines, was in that system which I found in Moscow among a small group of people, instructed by a certain Gurdjieff.'

R. L.: 'Do you mean the enigmatic Gurdjieff from Fontainebleau, whose name I constantly come across without however being able to locate or indeed to verify him?'

O.: 'I don't think there can be two Gurdjieffs. Many important truths, unknown to any other system, were explained through the system propagated by Gurdjieff—for of course it was not Gurdjieff's own discovery but an esoteric system which had been entrusted to him by others Gurdjieff lectured in Moscow, and, though I was living at the time in Petersburg, I soon decided to join him. When the Russian revolution came, I had no illusions about it, but decided at once to leave the country and to await the end of the war in some neutral place with the intention, when the war was over, of continuing my work in England.'

R. L.: 'Had you lived in England before?'

O.: 'No, but on my way back from India I had stayed in England while making preparations for the publication of some of my books. My connections with Gurdjieff made it impossible for me to leave Russia in 1917. He went to the Caucasus, and after a time several members of his classes, myself amongst them, joined him there, where we stayed for over two years. During 1918, however, I had begun to feel somehow out of touch with Gurdjieff. It seemed to me as though he were changing, but whatever the cause I could no longer understand him, and it appeared to me that he had drifted away from his original idea. Although I tried to concentrate on separating the system from his personality, and by keeping the two apart to go on working with Gurdjieff, it proved impossible, and eventually I had to leave him. He went to Tiflis, and I remained where I was, at Essentuki. I was liberated from the Bolsheviks by the Whites in 1919, and soon afterwards I left for Constantinople.'

R. L.: 'Did you ever come across Gurdjieff again?'

O.: 'Yes, during my lectures in Constantinople. I even tried to resume our work in common, but it was impossible. In 1921 I went to England and began to lecture there to people who were interested in such ideas as those with which I was concerned, and when Gurdjieff visited London I tried to help him—I even kept in close touch with him and with his work when he moved to France, and visited him there on many occasions. Early in 1924, however, I realized finally that we could not work together, and so I broke away from him entirely, and I haven't seen him since.'

R. L.: 'Do you think there still exist definite groups possessing esoteric knowledge?'

O.. 'There are several such esoteric groups in the East and a few even in the West. They are the only ones that can transmit higher understanding. You find higher knowledge of paramount importance in Christianity, though perhaps not in orthodox Church Christianity. You find esoteric knowledge in the Gospels, but hardly anyone knows how to read them. Does anyone know the real meaning of the Lord's Prayer? I doubt it. But the Lord's Prayer contains some of the deepest esoteric knowledge.'

R. L.: 'Do you believe in God?'

O.: 'I don't believe in anything. I believe only in the possibility of acquiring more and higher knowledge. I take nothing for granted—neither God nor destiny nor faith. What we usually call faith is nothing but a bundle of automatic emotional reactions, yet I know that besides such imaginary faith there is also *real* faith.'

R. L.: 'Do you believe in the existence of an individual "I" in each one of us?'

O.: 'I should myself have put that question rather differently. All I can say is that our "I" is for us practically non-existent at present, because we don't know it. Something we don't know of cannot exist for us—and so this becomes a purely philosophical and therefore useless question. We are thousands of "I's", all of which are imaginary. Our real "I" we can only discover through persistent effort.'

R. L.: 'Knowledge, I presume, is for you both the apex and the axis of all human existence?'

O.: 'Of course. The more we know about ourselves, the more we discover about other things. Things vary in accordance with our knowledge. They are just as much or as little as we know about them. They are neither material nor spiritual nor anything else. They are just what we know about them, their reality being merely the expression of our own understanding.'

175

THE ENGLISH ADVENTURE

R. L.: 'What is your attitude towards miracles?'

O.: 'They cannot happen unconsciously. Even the Transfiguration is not a magical but a mechanical happening. We can achieve miracles only with full consciousness.'

R. L.: 'What of magical language, of Eastern mantras, of invocations of Western religions, magical formulae, of mediaeval brotherhoods such as that of the Rosicrucians?'

O.: 'There is magical language: but only for people who know how to read it. Language, no matter how magical it may be, can have no influence over people who do not know. What we generally believe to be the magical power of language is simply its appeal to the emotions.'

R. L.: 'So you don't believe in any mechanical transmission of knowledge—through magic formulae, for instance?'

O.: 'I don't. Only conscious effort can achieve anything. Nothing can grow through the mechanical work of copying.'

R. L.: 'You don't believe in any mental exercises either, I take it?'

O.: 'All Jesuitical, Rosicrucian and similar exercises are useless for us. Exercises fix our present state of sleep so strongly that it will be only more difficult to overcome it. They can be compared to fixing a photograph before it has been developed. What is the good of fixing yourself before you have been developed? Fixation may be all right after you have developed certain qualities—not before.'

IX

During the following months I was regularly admitted to Ouspensky's lectures. His audience was not the sentimental, essentially self-centred and lazy crowd which was ready enough to support so many spiritual movements at that time; there was none of the happy-go-lucky optimism of cheapened religiosity, or of the blind devotion with which we meet in the case of so many teachers and their disciples. The very method of Ouspensky forced his listeners to think for themselves. At times it was almost painful to watch how they seemed to concentrate on each of his pronouncements, and how hard they were trying to think out certain problems for themselves.

Generally, Ouspensky would lecture for five or ten minutes, and then he would suddenly stop and say: 'Think about what I have just

176

said, and ask me questions about it. We must discuss it before I can go on.' Such a method compelled active collaboration on the part of his pupils. At the beginning there was always something rather frightening in the breathless pause before the first question was asked. Fear that a question might be irrelevant to what had been said during the lecture, or that it might disclose intellectual curiosity alone, prevailed even towards the end of a session. Mere literary or philosophical questions were not welcome, and the effect of such a question was invariably devastating. Ouspensky was never rude, nor even ironical—but he was cruelly matter-of-fact, and would not tolerate questions that did not betray an honest desire to know more.

Someone would ask, after Ouspensky had discussed the various states of consciousness· 'Is Buddha the seventh state of consciousness?'

Ouspensky, without even looking up to see who had asked the unfortunate question, would only answer: 'I don't know.' He then remained silent, and you felt that in his thoughts he probably continued, 'and I don't care'. There was nothing to be done, and the person who had put the question had to consider the answer satisfactory and could only try to hide the sudden blush that was covering her face—for women were the chief offenders in this way.

After Ouspensky had explained that a genius is not a being with a higher consciousness, but just a more perfect piece of machinery than ordinary people are, someone asked: 'Don't you think that a man like Beethoven was more than a piece of machinery?'

Ouspensky answered to this: 'I don't; and I am not interested in it, because I am only interested in my own or perhaps your state—that's why we are here.'

He forced his listeners to train their thoughts to keep to what was real, what was directly connected with the teaching that was given them. If someone tried to introduce a word that had a meaning in another psychological system, but was not used by Ouspensky he would not admit any compromise. Once a listener asked: 'Should we meditate?'

Ouspensky answered: 'I don't understand.'

'Should we not meditate?' repeated a more faltering voice.

'Meditation is a word that you picked up somewhere,' came the answer; 'you should know by now that it has no meaning whatever in the system that I am representing. So please try to refrain from using unnecessary words. We have got our own terminology, which is quite adequate to our purpose. If I should find that we need new words, I will introduce them myself.' All this was said without the slightest impatience or offence, very calmly and without any suggestion of a reprimand.

No matter what the value of Ouspensky's system, there can be no doubt that his very sternness was of the greatest value. People who found it hard to think were forced to keep their thoughts within a definite circle, concentrating on the knowledge contained within that particular circle so as to absorb it in such a way as to create their own thoughts out of that circle.

Ouspensky offers little to the imagination; but very much to one's power of thought; and there are no miracles, dramatic conversions, emotional confessions or *tours de force* in his method. He is never satisfied with one particular discovery but tries to go deeper and deeper. He takes nothing for granted and induces his listeners to establish every new fact for themselves. There is no evasiveness in his teaching or in his answers, and he is almost unattractively simple and sober in his pronouncements.

X

The whole of Ouspensky's system rests on the acknowledgement of the truth that man is not conscious but asleep. Most of us do not even know that we are asleep. We can only begin to wake up if we realize and admit that we function in a dream, automatically. We can only wake up through self-observation. Self-observation can only be produced through constant effort. One of the main barriers preventing us from waking up is our imagination,[1] which intrudes constantly into our thought. Imagination runs away with our thoughts and leads a thoroughly destructive existence within us. We are only rarely able to think beyond a certain point, and this point is generally very soon reached. Our thoughts are then taken over by our imagination, which runs amuck with them, without direction, aim or control. We can only stop the wasteful chase of our imagination by being

[1] The word 'imagination' in Ouspensky's terminology does not express creative imagination responsible for most scientific, literary, artistic or, in fact, any creative work. Such an imagination he calls by different names, according to the particular case. He means, by imagination, uncontrolled imaginary ponderings or daydreams, automatic and without effort.

attentive. The moment we are attentive the activities of our imagination stop, and thought can come into action. Imagination is a very violent destructor of energy; mental effort on the other hand stores up energy. We waste a lot of energy by the wrong use of our various centres. We allow our five centres to become mixed up, and one to do the work of another.

Good or bad can only exist if there is an aim. Without aim they are non-existent, and we merely accept conventional versions of them, created in the past by people who were as much asleep as ourselves. Reality can only be known in a state of waking. Real knowledge is creative knowledge. Without instruction, coming from people in possession of such a knowledge, progress is almost impossible.

Our ultimate goal is an objective consciousness in which all our former inner limitations cease to exist. In such a consciousness there are no secrets or mysteries. But we can never reach such a high level through increase of our knowledge alone. Knowledge and being must be perfected together. We must aim at growing into a harmonious whole in which bodily, emotional and mental functions are alike developed; where they perform all their duties; where they can collaborate at will; where, in short, both the man and his understanding function to perfection.

XI

Though from the ordinary man's point of view the psychological part was perhaps the most important, it formed only a fraction of Ouspensky's system, which embraced an entire cosmology, and necessarily dealt with such different subjects as mathematics, physics, sex, religion, the arts. But those branches required an even more direct study under him than the psychological part of his system.

As in most esoteric doctrines, the school idea plays a predominant part in Ouspensky's system. Certain things can, according to him, not be taught or learned from books or through individual study but require a school—a group of people who will work together under special guidance, evolving the same terminology, beginning to understand one another. Since times immemorial, from the ancient mysteries to the various mediaeval schools or monastic brotherhoods, the school method has always been considered as indispensable for the propagation of hidden knowledge. No man working by himself can obtain certain results, since these can evolve only through discussions between teacher and pupils. The truths contained in an esoteric doctrine cannot be realized as long as there is no school.

Never before have I met anyone working more directly and more logically to help people to conquer the phantoms of sleep and to lead them into consciousness.

CHAPTER VI

HARMONIOUS DEVELOPMENT OF MAN

Gurdjieff

I

The personality and the life of Gurdjieff are both shrouded in mystery. He has said or written little of his past, and is indifferent as to the accuracy or otherwise of the statements regarding his personality; but, though he considers that all that matters is his teaching, the reader may find some account of the many vicissitudes of his life equally interesting.

Even Gurdjieff's main collaborators, who worked with him for a number of years, were unable to testify as to the truth of some of the facts. They derived most of their knowledge from Gurdjieff's mother and brother, whose reports had to bridge the gaps between Gurdjieff's own haphazard utterances. Even his Greek nationality is questioned by some people one of his pupils told me that his master was an Armenian, while the majority of his pupils used formerly to call him, in the Russian fashion, by the patronymic George Ivanovitch. He is supposed to have been born in Alexandropol in the late 'seventies; but certain facts which I discovered during my investigations seemed to point to his having been born earlier. His father appears to have been a merchant; he himself had a rather superficial elementary education, and his knowledge was acquired almost entirely in later years. At one period in his life he was a carpet dealer, and for a number of years he travelled extensively in the Near East and in central Asia. He is reluctant to talk about those early adventures, and we can only guess at most of them.

A few years before the world war Gurdjieff suddenly appeared in Moscow. His lectures attracted considerable interest in certain intellectual circles. The background of these essays in education is clarified by some autobiographical material which he introduced into a later publication. It appears that he had been in contact with a number of people who devoted their time to the study of what Gurdjieff called 'theosophism', 'occultism', or 'spiritualism', and had eventually become an expert among them. After some years he abandoned these 'workshops', as he called them, 'for the perfection of psychopathism', and, 'with enormous and almost superhuman effort and heavy expenditure', organized in 'different cities three small groups of people of varying types'. He founded his groups in Russia, 'which at that time was peaceful, rich and quiet'. 'Arriving at this final decision', he began at once 'to liquidate current affairs, which were dispersed over different countries in Asia', and to collect together all the wealth which he had amassed.

The Russian Revolution brought an end to his groups. He left Moscow for Tiflis, whence he proceeded later to Constantinople. A certain number of his pupils followed him, and in 1920 he suddenly appeared in Berlin, which was at the time most promising ground for any unusual movement. A year or so later Gurdjieff moved on to Paris, and once or twice he visited London. His teaching, his strange power over a number of people and the help of various friends enabled him to collect enough money to acquire the Château du Prieuré, a fourteenth-century property at Fontainebleau, and establish a new school there.

The name of the new school was 'Institute for Man's Harmonious Development', and most of Gurdjieff's pupils at that time were Russian or English. The strong emotional appeal of his romantic personality attracted the Russians; while for his Anglo-Saxon followers it was the Rabelaisian exuberance of his whole personality and the mystery attached to him that provided much of the outward fascination.

The pupils generally came to live at the Château, and for the first week or two they would be treated as guests. Afterwards they had to share all the work, which included besides the ordinary housework such manual labours as gardening, felling trees, or chopping wood. Gurdjieff held very strong views on the necessity of an unconventional way of living and of activities likely to decrease old habits and automatic mechanical functions of his pupils. While performing such work as gardening, or chopping wood, his pupils were obliged to employ those of the muscular functions that had not yet been deadened by conventional use. Manual work revealed to them also a number of hitherto unknown things about themselves.

Though most of the pupils believed in Gurdjieff with the fervour of true discipleship, there were often quarrels and violent arguments, and those disturbances ran like a dark thread through the whole history of the Prieuré. Some of the pupils would at times complain

182

that they could no longer support Gurdjieff's violent temper, his apparent greed for money or the extravagance of his private life. On occasions these feelings so outweighed their admiration for him that they felt constrained to leave the Château indignantly. I have been assured that the quarrels were not due to a lack of self-control, but formed part of Gurdjieff's tactics. By rousing their anger he induced people to forget their self-discipline and thus reveal to him their real emotions. Possibly this was not the only reason for Gurdjieff's displays of temper; when he considered that a pupil was failing to make sufficient progress under his guidance, instead of asking him to leave the place, Gurdjieff preferred to provoke such storms as would force him to depart.

II

When asked what he was aiming at, Gurdjieff would answer: 'At developing people into human beings'. To achieve this, Gurdjieff used the picturesque expressions of a most unconventional French or an even less conventional English, a deliberately engaging intonation of his voice and the most varied gestures.

When asked what he meant by developing people into human beings, Gurdjieff would generally add that he wanted to make them become more conscious of reality. Though Gurdjieff, unlike Ouspensky, generally followed a system of evasiveness in answering the questions of his pupils, he gives us in his book some glimpses of his leading ideas. There he says that 'the modern man does not think, but something thinks for him; he does not act, but something acts through him; he does not achieve, but something is achieved through him.' This is, of course, the belief of most teachers. The root of all true religious endeavour, too, is the wish to get away from the misleading fancies painted by our imagination and to see that truth the very centre of which is God.

Gurdjieff's first rule for facing reality demanded that we should break away from the automatic, habitual manner of living common to people in general. According to Gurdjieff, while our physical centre is fully developed, the growth of the emotional centre has only just reached the stage of adolescence, while the mental centre has not developed beyond the stage of infancy. We ought to be able to control each one of the three by any of the other two centres. Gurdjieff considers that most of the characteristics commonly regarded as virtues are in truth vices. In his opinion man's fundamental sins are vanity and self-conceit, which are mainly the results of a wrong education. 'I categorically affirm', he says, 'that the happiness and self-consciousness, which should be in real man . . . depend in most cases exclusively on the absence in us of the feeling of "vanity".' There are two guiding principles for the attainment of that happiness: (1) 'To be patient towards every living creature', and (2) 'not to attempt by the use of any power of influence we possess to alter the consequences of the evil deeds of our neighbours'.

One of Gurdjieff's main methods is a queer system of dances, the aim of which is not to give the dancer a chance to express his subjective emotions, but to teach him the collaboration of his three different centres through 'objective' exercises. Every movement, pace and rhythm is minutely prescribed. Each limb has to be trained in a way that permits it to make independent movements, not at all co-ordinated with those of the other limbs.

We all know that our muscles act and react in certain ways because they have always been used to making the same kind of movement. This does not mean that such movements necessarily and always fulfil the real 'ambition' of the muscle. To illustrate this point, let us consider for a moment the difference between our own and the Eastern way of sitting. The Eastern fashion of properly crossed legs and straight spine is much more restful than that of sitting on chairs with our legs dangling down and with the weight of the body wrongly distributed. One can sit in that posture for hours without being interrupted by a restless body or aching limbs and one rests in it much better than by lying down on a bed. And yet hardly any of us can do it. Why? Because our muscles act in automatic fashion.

Gurdjieff's dances were meant to break the muscular conventions of the dancers. By creating independent movements instead, he endeavoured to attack the mental and emotional conventions of his pupils as well.

Gurdjieff himself wrote the scenario and the music of the dances. Some of the music was based on dervish dances, of which he seemed to possess a very thorough knowledge. He has written thousands of compositions, most of which served as music for the dances.

When in 1924 Gurdjieff took a group of his pupils to the United States, the performances of 'objective dances' roused a certain interest. Many people were attracted by their novelty, for these

184

dances had nothing in common with the methods of Dalcroze, Rudolf Steiner, Isadora Duncan, or any of the newer reformers.

The British author, Mr. Llewelyn Powys, described the visit of Gurdjieff to New York and the effect of his dances in a book, *The Verdict of Bridlegoose* (1927), in which he writes· 'The famous prophet and magician Gurdjieff appeared in New York accompanied by Mr. Orage, who was acting for him as a kind of Saint Paul. . . . I had an opportunity of observing Gurdjieff while he stood smoking not far from me in the vestibule. . . . His general appearance made one think of a riding master, though there was something about his presence that affected one's nerves in a strange way. Especially did one feel this when his pupils came on to the stage, to perform like a hutchful of hypnotized rabbits under the gaze of a master conjurer.'

I heard very similiar opinions from many different sources. People told me that the dancers looked like frightened mice; but they added that it was useless to judge the dances themselves by common aesthetic standards. And yet I came across people who had admired them even for their aesthetic beauty, though there were none of the usual attractions of stage presentation. The dancers wore simple tunics and trousers. One of them told me that the impression of being hypnotized came from the intense concentration that each performance required. Not only had their bodies to act: each one of their three centres had to be controlled consciously, and the required co-ordination of the three centres could only be achieved by the greatest effort of concentration.

Soon after his return from America Gurdjieff had a serious motor accident at Fontainebleau, and remained an invalid for many months. 'On account of my motor accident . . . which brought me near to death,' Gurdjieff says, 'I was forced to liquidate everything . . . that had been created by me with such unimagined efforts.' Regular work at the Institute had to be given up. Though occasionally pupils would still come to stay at the Château, Gurdjieff's main educational activities at Prieuré belonged to the past. But his teaching was spreading through America, where his main collaborator, the English writer, Mr. Alfred Orage, was holding special classes. Gurdjieff began to visit America regularly almost every year, and after 1930 he made New York his headquarters.

185

THE ENGLISH ADVENTURE

III

It was Gurdjieff's personality rather than his doctrine that so strongly affected many people in France, England and America. One of his pupils said to me one day. 'I imagine that Rasputin must have been like Gurdjieff; mysterious, domineering, attractive and frightening at the same time; full of an over-abundant vitality and of strange knowledge, inaccessible to other men.' Some people tried to explain away Gurdjieff as a charlatan and hypnotist. His hypnotic powers were never disputed, yet all his external methods constituted but an insignificant part of his far wider knowledge. It was not merely emotional women and certain types of semi-intellectual men who came under the spell of Gurdjieff. Men and women with pronounced critical faculties and a marked intelligence became his pupils. Many of them parted ways with him, but they all admitted that Gurdjieff was one of the real spiritual experiences in their lives. Katherine Mansfield was one of his followers, and she believed deeply in Gurdjieff, and even hoped that under his influence she might be able to conquer the disease that was raging within her. She actually went to work under Gurdjieff's directions at Fontainebleau, though too late to regain her health, for she died there after a few months.

A great number of men and women well known in the intellectual world came under the spell, and D. H. Lawrence apparently gave much thought to Gurdjieff, and was at one time on the point of entering his circle. Lawrence heard much about him from his American friend, Mrs. Mabel Dodge. He was extremely interested in Gurdjieff's ideas, and referred to him in many of his letters. But Mrs. Dodge's enthusiasm seems to have aroused his suspicions, and he wrote to her in April 1926: 'My I, my fourth centre, will look after me better than I could ever look after it. Which is all I feel about Gurdjieff. . . .' A month later he wrote from Florence: 'As for Gurdjieff and Orage and the awakening of various centres and the ultimate I and all that—to tell you the truth, plainly, I don't know . . . there is no way mapped out, and never will be. . . .' Eventually, when his friend pressed him to go and visit Gurdjieff, Lawrence became impatient, and wrote: 'I don't think that I want to go and see Gurdjieff. You can't imagine how little interest I have in those modes of salvation. . . . I don't like the Gurdjieffs and the Orages and the other little thunderstorms.'

HARMONIOUS DEVELOPMENT OF MAN

Mr. A. R. Orage, whom Lawrence mentioned in the last letter was Gurdjieff's chief assistant and lecturer. He had great intelligence and an attractive personality, and it was mainly due to him that Gurdjieff's ideas became so popular in America. A philosopher and writer by profession, he was a man of erudition. Before the war he owned the review *New Age*, and was the author of various highly acclaimed philosophical, economical and critical books.

IV

I had for long been anxious to meet Gurdjieff, and at last, when I was in New York, it was arranged that I should see him. I asked Mr. Orage to give me an introduction, but, as at the time the two men were barely on speaking terms, Orage considered that his introduction would only shut Gurdjieff's door against me. Eventually, however, I was given a letter of introduction to a very old friend of Gurdjieff's in New York, who was only too willing to arrange the interview, and who asked me to ring him up three days later to find out the exact date of the meeting When I rang him up on the appointed morning he advised me to get into touch with Mr. Gurdjieff's secretary.

I asked him whether I should mention his name. 'Oh no,' came the answer, 'that would not be a recommendation. But you might say that a Mr. L advised you.'

'But I don't know Mr. L.', I replied.

'Then just say that you had been told that Mr. L. was going to talk to Mr. Gurdjieff about you, and to arrange for your interview.'

I rang up the secretary. She knew nothing at all about a conversation between Mr. L. and Mr. Gurdjieff; but she said that if I wrote a letter, giving all the reasons for my proposed visit and stating in detail who I was, she would take it to Mr. Gurdjieff. I wrote the letter and two days later the secretary rang me up: Mr. Gurdjieff would see me at 2.30 p.m in his rooms, numbers 217 and 218 at his hotel.

Before my interview I had lunch with a distinguished American writer who was supposed to have known Gurdjieff for many years, and I asked him about Gurdjieff. 'I have never actually spoken to him,' he said; 'but I often went to his classes and to his dances. I must confess that he is an enigma to me.'

'Do you think it is true that he sometimes uses his strange faculties for other than spiritual purposes?'

187

'It would be unfair to affirm this. All the unorthodox things we hear about him may be parts of a system of deep spiritual significance. You must not forget that Mme. Blavatsky, too, often tried to obtain genuine reactions from her pupils by shocking and antagonizing them. Gurdjieff may perhaps be doing something of the sort. There was a time when Orage and others of Gurdjieff's followers tried to induce me to join them and to become one of Gurdjieff's assistants. I refused persistently for a number of years, and I must say I am glad that I was never intimately associated with them.'

'Is it true that Gurdjieff has changed thoroughly since his motor accident?'

'He certainly seems to have done so. He was almost dead for a very long time, and it may be that such a deep experience has transformed him. As you may have heard, his first book came out quite recently. It surprised me, for it showed me a new, more altruistic, less materially minded Gurdjieff.'

'Where can one get this book?'

'I fear nowhere. It has been printed privately, and Gurdjieff sends it only to those he considers worthy of being instructed by him. He happened to send me a copy, but its style is so atrocious that I had the greatest difficulty in getting through it.'

'Have you seen him recently?'

'Yes, at a reception last spring. I must tell you of an interesting incident which occurred that day. A friend of mine, who is one of our great novelists, was sitting at my table. I pointed to a table at which Gurdjieff was sitting, and asked her whether she knew him. "No, who is he?" she replied, looking across. Gurdjieff caught her eye, and we saw distinctly that he suddenly began to inhale and to exhale in a particular way. I am too old a hand at such tricks not to have known that Gurdjieff was employing one of the methods he must have learned in the East. A few moments later I noticed that my friend was turning pale; she seemed to be on the verge of fainting. And yet she is anything but highly strung. I was very much surprised to see her in that strange condition, but she recovered after a few moments. I asked her what the matter was. "That man is uncanny", she whispered. "Something awful happened", she continued, but began after a moment to laugh in her broad natural way. "I ought to be ashamed, nevertheless I'll tell you what happened. I looked at your 'friend' a moment ago, and he caught my eye. He looked at me in such a peculiar way that within a second or so I suddenly felt as though I had been struck right through my sexual centre. It was beastly!"' My host stopped for a second, and added smilingly: 'You had better be careful. The man you are going to see can certainly make use of strange powers: he had not learned them in Tibet for nothing.'

'I so often hear about his experiences in Tibet,' I replied: 'but I am somewhat suspicious of those Tibetan tales. Every other messiah, from Mme. Blavatsky onwards, claims to have gathered knowledge n the mountains of Tibet. How do you know that Gurdjieff has actually ever been there?'

'I happen to possess first-hand proofs. Some years ago there was a luncheon in New York, given, if I remember aright, for Gurdjieff. A number of distinguished men had been invited, among others the writer, Achmed Abdullah, who told me that he had never seen Gurdjieff before, but that he was very much looking forward to meeting this unusual Armenian. When Gurdjieff entered the room Achmed Abdullah turned to me and whispered: "I have met that man before. Do you know who he really is? Before the war he was in Lhassa as an agent of the Russian Secret Service. I was in Lhassa at the same time, and in a way we worked against each other." So, you see, it is quite true that Gurdjieff had been at the very fountain of esoteric knowledge Some people say he was in Lhassa as a Secret Service agent, in order to disguise the real purpose of his visit, which was to learn the supernatural methods of the Lamas. Other people maintain that his esoteric studies were only a pretext behind which he could hide his political activities. But who can tell?'

V

Gurdjieff lived in one of the smaller hotels in 57th Street. When the reception clerk at the hotel desk telephoned up to announce my visit, I was told to go 'right up' to number 217. I knocked at the door, and entered a small darkish room. A tall young man with a cigarette in his mouth was standing at the door to receive me. 'How do you do', he said; 'he will be with you in a moment; please sit down.' He looked presentable and cultured; but I have hardly ever seen a pair of more frightened eyes. I admit that it was not difficult to allow one's imagination to detect features that may not have existed in reality. Yet I had come to this meeting determined not to dramatize it, but to observe as keenly as possible and to gather

189

firsthand knowledge. The story of Gurdjieff was dramatic enough as it stood. There could be no doubt about the expression on the young man's face. He was very pale, his eyes glowed feverishly, and he gave me the impression of someone who had just seen a ghost. He smoked his cigarette nervously, with his eyes focused all the time on the adjoining room. There was no door between the two rooms, and I could discern in the far one a bed and some luggage. The reception room in which we were sitting was, in comparison with those of most hotels of the district, shabbily furnished. Several cheap black suitcases were lying on the floor in front of an empty fireplace. I heard someone opening the door from the passage to the bedroom, and a moment later Gurdjieff joined us.

'How do you do', he said in very bad English and with a strong oriental accent. I was particularly struck by the way he pronounced the 'h'. It was not the light English 'h', but the deep, guttural 'ch' of some German words, or rather the 'chr' of Eastern languages. Gurdjieff was wearing a waistcoat half unbuttoned, no coat, dark trousers and bedroom slippers. You could see the braces under his waistcoat.

'Excuse this costume', he said; 'I have only just finished lunch.' He then pointed at me and said to the young man: 'This Englishman very precise.' He obviously meant punctual. 'He really English', he went on, without allowing me to contradict; 'not like you all, half-Turks, half-Turks.' He turned towards me: 'Americans are not English, for me they are only half English and half, half'—he was trying to remember the word—'half Turkish.' He laughed and continued instantly, 'You excuse my English. It awfully bad. I speaking my own English, you know—not modern, but pre-Shakespearian English. It awfully bad, but my friends understand. And I understand everything in real, modern English, so you go and speak. This man'—he pointed to his pupil—'will translate my pre-Shakespearian English for you. He knows.'

'Oh, it is perfectly clear to me, Mr. Gurdjieff,' I tried to contradict; 'I understand everything you say.'

'Then have a cigarette.'

'Thanks, I am afraid I don't smoke.'

'Oh, not smoke one of those Americans! No, I give you wonderful cigarettes, real cigarettes, Turkish and Russian. Say what?' He placed a large box of Russian cigarettes in front of me.

'Thanks all the same,' I said; 'but I really do not smoke.'

HARMONIOUS DEVELOPMENT OF MAN

'Come, come, they good, *prima, prima*. If not smoke these, I can give
you ... what calls itself non-smoking cigarettes. What call you?' he
turned to the young man who explained: ' Mr. Gurdjieff keeps special
cigarettes for non-smokers, perhaps you would care to take one.'

I was beginning to feel slightly uncomfortable, but I tried to treat
the whole matter as a kind of a joke, and I said light-heartedly:
'Thanks awfully, I am sure I should be sick straight away if I smoked
any of your cigarettes; and no-one here would enjoy that. I have
never smoked in my life', I lied.

I sat down on a little sofa not far from Gurdjieff, who was reclining
comfortably in a big chair. The young man had remained all through
our conversation on his chair near the fireplace. He kept on glancing
nervously towards Gurdjieff, and it was impossible to imagine that
he could ever laugh or smile. Terror seemed the only expression
of which his face was capable—or was it some hysterical form of
expectation?

Gurdjieff's face was manifestly Levantine. The skin was darkish;
the twisted moustache was black, though distinctly greying; the eyes
were very black and vivid. But the most Levantine feature of his face
was the mouth: it never remained quite shut and it exposed the teeth,
one or two of which had been darkened as though by constant
smoking. He was quite bald and slightly stout; yet you could see
that he had been good-looking in his earlier days, and it was obvious
that women must have been very susceptible to this virile Levantine
type of man.

He was very obliging and smiled constantly, as though trying to
show me his most attractive side. Nevertheless I began to feel very
queer I am not easily influenced by 'telepathic' enticement, and am
not at all what is called a 'good medium'; no doctor or hypnotist
has ever succeeded in hypnotizing me. On this particular occasion I
was very much on my guard and prepared to counteract any possible
psychic influence. And yet I was beginning to feel a distinct weakness
in the lower parts of my body, from the navel downwards, and mainly
in the legs. This feeling grew steadily every second. After about
twenty or thirty seconds it became so strong that I knew I should
hardly be able to get up and walk out of the room.

I had been specially careful not to look at Gurdjieff and not to
allow him to look into my eyes. I had avoided his eyes for at least
two minutes. I had turned all the time towards the young man, to
whom I had said: 'I shall talk to you, and perhaps you will be so

kind as to translate my words to Mr. Gurdjieff in case he does not understand me.' The young man had agreed, and I remained facing him, with Gurdjieff on my right. And yet the feeling of physical weakness pervaded me more and more.

I was intensely awake and conscious of what was going on within me, and I was observing this fascinating new experience with the keenest awareness. The feeling inside my stomach was one of acute nervousness, amounting almost to physical pain and fear. This weakness did not upset me above the navel: it was limited to the stomach and legs. My legs were suffering from the sensation similar to that which people experience before a trial at court, an examination, or a visit to the dentist. I was sure that if I tried to get up my legs would sag under me and I should fall to the floor.

Though I had not the slightest doubt that my queer state had been produced by Gurdjieff's influence, I was perfectly composed and determined to get out of it. I concentrated more and more on my conversation with the young man, and slowly the feeling inside seemed to melt away, and I began to feel normal again. After a couple of minutes I had definitely left Gurdjieff's 'magic circle'.

There are several explanations of my queer experience. It might have been a form of hypnosis or even auto-hypnosis which, for certain reasons, could affect only the lower half of my body without touching the brain and the emotional centre. But I doubt if it was either. It may have been a form of electric emanation such as Rasputin is said to have possessed in a high degree. This form of radiation seems to act even if its owner is hardly conscious of it, and it belongs to him almost in the way that certain odours belong to certain coloured races.

There may have been another reason for my strange experience. According to clairvoyant people, who have disciplined their gift to such an extent as to be able to use it with the fullest consciousness, a clairvoyant examination may produce effects similar to that which I had just experienced. Rudolf Steiner examined people occasionally in that way, the object of such an examination being to see the person's spiritual instead of his merely physical picture. But Steiner was always fully conscious of what such an examination entails. 'The thought that a human being could be merely an object of observation,' he said in one of his books, 'must never for a moment be entertained. Self-education must see to it that this insight into human nature goes hand in hand with an unlimited respect for the personal privilege of each individual, and with the recognition of the sacred and inviolable nature of that which dwells in each human being.'

Of course I could have protected myself against a 'clairvoyant examination' Had I come to meet Gurdjieff in an open instead of a defensive state of mind he would probably not have succeeded in achieving whatever he was aiming at. No 'psychic' power is strong enough to affect a loving, human attitude, and there are other methods by which it is possible to protect oneself against an unwanted clairvoyant scrutiny.

When the feeling of nervousness and weakness in my legs had disappeared, I turned towards Gurdjieff. 'I was told', I said, 'that you had lately published a book. As to my knowledge you have never published anything before, everything I know about your ideas is secondhand. I should be grateful if you would tell me where I can buy your book.'

My host got up, went to one of the black suitcases on the floor, took out of it a thin book, and came up to me. 'Here it is, and, you know, no money can buy it. It is only for a few. But I present it to you. You find all in it you want.'

I thanked him and went on: 'I was told you were preparing a large book that will contain all your teaching and your experience of many years.'

He waved his hand as though the big book I mentioned meant nothing to him. 'I writing nine books always, they thick so—so.' He showed with his fingers that each one of these books was at least three or four inches thick.

'There seems to be a manuscript of one of your books in the possession of one of your former pupils in London. Is it one of the proposed nine volumes?'

Gurdjieff made a contemptuous gesture: 'That nothing, just nothing. They all have my visions.'

I looked enquiringly at the young man. 'He means versions', he whispered.

'I always write three visions. Only last is for publication. No-one knows last one only myself. Others are here and there and here. They all have them, and then begin their own teaching on them. But that mean nothing. I have pupils all across the world, in all countries, groups are everywhere. In England alone fifteen, in fifteen cities. And all try to do new teaching on my teaching. Ach, but means nothing, just nothing.' He snapped his fingers in a gesture of contempt.

THE ENGLISH ADVENTURE

'Is it true that you are preparing a group of disciples who will eventually become a sort of esoteric school, out of which your knowledge will radiate into the world?'

'You find everything in this book, everything.' He pointed to the little volume in my hand. 'Everything is there. No good you now speak to me. You not know me. You first read this book and then come to me. Then we speak together. But now you not know what ask. First read this book, everything in it.'

I understood that Gurdjieff had no wish to answer my question and that he considered the conversation finished But I was determined to stay on for another few minutes and to see more of him. 'Is Ouspensky's teaching in your opinion original or based on yours, and do you consider him the most important of all your former followers?' I continued as though I had not noticed his impatience.

'He just been one of my pupils, one of thousand, ten thousand.' He again made one of his deprecatory movements with one hand. Whenever he made one of these gestures he looked the perfect Levantine: evasive in his answers, hyperbolical and anxious as to what effect he was producing. It may be that all the mannerisms and inconsistencies of his behaviour were parts of a method and that by employing such a system of 'tricks' he was able to discern my 'reactions' more clearly than he would otherwise have discerned them. Nevertheless I could not make myself believe that the pursuit of truth need ever require such a bewildering method of approach. Why should a man with great knowledge and experience require a technique of rudeness, of antagonizing his pupils, of constant evasiveness? Did not his knowledge suffice to 'look' into me and to examine my 'natural reactions' on a basis of ordinary human relationship? And yet some serious-minded people had been under his spell. He had treated some of them like slaves, and yet they had forsaken all their former beliefs and blindly followed him. His hypnotic powers, the physical attraction he must once have possessed, the fire in his eyes could not alone have produced such effects. Ouspensky had undoubtedly been right when he had told me that one had to separate the system represented by Gurdjieff from Gurdjieff the man.

Now that I had seen and apprehended Gurdjieff the man, I felt I could leave him. For once the original had been true to the accounts of him.

I got up, and Gurdjieff said: 'You first read this book. It has everything, and then you come to me again. We then talk.'

'When and where can I see you again?' I enquired.

'My office, Childs.'

I looked up without understanding. The young man near the fire-place helped: 'He means the Restaurant Childs in Fifth Avenue and 56th Street.'

'I have three Childs, they all my office. Here I work in the morning. But evening my office Childs. You come and we then drink coffee together and speak more. I there every evening six to eight.'

'Thank you, Mr. Gurdjieff. I shall certainly visit you there after I have read your book.'

I went straight to my hotel, which was no distance away, and when I reached my room I became conscious of a strong desire to wash my hands. I washed them in very hot water for about five minutes, and then felt better, and sat down to record my strange experience.

VI

The book that Gurdjieff had presented me with was bound in a most curious sort of paper: it resembled suede leather and yet gave a harshness to the touch that almost set one's teeth on edge. I felt that this binding was not chosen without a purpose. On its cover were the words:

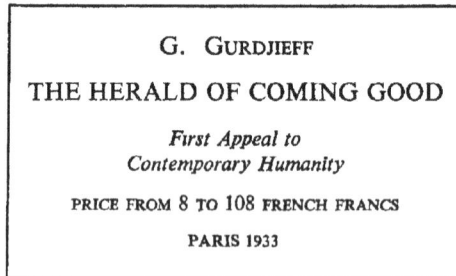

G. GURDJIEFF

THE HERALD OF COMING GOOD

First Appeal to
Contemporary Humanity

PRICE FROM 8 TO 108 FRENCH FRANCS

PARIS 1933

Inside the book there was a green registration blank with the number of my copy and a space for supplying such details as to whether it was 'acquired accidentally or on advice', the sum paid, and name and address of the adviser. As I had been presented with my copy I escaped this procedure.

The book was an announcement of what Gurdjieff called, without undue modesty, 'Coming good'. By this he meant the books that he was promising to place before the world in the near future. The little book was an amazing publication. It gave you in many instances the impression of the work of a man who was no longer sane. And yet it was impossible to sweep aside Gurdjieff's statements as the self-adulation of an insane mind. (Some of the statements quoted in the earlier pages of this chapter have been taken from *The Herald of Coming Good.*)

Gurdjieff here promises to disseminate the whole of his knowledge, which seems to include many esoteric secrets. He announces the publication of three series of books, comprising ten volumes, the title of the whole series to be 'All and Everything'. The first series will be called 'An Objective Impartial Criticism of the Life of Man', and will contain such subjects as 'The Cause of the Genesis of the Moon', 'The Relativity of Time Conception', and 'Hypnotism', the second series will be called 'Meetings with Remarkable Men'; the third will be 'Life is real only when "I am"'. We are told that the original manuscript is written in 'Russian and Armenian', and that 'the first book of the first series is already being printed in the Russian, French, English and German colloquial languages', and that 'translations are already being finished in the Armenian, Spanish, Turkish and Swedish languages'. Only the three books of the first series will be universally accessible. The contents of the second series will be made known 'by means of readings, open to those who have already a thorough knowledge of the contents of the first series'. 'Acquaintance with the contents of the third series is permitted only to those people who ... have already begun to manifest themselves ... in strict accordance with my indications', Gurdjieff explains, 'set forth in the previous series of my writings.'

The style itself exhibited the same signs of strangeness, amounting almost to insanity, that were manifest in the subject matter. Reading the *Herald* was like the progress of a cart over cobblestones. Most sentences ran on endlessly. The first sentence contained no fewer than two hundred and eighty-four words.

I was more interested in certain personal data than in the fantastic announcement of the coming books. Certain facts of that mysterious life were disclosed here for the first time, though hardly any of them was very clear. Gurdjieff admitted having spent some of his life in an Eastern monastery in order to acquire certain occult knowledge. 'I decided one day', he says, 'to abandon everything and to retire for a definite period into complete isolation ... and to endeavour by means of active reflection . . . to think out some new ways for my fertile researches. This took place during my stay in Central Asia, when, thanks to the introduction to a street barber, whom I accidentally met . . . I happened to obtain access into a monastery well known among the followers of the Mohammedan religion.' Gurdjieff admits that he also devoted himself to the study of 'supernatural sciences', that he learned how to perform the usual supernatural tricks, and he relates how he acquired the gift of hypnotism. 'I began to collect all kinds of written literature and oral information still surviving among certain Asiatic peoples, about that branch of science, which was highly developed in ancient times, and called *mekheness*, the "taking away of responsibility", and of which contemporary civilization knows but an insignificant portion under the name of "hypnotism" . . . Collecting all I could, I went to a certain dervish monastery . . . in central Asia . . . and devoted myself wholly to the study of the material in my possession. After two years of thorough theoretical study . . . I began to give myself out to be a "healer" of all kinds of vices and to apply the results of my theoretical studies to them. . . . This continued to be my exclusive preoccupation . . . for four or five years . . . I arrived at unprecedented practical results without equal in our day.'

Gurdjieff discloses that both through nature and inheritance there had been in him a predisposition towards supernatural knowledge. 'Great Nature', he writes in his pompous style, 'had benevolently provided all my family and me in particular . . . with the highest degree of comprehension attainable by man. . . .' From his earliest days Gurdjieff appears to have had access to a knowledge not open to most men, and this may be partly responsible for his belief in his own infallibility. 'I had . . .', he says, 'the possibility of gaining access to the so-called "holy of holies" of nearly all hermetic organizations such as religious, philosophical, occult, political and mystic societies . . . which were inaccessible to the ordinary man . . . I had read almost everything existing about these questions . . . a literature accessible to me because of quite accidental circumstances of my life far beyond the usual possibilities of the ordinary man.'

Speaking of his former possessions Gurdjieff says that he had accumulated enormous wealth. It is not disclosed by what means, but he states: 'I began to liquidate my current affairs, which were dispersed over different countries in Asia, and collecting all the wealth which I had amassed during my long life. . . .' This reference

197

to a long life as far back as 1912 focuses our attention on the subject of Gurdjieff's age. In another place he speaks of having finished certain researches before the year 1892. Both these facts indicate that in 1933 he must have been at least seventy, this being the year of the publication of his book. And yet the man to whom I had spoken that afternoon seemed little more than fifty years old. His looks, his figure, his voice—everything about him suggested that age.

VII

Though Gurdjieff had adherents in England and in France, most of his credulous followers were in America. I was surprised at the number of people there who had attended his classes or seen his dances. Often when I mentioned his name, someone would come forward and give me some dramatic account, illustrated by a personal experience. Though these accounts varied, though some of the speakers swore by Gurdjieff and others almost cursed him, though some considered that he possessed greater and deeper knowledge than anybody alive and others called him a charlatan and a madman, they all agreed that there was something powerful and uncanny about him. Stories were reported to me of people who had given Gurdjieff their whole fortunes in order to help him with his work, and of pupils who were unable to tear themselves away from him, and felt happy in his presence even if they had to suffer from his abuse. I have never heard the word 'possessed' used so often in connection with any other teacher.

And yet there could be no doubt that the man who exercised such a strong influence over his pupils had ceased to be the power he once was. Evasiveness, contradiction and bluff—formerly the weapons in a most complicated system—seemed to have become part of Gurdjieff's very nature. When his mother died in 1925 at Fontainebleau Gurdjieff placed on her grave a huge tombstone with the fantastic inscription:

'*Ici Repose*
La Mère de Celui
Qui se Vit par
Cette Mort Forcé
D'Écrire Le Livre
Intitulé
Les Opiumistes'

HARMONIOUS DEVELOPMENT OF MAN

('Here lies the mother of one who sees himself forced by her death to write the book *Les Opiumistes*.') Mme. Gurdjieff was well over eighty at the time of her death, her end was not unexpected and could have hardly been a great shock to her son. The book which he saw himself 'forced' to write has never been heard of.

It suddenly occurred to me that there was among Gurdjieff's present pupils not one of those who had gathered round him in Russia before the war. This was indeed of utmost significance, and it showed, too, why in his early days those who knew him had nothing but praise for him, while the opinions of his later pupils were, to say the least, most conflicting.

It was not only in New York that I met people who had been in touch with Gurdjieff. I came across them in several smaller towns and, of course, in California, where every uncommon metaphysical theory finds adherents. There were groups of people who had once been instructed by Alfred Orage, and who now tried to follow Gurdjieff's chaotic teaching. Even if people had no longer any contact with Gurdjieff, they would become intensely interested the moment I mentioned his name. His indomitable personality never failed to exercise a strange fascination even over people who had denounced him long ago.

VIII

I suspected that Gurdjieff had no intention of giving any precise answers to the questions I had put to him, even supposing I were to meet him again. I could not conceive how a conversation of any significance could be successful in the atmosphere of an eating place in Fifth Avenue, with all its noise and bustle. The presence of Gurdjieff's pupils, whom I did not know, would be of little help in such a conversation Nevertheless I decided one evening to visit him at his restaurant.

The Greek was sitting at a table quite near the entrance. Dressed in a dark suit, he looked more commonplace than on the first occasion I had met him. He was smoking a cigarette and writing in a copybook in front of him. The page was covered with large, slightly unformed English calligraphy. On another page the writing looked rather exotic and I assumed that it was Armenian. Gurdjieff did not recognize me at first, and I had to stoop down to him and explain who I was. After a few seconds he remembered me and asked me to sit down next to him. One of his pupils was with him.

199

THE ENGLISH ADVENTURE

I tried from the very first to ask Gurdjieff precise questions about his teaching. This would save time, and it would reduce the possibility of evasive answers. But I had hardly finished speaking when he got up and walked over to a lady who must have been standing there for some time, anxious to catch Gurdjieff's eye. In her face there was the same expression that I had seen in the face of the disciple during my first interview. When Gurdjieff had returned to our table I made another attempt to talk to him, but this time we were forestalled by a middle-aged man who came up to us. It was another of Gurdjieff's pupils. We exchanged names and the man sat down. Meanwhile Gurdjieff ordered coffee with lemon. This seemed to me a strange drink, but the waitress must have been used to the order, for she showed no signs of surprise, and returned with the drink a few minutes later. Gurdjieff squeezed out the juice of the lemon into the black coffee, and then dropped the lemon into the cup.

Within ten minutes several other pupils arrived, and our party now occupied three or four tables in a row. Gurdjieff was for ever getting up, walking towards the door, and talking to people who were coming and going. It was impossible to begin a connected conversation. Nevertheless I had a more favourable impression of him than at my first visit. He seemed simpler and less sinister. I noticed now for the first time a certain human quality in him. Even his English seemed better, and I began to suspect that its inferior quality during my first interview had been partly assumed. Had it been a part of Gurdjieff's method of provoking 'genuine reactions'? I limited myself after a while to questions about his plans with regard to his new school, to the publication of his books or to other details of his work But even so he remained evasive, and I could not record a single definite answer.

During one of his frequent absences from the table I began a conversation with the gentleman opposite me. He seemed Gurdjieff's main assistant, and I noticed that the questions I had been asking his master were making him uncomfortable. Eventually he expressed his anxiety: 'I am afraid you have chosen a wrong method of questioning Mr. Gurdjieff. By asking him in such a direct and precise way you almost force him to answer yes or no. He is not used to that, and he does not care for such a form of conversation. Anyhow, I don't think you'll succeed very much. You ask him in a conversation of twenty minutes questions for the answers to which many of us have been waiting for a great many years. None of us dares to put to him such questions'.

I thanked him for the information and decided that it would not indeed be of much avail to remain here any longer. As I was leaving for England in a few days' time, and had no chance of following the method of the disciples, it seemed that I should have to depart without receiving answers to my questions—but the frightened faces of the eight or ten people sitting round, and the hushed atmosphere the moment Gurdjieff addressed any of them, had been more explicit than any conversation could have been.

Gurdjieff's pupils did not try to disguise their feelings towards me. They probably considered me an intruder, and my presence was anything but welcome. When they had met me at the beginning of the evening they had cast inquisitive glances in my direction as though fearing that a new disciple had arrived, upon whom their master might waste some of those favours that had hitherto been bestowed exclusively upon them. Once they were reassured that I was not a disciple, they seemed to feed their antagonism on my attitude towards Gurdjieff. They probably expected me to worship their hero, and were deeply offended at my failure to do so. Not one of them had given me even the conventional smile generally offered to a newcomer. Not one of them asked me the habitual questions which are put to break the ice, and they avoided helping me when they noticed my occasional difficulties in understanding Gurdjieff's English. It may be that their antagonistic reserve was affected by the presence of their master, under whose influence they were unable to show common politeness to a stranger. There was no doubt: I had overstayed my welcome, and I rose to go. No-one tried to persuade me to stay on, and even Gurdjieff did not utter a word of encouragement. I thanked him, bowed to the assembled company, and walked out into the bracing air of an autumn evening in New York.

IX

When I arrived back in London I went to one of Gurdjieff's former followers in Europe. He was a fairly intelligent man, and earlier in the year I had had some interesting conversations with him about Gurdjieff. I told him of my experience in New York.

'Your account', he replied, 'does not surprise me. I have often heard stories like that. Even to me certain things about Gurdjieff were always as inexplicable as they must be to anybody unaccustomed to his wanton methods. And yet he has brought me—and many other people—nearer to truth than anybody else. Mind, emotions and body are no longer antagonistic. Though it is true that many of the things Gurdjieff does and says seem meaningless, yet while you are in the midst of your work, he will say something to you that will give you the answer to questions you have been long pondering. His sense of your problem of the moment and his knowledge of the moment at which you are ripe for the answer are uncanny. At times we had to wait for years, and it was as though Gurdjieff knew exactly how many doubts we had to conquer before we were ready for his answers. You would be wrong to judge his conduct according to ordinary human standards. There seems a richness within Gurdjieff which allows him to do things that would be wrong for our own limited selves. In a way he reminds me of the god Siva.'

'The god Siva?' I interrupted with surprise.

'Yes, Siva, the destroyer-god of the god-trinity, the god of many functions, the lord of the spirits of music—and, don't forget, the god of dancing.'

This conversation only renewed and strengthened my conviction that the very teacher who may be of great help to one person may utterly fail to disclose himself to another. Even in the more recent years Gurdjieff's methods seemed to have been of some assistance to various people. Others were enlightened—where I was merely puzzled.

I could dimly discern that the essence of Gurdjieff's teaching contains a truth that everyone in contact with spiritual reality is bound to preach. But I failed utterly to accept his methods in that spirit of trust, of faith or of understanding, any one of which is essential for the absorption of spiritual knowledge. Sometimes the personality of a teacher is more impressive than his teaching—at other times the reverse is the case. If I found it impossible to accept Gurdjieff and to let him help me in moulding myself, it was because his personality, however strong, failed utterly to convince me. I had been unable to perceive in the man George Ivanovitch Gurdjieff the harmonious development of man.

X

Just as the manuscript of this book was going to the printers I received the following letter:

HARMONIOUS DEVELOPMENT OF MAN

Captain Achmed Abdullah.   *Fifth Avenue House,*
Sunday.   *New York City.*

DEAR SIR,

As to Gurdjieff, I have no way of proving that I am right—except that I know I am right.

When I knew him, thirty years ago, in Tibet, he was, besides being the young Dalai Lama's chief tutor, the main Russian political agent for Tibet. A Russian Buriat by race and a Buddhist by religion, his learning was enormous, his influence in Lhassa very great, since he collected the tribute of the Baikal Tartars for the Dalai Lama's exchequer, and he was given the high title of *Tsannyis Khan-po*. In Russia he was known as Hambro Akvan Dorzhieff; to the British Intelligence as Lama Dorjieff. When we invaded Tibet, he disappeared with the Dalai in the general direction of outer Mongolia. He spoke Russian, Tibetan, Tartar, Tadjik, Chinese, Greek, strongly accented French and rather fantastic English. As to his age—well—I would say ageless. A great man who, though he dabbled in Russian imperialistic politics, did so—I have an idea—more or less in the spirit of jest.

I met Gurdjieff, almost thirty years later, at dinner in the house of a mutual friend, John O'Hara Cosgrave, former editor of the *New York World*, in New York. I was convinced that he was Lama Dorjieff. I told him so—and he winked. We spoke in Tadjik.

I am a fairly wise man. But I wish I knew the things which Gurdjieff has forgotten.

Very faithfully,
A. ABDULLAH.

PART THREE

FULFILMENTS

'And ye shall know the truth,
and the truth shall make you free.'
ST. JOHN viii. 32.

INTRODUCTION

ARYAN GODS

I

Almost fifteen years lay between the time at which I began my search and the moment at which I decided to write of it. New creeds had appeared beside the old, and had, in some cases, replaced them.

In 1934 I decided to revisit the men through whose influence I had once learned so much. I had begun my search in Germany and it was obvious that Germany should be the first country for me to revisit. I was anxious to see what had become of the work of Stefan George, Rudolf Steiner and Keyserling under the Third Reich.

It became evident to me during the very first days that there was as little room in the new Reich for the old spiritual influences as there was for those of such men as Thomas Mann or Albert Einstein. My search reduced itself therefore to a study of those influences outside German life, to the question as to how it was possible for the influence of men who had once been hailed by many representative Germans as their true leaders to be swept away by tendencies entirely opposed to their own and to a search for the new gods that had replaced the old ones. What is the practical value of spiritual doctrines if they have no influence upon the conduct of a nation? I soon discovered that such doctrines can only affect a small group of people, who in their turn have to disseminate the new message. Doctrines that are adopted immediately seldom have a deep influence. The conduct of a nation is not directed by discoveries made by the spiritual leaders of the day.

Even the name of Stefan George, the man whose only medium was the German language, seemed to evoke a more enthusiastic echo among young men in Paris than in Berlin; the fame of Steiner was growing in Switzerland, Holland, England and other countries, rather than in Germany; and Keyserling, whose name was hardly mentioned in Germany, had become something of a hero in Spain, South America and in France. Even Rilke, one of Germany's most distinguished poets, worshipped by pre-Nazi Germany as were few others, seemed almost forgotten. This was not surprising. The message of each of these men was in no way limited to his own particular country, and affected all people alike. Those Germans for whom those names still had a deep meaning—and they hardly cared to speak loudly about them—formed an infinitesimal minority.

II

In the case of George, the hero of yesterday was nearly made the hero of to-day. The Nazi government acted in the spirit of Napoleon's remark, 'They tell me we have no great literature; I must speak to the Minister of the Interior about it', and were anxious to make George the figurehead of German literature.

George's visionary appeals to the native instincts of the German people could easily be misinterpreted as being identical with the new racial doctrine. But he soon dispelled the notion that his teaching could be adopted as a topical political doctrine, and when the Government offered to make him President of the new German Academy he declined. Soon afterwards he left the country—on account of his health, it was stated, though his decision is thought to have been affected only partly by this consideration—and went to Locarno.

He died in Locarno in 1934, away from the country whose language and many of whose spiritual values he—more than any man since Goethe—had helped to re-create. His friends arranged that his funeral should take place with no loss of time, before an official representative of the German government could arrive.

III

Before I left England on this visit to Germany I had been given introductions to some of those Nazi leaders who would be able to answer my questions. I went to see several of those men, but they spoke only of politics, social reforms and their victory over economic difficulties. They could tell me nothing about that spiritual power that had inspired the strange upheavals in Germany during the last few years.

I was advised that nowhere should I see a more distinct manifestation of this new spirit than at a demonstration at which the 'Leader' would be present. I was assured that wherever the 'Leader' appeared the love of the masses would show me the mystical powers that guided Germany's new destiny. The best place would be outside the Chancellor's palace, from whence the 'Leader' usually emerged in the early afternoon.

I went to the Wilhelmstrasse and joined a crowd of people waiting opposite the courtyard of the Chancellor's palace. It was the same palace in which the aged Disraeli had signed the Treaty of Berlin; in which Bismarck had tried to stabilize the new Reich, and in which the courtly Bülow, the cautious Stresemann and the hesitant Bruning had ruled over Germany. Under the roof of the palace two floating ladies in classical garb supported the Eagle of the Reich. All three of them were made of a stucco which had acquired the charming patina reminiscent of the days when Berlin was only the capital of the Kingdom of Prussia. At the entrance gates there were policemen with steel helmets and the men of Hitler's personal bodyguard. They were all over six feet tall, and wore black uniforms with black steel helmets and, round their sleeves, a yellow band with the words 'Adolf Hitler'. They had short modern-looking rifles, and a dagger and a revolver were stuck in the belt of each of them. The floating ladies under the roof seemed, all of a sudden, very old-fashioned.

It was a hot sunny day. I was one of a group of about a hundred people. There were a number of middle-aged 'Hausfrauen' perspiring heavily under the midday sun, and munching sandwiches that they had brought with them. There were boys of the 'Hitler Youth', healthy-looking with tanned legs and sunburnt faces, and with a red swastika armlet round the sleeve of their brown shirts. There were young girls, slim, unselfconscious and typical of the new German *Mädchen*. They had little in common with their less prosaic, less good-looking and more womanly pre-war sisters. There were also a few men without coats and with those indispensable attaché cases which under the Nazis seem to form a part of German masculine attire just as much as they had done under less militaristic rulers.

Many members of both the younger and the older generations

were casting longing glances in the direction of a stout little fellow in a white apron, offering ice creams and shouting with the squeaky voice of a third-rate comedian, 'Eskimo, meine Damen und Herren, Eskimo!' It was very hot indeed.

Suddenly the blue policemen and the black bodyguard seemed turned to statues. A very long open motor car drove slowly out of the courtyard. The man at the wheel and his neighbour were both wearing black uniforms adorned with silver. In the rear of the car and next to a third man in black was the 'Leader'. He wore an incongruous pale mackintosh and no hat. With a rigid gesture of his right arm he acknowledged the greetings of the crowd. The thin mouth under the little black moustache was shut tight and the face bore a strained and self-conscious expression.

The people round me raised their arms and shouted 'Heil Hitler'; some of them waved handkerchiefs, two or three women threw little bunches of flowers into the car. There could be no doubt as to the warmth and the spontaneity of their enthusiasm. I had, however, seen a similar and much more passionate display of fervour when Mussolini appeared at a window of the Palazzo Venezia to raise his arm in Roman salute. Over and over again have I seen crowds whose emotions were focused so strongly on the hero of the moment that it looked like some voluptuous self-sacrifice. The enthusiasm in the Wilhelmstrasse failed to disclose to me the nature of the specific Aryan gods.

For a certain time I hoped to find those gods among the people I met in daily life. But these people showed either the blind fanaticism of soldiers who obey without questioning, or the disappointment of those who had expected the Third Reich to bring them Paradise and now grumbled over their unfulfilled dreams; they tried to persuade me with fair-sounding propaganda and ready-made speeches or they refused to take any interest in issues outside their own sphere.

IV

Finally I was advised to go and see the leading young workers within the party. I visited in important Government and Party offices several young organizers, propagandists and private secretaries. They had a blind faith in their new gods and in the *Fuhrer*. Though their names were little known to the man in the street, they were supposed to be at the very core of the Third Reich.

FULFILMENTS

I was impressed by their enthusiasm, and so I asked them outright: where are your new gods; where are the mystical forces of which your manifestos and books speak so loudly? The young men were obliging and answered in unison: the mystical forces are to be found in Hitler's life and achievement, in his mission and his success. When I pressed them for more exact answers, they said:

'The gods you are looking for are in the fellowship that the Leader restored to German life. The Germans had learned real friendship in the trenches; but they were forced to forget it in the immoral years between 1919 and 1933. The Leader gave them back fellowship.

'The gods you are looking for are in the strength of the Leader. Before him there was no leadership, and Germany was a toy in the hands of private interests or foreign powers. The Leader brought strength and unity of purpose, and he thus inspired youth.

'The gods you are looking for are in the faith of the Leader in his people. Before him politicians relied on the workmen or the bankers, the army or the trade unions, industry or the priests. For the Leader the whole nation is one, and all classes worship him as their only idol.

'The gods you are looking for are in the purity of the race that the Leader is giving his people, and in his care for their health. To-day the people know that there is someone who perceives the mystical power that is in their blood, and who prevents them from stooping down below themselves and from allowing that blood to be mixed.

'The gods you are looking for are in the pure character of the Leader. Before him, champagne flowed through the Wilhelmstrasse. To-day ours is a Leader who is a vegetarian, a teetotaller, a non-smoker, and whose only relaxation is listening to Wagner and Schumann. His life is so pure that even his enemies cannot find the slightest blemish in it.

'The gods you are looking for lie in the deep religiosity of the Leader. He is not a churchgoer, for the whole nation is a church for him, and to serve his people is his holy service. His Christianity is not theoretical but truly active, and that fascinates the masses. It brings them a direct message from the gods you are looking for.'

After the young men had spoken with such enthusiasm and fervour, I understood that spiritual truth only discloses itself to a few in profound thought or through native wisdom, which is, perhaps, the highest of the divine gifts.

V

And so I went to a very wise man. He had no prejudices, political or otherwise, and he had reached that maturity where such things as success or enmity no longer exist. Never in the past have I found his pronouncements to be wrong. I begged him to tell me of the spiritual currents that run invisibly under German events.

'The Nazi revolution', the wise man said, 'is a confirmation of the Old Testament. That is its fate. You can compare Nazism only with ancient Judaism. No other two movements in history have been so similar one to the other as those two. They are both based on purity of blood, they both stress the importance of race and family and are both convinced of their own exclusiveness; they both believe that God bestowed a special mission upon them, and they both see a holy, mystical quality in the soil on which they live. You find the whole of the Nazi attitude in the sentence of *The Mythos of the Twentieth Century*, the Nazi Bible written by our official cultural leader Alfred Rosenberg: "Besides the mythos of the free soul," he says, "there is the mythos of the religion of blood."

'The idea of purity of blood—for to-day it is no more than an idea—is responsible for much of the Nazi success. Not the powers of the spirit win victories on this earth. It is blood that wins them.

'The ancient Jews adhered to the principle of purity of blood with even greater insistence than do the Nazis. Only through purity of blood could they obtain their highest achievements, which could come to them through the brain alone, and through that brain only if it were fed by the purest of blood. No Jew in possession of spiritual truth was allowed to wed a stranger, for only in purity of blood could a truth, indispensable for higher achievement, be preserved. The body of the ancient Jews was meant to be a chalice for the reception of the wisdom that came from God. And their blood had to be kept pure so that the physical body of the most Perfect of men might be born out of it.

'To-day blood plays a different part. Through the teaching of Christ all men on earth have become equal, and every one of them can partake of a knowledge that could formerly manifest itself only in those of pure blood. Purity of blood as a spiritual necessity has no longer any meaning. Anyhow, as a nation we have become so mixed that it will take centuries before we can claim to be pure in blood. I fear that the modern idea of purity of blood is an intellectual

o   209

construction without spiritual roots. It is effective, because it evoked certain powers within the nation that should have been made use of for years but have been neglected by our former leaders. The fourteen years before the Nazi revolution were the years of intellectual and other experiments and of contempt for the power of the blood. This was bound to claim revenge, and so we see that to-day appeals to the blood adorn almost every German government decree, and serve as subject for well-nigh every speech and manifesto.

'But this idea of blood implies more than purity of blood alone. Blood is the opposite of spirit. Thus the idea of blood is one of physical ties, of heredity, of the soil, of property, of possessiveness. It is the last legacy of the nineteenth century, which believed blindly in the reality of matter.

'Was it Germany's mission to strengthen the power of the last century? I believe that Germany had a mission to fulfil. People who say that we are of the country of Lessing, Goethe and Schopenhauer, remind us that we are chosen to introduce spiritual understanding into the modern world. In pre-war days the blatant contradiction of that mission was our Kaiser. Though Germany's mission is a general European mission, it seems that through our geographical position and historical inheritance we were especially predestined to fulfil it. It is the mission of making Christianity a reality in our age. Christ demolished the frontiers that existed between men; spiritual equality of men should at last be extended to nations. We have reached a moment when this has to be done, and when economics will force the world to do it. We must not be deceived by temporary economic barriers. Whether they survive twenty or thirty years is immaterial, for they are only temporary. Even to-day nations begin to pull them down and to collaborate through barter. Germany's mission, I think, was to foster such a *rapprochement* of the various nations, and to extend it to other fields besides economics. To fulfil that mission of the twentieth century we had to break away once and for all from the laws that had governed the nineteenth. A new conception of political and national life was necessary. And it was in our power to introduce it and thus to fulfil Germany's destiny.

'Where did the powers of materialism come from, that reigned so vigorously over the last century? They are the last manifestation of the principle contained in the Old Testament. This principle is not limited to the religion of the Jews alone. It is the principle of all pre-Christian religions in which the forces of blood are predominant.

In the Old Testament we find them more clearly defined than in any other religion, and they affected the Western world primarily through the medium of the Old Testament.

'Purity of blood had enabled the Jews to provide the perfect body for the Son of God and to give the world the most perfect form of materialism. Since the first task has been accomplished, and since the forces of materialism have fulfilled their mission the principle of the Old Testament is no longer needed. And yet Hitler's victory is a victory of that principle. Lack of spiritual individualism with blind obedience to one law alone, and the corresponding separation of nations, the stressing of family ties, of purity of blood—all these are principles of the Old Testament.

'Hitler as the instrument of certain powers must have heard dim voices that told him of the approaching end of the old principle. But he misunderstood the voices. Instead of replacing the old principle by a newer gospel, he attacked the religion contained in the Old Testament. Instead of forgetting a unity with the soil which in our age ought to be a unity with all and every soil and not one in particular, instead of forgetting blood and race, he strengthened those powers. Instead of opening our frontiers and letting the world come to benefit from the new springs of German spirit, he antagonized the world. Instead of inviting the whole world to collaborate he withdrew from the League of Nations. He is the only European leader who can afford to adopt any policy he wishes He could have led our country out of limited national issues into truly spiritual ones. Several of our statesmen with much less power had begun to do it in the last few years. Hitler merely emphasized such issues as rearmament, as the fictitious equality of status, as racial pride. Instead of destroying the principle of the Old Testament he destroyed some of its racial representatives. The Third Reich might have become a truly *Holy* German Empire. . . .

'The power of destiny proved too strong in one instance only. I am referring to the exile of many of our best men. Thousands of them were forced to go into the world and thus the spiritual frontiers between Germany and other countries are breaking down, though not in the way many had hoped they would.

'People who claim to know more than most mortals say that, though in a different form, another nation has begun to fulfil what might have been Germany's mission. Great Britain is that nation. She is establishing at present within her own Empire the most perfect example of practical Christianity through international collaboration spreading over five continents. She may not be conscious of what she is doing—though I doubt it. What matters is that Great Britain introduced into the modern world the Christian idea of deliberate collaboration and elimination of narrow nationalist elements in all important issues of her life. Germany had the knowledge and the opportunity for fulfilling that mission England was guided merely by her indefinable "sense" that perceives truth without knowing it. Politically the British Empire has become a much looser entity than it has ever been before, and one part after another is making itself politically independent. Economically, however, each individual part is trying to collaborate with the others, to readjust itself to their needs, to take of their best and to give them of its best in return. The British Empire is experiencing a rebirth through free collaboration instead of through conquests. Only in organic unity and in spiritual freedom can the modern world escape a premature death.'

CHAPTER I

THE LONELINESS OF HERMANN KEYSERLING

I

Though I had not seen Keyserling for some twelve years or more, I had followed his career with enough interest to know that his reputation had been fast increasing. The *Tagungen* in Darmstadt, which had been continued for several years, formed only a small part of his activities. Almost every year he had published a new book—provocative, stimulating, full of new light on old truths and displaying a lively imagination. After the *Travel Diary* there appeared a book called *Schöpferische Erkenntnis* ('Creative Understanding'), which contained a synthesis of his main philosophy of 'Significance'. The next book was *Recovery of Truth*, which was partly a continuation of its predecessor. Then came *Menschen als Sinnbilder* ('Symbolical Figures'), a very personal collection of essays, and *Die neuentstehende Welt* ('The World in the Making'), one of the author's most successful books. With his next book, *Das Spektrum Europas* ('Europe'), Keyserling offended most of the nations he had ever visited. His brilliant but superficial analysis of most of the European countries earned him new fame and fresh abuse. The result of a lecture tour through the United States was a bulky volume *America Set Free*. It is an entertaining book, full of unusual matter; and written—such is Keyserling's linguistic facility—in English. But it was too absurd and unflattering and was in consequence banned throughout the United States After a prolonged visit to South America, Keyserling wrote *South American Meditations*, which he called the essence of his spiritual maturity. As he said later: 'This book gave to South America its soul.' No other man could have made such a statement. But who else could have written this extraordinary book, each one of its five hundred closely printed pages full of startling ideas and bursting with imagination? Edmond Jaloux, the eminent French publicist, wrote of the author of this book: 'He has an almost fabulous volubility of thought. Original ideas, profound reflections, unexpected points of view, varied knowledge, all come from him in almost torrential form. . . . The reader feels slightly dazed before such a formidable abundance of thought.'

213

FULFILMENTS

More important than the *Tagungen* and the books were becoming Keyserling's lectures. He lectured with the same ease in German, Russian, French or English. He also began to learn Spanish, a language that particularly appealed to him. After a few months he could even lecture in it. What is more, he began to coin his own Spanish words just as he formerly used English, French or German words that were of his own creation. In 1931 he engaged the huge Trocadero in Paris and delivered three lectures in French, and the experiment proved successful, some six thousand people filling the hall every evening. Keyserling continued to enlarge the scope of his international activities. He accepted an invitation from his Spanish friends to hold a congress at Mallorca in the form of a *Darmstadt Tagung*. Most of the leading Spaniards were present, and the congress was considered one of the most outstanding events in the intellectual life of Spain.

Keyserling's linguistic and geographical possibilities enabled him to exercise a certain intellectual influence over people in many different countries. With characteristic self-assurance he would say: 'In my childhood I had a gift for sculpture. But to-day I don't need to sculpt in stone, I can sculpt nations.'

His fame was greatest outside his own country. Before the Americans realized that Keyserling had shocked them by his unconventional behaviour and offended them by his provocative book, he could claim to be one of the most popular foreigners in the United States. He was famous enough to induce a casual acquaintance to have his visiting cards printed:

Carol Brent Chilton

Friend of Keyserling

But Keyserling's unbalanced criticism of the United States alienated many Americans, and hero worship was soon replaced by unflattering stories, concocted by important hostesses whose lion-hunting proclivities had not been satisfied by the philosopher. Keyserling's philosophy was too manysided to be put into a nutshell and served round dinner tables as a subject for amusing conversation. On the other hand he was too striking a man to be neglected as a subject of table talk. The real issues of his personality were overshadowed by unimportant details. The less frivolous naturally continued to appreciate him for his intellectual achievements. Keyserling,

214

however, never pretended to be a philosopher addressing a small circle of specialists; he was, rather, a 'spiritual inspirer'. He could not possibly limit himself to the select few but had to consider the big majority.

In the autumn of 1933 he was invited to Paris to speak at a big international congress. The French Minister of Education presided over the opening lecture, and the Archbishop of Paris was also present. Paul Valéry was in the chair, and among foreign listeners there were Salvador de Madariaga from Spain and Aldous Huxley from England. Keyserling spoke about *La révolte des forces telluriques et les responsabilités de l'esprit* and at the second lecture about *La communauté des esprits*. The essence of those lectures can be found in a few highly topical sentences in which Keyserling expressed his beliefs in real spiritual leadership. 'How does the spiritual guide act?' he asked his vast audience, and answered himself immediately: 'Not by suggestion like the mass leader, the lion tamer, but like a model, a mould or a fruitful symbol. He does not need the slightest material power. The proper formula or image, be it that of a living being or of an eternal truth, if only it is duly meditated upon, suffices to start a process of realization. It is in this purely spiritual creative activity that I see all the high future mission of the European spirit.'

Keyserling had just published two new volumes written in French, and among those who had praised him enthusiastically were Edmond Jaloux, André Siegfried, Guy de Pourtalès, Havelock Ellis, Thomas Mann, Siegmund Freud, Count Apponyi, Henri Bergson, José Ortega Y Gasset.

While looking through the window of my railway carriage at the shifting scenery of southern Germany I felt that I was indeed on my way to meet a celebrity of the very first water. His fame would have been impressive if he had been a film star or a boxing champion. For a philosopher it was unique.

II

Though I arrived in Darmstadt early on a Sunday morning, I rang up Keyserling without delay. I was asked to come and see him as soon as I wished. I had been warned by several people that he might be rude, that contradiction would make him lose his temper, and that I should be obliged to listen only to what he might care to

215

tell me. I well remembered his attitude ten or thirteen years earlier, and approached his home not without apprehension.

The house was situated at the bottom of the hill called *Mathilden-höhe*, which the Grand Duke Ernst Ludwig had presented thirty years ago to the young artists of his day. They had covered it with pretentious 'art' villas in the 'new' style. There were windows flanked by slender lilylike ornaments, and chimneypots covered with green or mauve tiles.

When I reached my destination I found on the gate an unpretentious enamelled plate with the words *Gesellschaft fur Freie Philosophie* ('Society of Free Philosophy'). On the door on the second floor the plate was smaller, but in brass, and it bore not only the words I had found on the gate but also *Schule der Weisheit* ('School of Wisdom'). I must confess that my memories of Darmstadt had led me to expect something much grander.

I rang the bell Keyserling, wearing white ducks and an open cricket shirt, himself came to the door. As it was a Sunday there was no secretary or servant. Keyserling seemed even bigger than I remembered him; he had grown fatter, but his eyes were still as sparkling, and his vitality seemed, if possible, even greater than ever. We crossed a small ante-room, entered the study and sat down in two leather chairs on either side of a table. Keyserling began to talk without any preliminaries, and I had hardly time to take stock of my surroundings. When, however, I was able to mention that I had just been in Berlin and that I had seen several members of the Government and had discussed topical questions with them, he immediately began to talk about his own troubles.

I could see from the very beginning how anxious Keyserling was to talk At first I could only understand part of what he was saying: his words chased one another as of old, and before one syllable was finished the next came tumbling out of his mouth. I found listening so strenuous that I decided to concentrate on watching Keyserling himself. His hair and his beard were distinctly greyer; and there was a disorder about his clothes which corresponded to his nervous and erratic speech. The room was small and rather simple. In front of the window there stood a homely writing table with a few manuscript sheets lying about; on one side of the room there was a bookcase, on the other a large table covered with books and newspapers. Through the window beyond some trees I could see a large and ugly church of uncompromisingly Protestant appearance.

THE LONELINESS OF HERMANN KEYSERLING

Slowly I gathered from the flood of words that Keyserling had become one of the most hated men in Darmstadt. It was by no means an enmity of the leading men in Berlin but came from some local authorities. For the last fifteen years Keyserling had been the most famous citizen of Hesse, but unfortunately his fame was international and thus anathema to the local men of power. He possessed most of the qualifications for unpopularity among the local satraps, who prided themselves on their independence and great power. The new idea of leadership (*Führerprinzip*) and of the final responsibilities of a leader only rarely prove successful. Had the name of Keyserling not been famous and had his wife not been the granddaughter of Bismarck, there can be little doubt that the local leaders would have tried to harm him even more than they had yet done. A year ago they had forbidden him to go to Spain on a lecture tour which would have brought him a large sum of money. As lecture tours were his chief means of earning his living, and as a prophet is but rarely listened to in his own land, this refusal caused a great loss of income to him. Most of the means of injuring him seemed exhausted, so finally the local men of destiny decided to deprive him of German citizenship. This matter, being of capital importance for the proper understanding of Keyserling, must be treated in some detail. Officials had arrived at his residence a fortnight earlier and had forced him to give up his passport, so that he was left legally unprotected.

'I, a Keyserling, who lived in my land like an independent king, I, father of two greatgrandsons of Bismarck, am treated like a pariah in a town which became famous through me. The local authorities offered to give me one of those certificates that are given to eastern Jews residing in Germany nowadays. And I, Hermann Keyserling, came to this country in 1918 because I believed I could help Germany; because I thought people like myself were needed here. I came to help, and all I get is hatred. I am getting proofs of admiration from the rest of Germany, from France, Spain, South America to this day; here—I am treated like an outcast. After the war I could have gone anywhere I wanted; I had friends in Paris, in Rome, in Vienna; Arthur Balfour and Lord Haldane were intimate friends of mine; I had better connections in England and France than in this country; but I considered it my duty to settle down here and to do my share whenever I could. And I always loved doing it.'

Keyserling would be put in a very dangerous position if he were deprived for good of his passport. He had sent telegrams to the responsible ministers in Berlin; he had telephoned to Berlin almost daily; he had fought with all his old fighting spirit. The central authorities in Berlin had telegraphed to the local leaders, ordering them to return him his passport, but the principle of local leadership had become such a powerful weapon that the local men felt strong enough to disobey the orders of their superiors in Berlin. Keyserling's denaturalization was to become effective the moment the police should deliver the official document in which the announcement of his loss of German citizenship was to be made. This would legalize his unprotected status.

'It has always been the same throughout my life—one long chain of tragic climaxes I must always fight to the very end, and I win my victories only when it is almost too late. I assure you it will be the same this time. I have a certain gift of foreseeing things; and I can almost see how it will all turn out now. I have often been faced with the danger of death during a revolution, but each time something has happened at the last moment to save me. It is as though death were still shy of touching me. Look at this wound!' he exclaimed, as he opened his shirt with a gesture. Across his chest there lay a deep scar—the result of a duel more than thirty years earlier. 'Hardly anyone has ever survived such a wound. I have. I shall survive many more wounds and fights including this one.

'Do you realize that I can claim to be one of the real prophets of the Third Reich? Do you know that I was one of the first to predict all that happened in this country in the last two years? Wait a second!' He jumped up from his chair, opened the bookcase, took out from it a couple of yellow-bound pamphlets, and opened one of them. 'This is an article I published last year. Listen to it.' He put on a pair of spectacles and began to read: 'Is it not true that I was one of the first who had foreseen the future evolution of Germany? ... In an essay I wrote in 1918 I drew a picture of what is happening to-day. ... My essays were one long evocation of national communal life and of a national rebirth. ... My lectures between 1920 and 1926 were one constant praise of heroism. ...' He interrupted his readings and said: 'Isn't that exactly what Nazism is doing?' Then he went on quoting from the pamphlet: 'As far back as 1925 I have predicted the present wave of nationalism ... One has to count me among the founders of the New Germany. ...'

THE LONELINESS OF HERMANN KEYSERLING

Keyserling put aside the pamphlet, and went on: 'It is known in Berlin that I am absolutely loyal to the Nazi régime and to the men who represent it. That is quite natural, for I am a German above all. Berlin has always treated me with the greatest consideration and has supported me. But the local pygmies harm me whenever they can. They hate me because I am not afraid of them; because my loyalty to the Third Reich is really much deeper and more seriously founded than theirs, because I am *grand seigneur*, famous, a Keyserling.'

I was becoming accustomed to the strenuous style of my host and to the speed of his words, and I thought I might venture a question. 'Do you think the German people are religious?' I asked.

'Not at all. We Germans do not believe in something that is beyond the rational, but in a *Weltanschauung*—a philosophy. Thus we are bound to change our beliefs more frequently than other nations. This, however, is not disloyalty, for we believe deeply in the superiority of a new *Weltanschauung* for which we had sacrificed an old one. The English with their intellectual laziness do not care for any *Weltanschauung*, whether old or new. But the Germans must have new ones all the time. That's the reason why we were so impressed by Martin Luther's words: "Here I stand. I cannot do otherwise." The English would have hardly noticed such an evocation; to them it is natural that once you make up your mind about something you stand by it. To the German imagination Luther's words appeared as verging on the miraculous.'

'Do you consider that the Germans have a political instinct?'

'Not as a whole, but we produce many outstanding exceptions. Take Germany's past history alone: Frederick the Great, Freiherr vom Stein, Bismarck—these men are among the greatest statesmen the world has ever known.'

'I seem to remember that somewhere or other you wrote in 1933 about various aspects of the last German revolution. You said that the passion of the German revolutionaries of the last year or two was not political but religious. You also said that the power of Germany's leader is based not on force but on faith. How do you explain such things about a nation that does not believe in what is beyond the rational, that believes more in a *Weltanschauung* than in a religion?'

Keyserling got up from his chair, approached me and looked straight into my eyes, narrowing his own in a sort of half-smile as though apologizing beforehand for his answer. I realized later that he did it often and that the grin was only a trick by which he was trying to tone down some of his replies. He said in a most conciliatory voice: 'How can any intelligent person rationalize about politics? Most political happenings are irrational and inexplicable. It is the same as with ourselves: nine-tenths of what happens within ourselves and of the reasons why we do certain things cannot be explained. You can understand happenings outside yourself only if you try to compare them with the experiences within yourself. Everything outside of ourselves is only an image of phenomena within.'

'I always imagined that the only inexplicable thing in life is death.'

'In a way death is the only thing in German life you can explain', Keyserling answered, as though roused to opposition. I could almost watch a theory entering his restless brain on the spur of the moment and in violent jumps. 'Do you realize that death is the real goal of all Germans? Germans see in death their final fulfilment. You must not forget that in Germany death is the highest virtue of the hero. To sacrifice a son on the altar of death is for a German mother a greater honour than to have borne even a genius. This is what distinguishes her from other mothers To enter Valhalla is for the German almost deification. Few of the great mysteries appeal more to the German imagination than the death of the Niebelungen. It is the highest deed in German mythology, the highest ideal—but few foreigners can understand that.'

'Doesn't the idea of purity of blood and health of the race contradict your statement about death?'

'Blood and race come from telluric depths. An appeal to blood is essentially an appeal to the instinct of the earth in man. That is the reason why appeals to the idea of race are so successful. In the domain of worldly success, "earthly" appeals are bound to succeed.'

'I don't quite follow.'

'Look here', Keyserling rose once again as though growing impatient; 'the spirit is the one thing that cannot have direct power on earth. Spiritual power and earthly power are of two entirely different dimensions on two different levels. The spirit cannot act on a level that is first and foremost a level of the earth; it is a force in itself, unconnected with the earth or with any of its expressions. It acts even outside the intellect. That's why it can appeal only to a few people, to those who are capable of producing spiritual reactions within themselves. A nation as a whole cannot possibly follow such an appeal; but it can follow the magnetic power which is contained in the idea of earth and blood. You evoke with them instinctive reactions that do not require any "sublimation" but can manifest themselves spontaneously. It is wrong to oppose the message of blood with that of the spirit as is being frequently done abroad. You must not try to mix up spirit and blood. They are of different dimensions. No epoch understood that contrast better than the Middle Ages. Spirit was embodied for them in the personality of the Pope, and flesh in that of the Emperor.'

'Do you consider men or women as the more adapted to carry what you called the message of the spirit into the world?'

'Why, women of course! While men concentrate on activity and achievement, women are always ready to become receivers for a spiritual message. Twice in modern history women have carried the message of the spirit into the world. In the days of earliest Christianity Roman women became Christians while their menfolk remained heathen. It was through their wives and daughters that they were slowly converted to the Christian faith. In the early Middle Ages, in the days of the Provençal troubadours, women created in their lives a refinement that carried spirituality among men. Men were rough and ready to violate women. In order to protect themselves, women built up an atmosphere of culture and refinement that kept men at a distance. Distance itself is congenial to spirituality. Spirit acts on the whole better from a distance than in direct contact.'

Almost three hours had passed. I was no longer able to follow the intellectual contortions of my host. He jumped from subject to subject with the rapidity of an acrobat, and my own brain refused to follow him. I rose. 'Must you leave? We were just beginning to have an interesting conversation. Do come to-morrow morning to continue our talk. Meanwhile I want you to meet my wife. She plays such an important part in my life that you cannot possibly understand me without knowing her. Can you come and have tea with her in the afternoon?'

Someone knocked at the door, and a tall and slender woman entered the room. Countess Keyserling had dark hair and eyes, a soft, light complexion and an engaging smile.

FULFILMENTS

III

When I returned in the afternoon Countess Keyserling was sitting in her drawing-room preparing tea. The room with its many lamp-shades, photographs, cushions, cigarette boxes and flowers was most decidedly a woman's room. We sat by a window looking out on a little garden with rose bushes and multi-coloured dahlias. Countess Keyserling began a conversation as though she had known me for a long time. How difficult it would have been to get over these first twenty minutes, had we been in England! We should have spent a lot of time with questions that required no answers and answers that were not listened to. I did not need to inform my hostess of the crossing I had had, or whether the drought in England was quite as bad as in Germany. She knew what I was interested in and she began to talk about it at once; about how her husband lived and worked, about her children, about her own part in Keyserling's life. She spoke English fluently, though with a German accent. Her womanliness was emphasized by a self-consciousness that made her blush frequently. The shyness was outbalanced by intelligence and self-assurance evidently developed through long experience. She must have been considerably younger than Keyserling and, while his appearance showed little care, Countess Keyserling was dressed immaculately.

'You will be surprised when I show you my husband's bedroom,' she said, 'not because of its ugliness—it is the ugliest room in the house—but for the library which you will find in it.' We went up-stairs. Indeed it was an ugly room, small, high and ill lit and cluttered with obsolete pieces of furniture. The most noticeable features of the room were countless bookshelves filled with books—nothing but detective stories—there must have been hundreds of them. 'It is the only relaxation my husband can find. He does not care for games or the cinema; music interests him much too much; at times he spends entire evenings at the piano improvising, but afterwards he feels more stimulated than before; detective stories are the only natural relax-ation that gives him peace. Often I have to read to him while he is in bed, and that sends him to sleep.'

We returned to the ground floor, where I was shown Keyserling's study. It was an odd, chapel-like room, dimly lit, and thousands of books lined the walls. One side of the room was transformed into a sort of Eastern shrine with a bronze Buddha in front of an ancient silk hanging from China and several Chinese and Japanese pictures.

THE LONELINESS OF HERMANN KEYSERLING

This was the chapel of the parish priest for whom this house was originally built. My husband hardly ever uses it now, spending most of his time in his office.'

'Does your husband work very systematically and according to a definite plan?'

'No, when he writes he almost appears to become a medium, driven by some power from outside or rather from within himself. He hardly knows what he is writing, and afterwards no one is more surprised at the results than himself. The writing simply pours out of him.'

Was it not the same with the method of his entire philosophy? There was an astounding wealth of thought, but everything in it appeared to be chaotic. Both in his conversation and his books I missed the continuity of a clear structure: the relative positions of chapters might easily be altered without doing much harm to the book; a theme might be treated in far greater or much less detail without affecting the whole. I had the feeling that ideas came to Keyserling incessantly, and that he put them more or less automatically on to paper, bothering little about their form. His artistic temperament must have been alien to a proper method in his work. Keyserling's combination of an obviously artistic disposition in his philosophy, and of an over-abundance in its formal structure, seemed to me one of his outstanding characteristics. It stimulated the reader's thoughts constantly, yet it did not allow him to put the newly-found truths into some helpful order.

When we returned to the drawing-room I asked: 'Does your husband read his manuscripts to you?'

'Practically never. I only read his books after they have been published. I have nothing to do with his professional work and we are both absolutely independent. That's probably why we are so happy together. When he goes abroad, especially to a new country, I hardly ever accompany him. He likes to learn a new country by opening himself to its impressions. In order to do that successfully he must not feel his usual atmosphere around him. My presence would handicap him. I am, as he calls it, his foreign and home secretary and his exchequer. I give him ten marks a month for his personal expenses which he generally brings back at the end of the month.'

'How do your two boys like being the sons of a famous philosopher?'

'They hardly ever think about it; but they consider him the most amusing companion they know. He treats them as friends and on the other hand he belittles their worries and troubles and develops in them a feeling of detachment and even irony that makes some of the worries of a modern German child more bearable.'

<h1 style="text-align:center">IV</h1>

When I arrived next morning at Keyserling's office, a young girl, obviously a secretary, opened the door. I was shown instantly into Keyserling's room, and even before we shook hands he exclaimed: 'I have just heard from Berlin. Orders from the various responsible ministers have been sent to the local leaders; and yet they still refuse to give me back my passport. A few weeks ago they published a declaration that both my sons and myself had been deprived of the Hessian and thus automatically of the German citizenship. Do you know what that means? As they don't deprive my wife of her citizenship, we shall no longer be legally married. For all you know, I am living now with a mistress and not with my wife. They try to catch my wife and myself where they think they can hurt us most, for they know well how devoted we are to one another. But they don't know me; I shall fight them to the end. They will have to use brute force to expel a Keyserling and the grandchildren of Bismarck.'

'Do you really think they will dare to do that?' I interrupted.

'It is difficult to say; but experience teaches me that I am spared nothing before my trials are over. That is my destiny.'

'So you believe in destiny?'

'Yes, but destiny is the privilege of only a few people: those who have a definite individual life line. The lives of most people are so intermingled with others—so little individual—that they can only have a *Massenschicksal*, which in each particular case is just fate.'

'Do you also believe in such signs of destiny as, for example, astrology and handwriting?'

'I somehow believe in astrology, but it seems to me wrong to think about it or to consult it. A disinterested belief in it is all I want for myself. It is different with graphology. For years I have known the man who is the real inventor of the art of graphology. His name is M. J. Crépieux-Jamin. He is a Frenchman, still alive, though he must be nearly eighty. He was in turn agriculturist, clockmaker and dentist. But his main claim to fame is his wonderful gift for graphology. I am praising him not because of what he said of my terrible writing [indeed, I knew only too well how "terrible" this writing was, and that it generally took me an hour to decipher a letter by Keyserling], though, I confess, I am sensitive to flattery. He said that my handwriting reminded him both of Napoleon's and of Pascal's. I was very pleased with this analysis, especially as I see myself as a mixture of active vitality and sharpness of thought. Of all the many handwritings M. Crépieux-Jamin has seen, he was most impressed by two that I had shown him—those of Annie Besant and of Rabindranath Tagore. He was so moved by the characteristics of Annie Besant's writing that he had tears in his eyes when he analysed it.'

The only photograph in the room was a photograph of Annie Besant with a long dedication.

'You knew Annie Besant well, didn't you?' I asked.

'I met her at Adyar in India during my trip round the world. When we met for the first time Annie Besant approached me with all the priestliness and paraphernalia that were expected from her by her theosophical followers, and she asked me: "Do you know what you were in your previous life?" To which I answered: "I am afraid my memory is so bad that I often have the greatest difficulty in remembering my present life." She looked at me for a second, and then she laughed. We became friends for life. Often in later years, when she was in some difficult or unhappy situation, she would write me a letter, asking me to send her just a line: it would cheer her up. I consider her the greatest woman politician in the world, to whom the Indians will owe a greater debt for their Home Rule than to anyone else. She had a greatness and unity of purpose which were quite unique. She became President of the Theosophical Society only because she could not become Queen of England. Yet I don't believe in her occult powers; I never took that side of her activities seriously. She knew that, and that was probably the reason why we were such good friends.'

I could not refrain from asking, 'Have you ever met Krishnamurti?'

'I met him at the same time that I met Annie Besant. He was then only a boy and a lot of nonsense was being said and done about the little chap. I consider it his greatest achievement in later life to have lived down the reputation of being the vehicle for the "World Teacher",—for Christ and goodness knows what. He was a delightful boy, and I was very fond of him. It was most amusing to watch the anxiety of the theosophists, who were frightened lest I should

P 225

enlighten the boy to such an extent as to make him renounce his claim to the throne of Christ. They always tried to prevent us from conversing without witnesses. I haven't seen him since.'

'What is your opinion of him to-day?'

Keyserling got up, and took from the bookcase another of the yellow pamphets that I had seen the day before. 'This is what I wrote about Krishnamurti a few years ago', he said, and began to read: 'Serious people have assured me in the last few years that though Krishnamurti may not be very great or very deep there can be no doubt about the beauty and purity of his soul. His renunciation of his throne showed me clearly that he is really quite an extraordinary personality of highest moral integrity. The philosophical insufficiencies of his doctrine leave me rather helpless. . . . Judged as an Indian he seems to me to be standing close to the spirit of Moscow. This is also true of Gandhi, and, *mutatis mutandis,* even of Buddha. On the other hand, Krishnamurti is strangely unintellectual for an Indian. This is why he does not like to make any spiritual decisions. If he wants to be the teacher of the whole world his attitude to-day must be one of antagonism against religion, metaphysics, occultism. . . . In his own way he is a leading representative of the religion of godlessness.'

'You mentioned Tagore before . . .'

'Oh, *welch ein Mensch!* I simply adore him. I don't care for his poems, because lyrical poetry at its best bores me; the only form of poetry I can cope with must be dramatic or heroic. But Tagore's genuine spirituality always showed me how great and beautiful his character was. Nevertheless I no longer have a desire to see him; I prefer to love him from a distance.'

Another obvious question came into my mind. It was not tactful perhaps to examine Keyserling as to his attitude towards men who might be considered his 'competitors'; but I considered it my duty to know his opinion about several of those men. I asked: 'What about Rudolf Steiner?'

'I have never met him, though you may have heard the gossip about some quarrel between us more than ten years ago. That, however, does not alter my admiration for his enormous gifts. He possessed a genuine second sight, real occult powers and a tremendous intellectual and spiritual knowledge; ultimately, however, I see in Steiner the acting of an evil power.' Keyserling's words surprised me greatly, but before I could find time to interrupt him, he continued:

THE LONELINESS OF HERMANN KEYSERLING

'In the last years of his life Steiner developed a tremendous lust for power, and finally he was eaten up by it: the cancer from which he died was nothing else than the expression of the lust for power that destroyed him. Cancer is a symbolical disease, and lust for power becomes in spiritual regions black magic. Steiner's occult activities were full of what you may call white magic; it is therefore not easy to see a clear spiritual picture of him. I personally "feel" him as ultimately bad.'

Though I knew that Keyserling's statements were utterly unfounded, and terribly malicious, I did not care to begin a discussion which on Keyserling's part would have been based mainly on assumptions and not on knowledge. Keyserling's information was obviously inspired by malignant gossip, and I knew how dangerous it was to judge a man whom one did not know personally. I went on with my enquiries.

'What do you think of Mme. H. P. Blavatsky? Was she the fraud that some recent books on occult subjects make her out to be?'

'Nonsense, she was incredibly gifted. Yet it is most difficult to understand people like her, people who are, foremost, mediums of greater spiritual forces. In their ordinary conscious state they often have to lie and to be frauds. Mme. Blavatsky undoubtedly often produced false tricks with which she tried to satisfy the occult greed of her followers, constantly awaiting miracles. But she was a genuine occult power.'

'And Leadbeater, Annie Besant's notorious collaborator—did you know him? . . .'

Keyserling smiled as though reminded of some amusing situation. 'Indeed, I did. He, too, had genuine occult powers—infinitely more than Annie Besant—and it was quite true that he suddenly "saw" occult colour images of your character, a country or an event. But it was just like having a fine voice or eyes of a particular colour. He was stupid, yet I liked him for his quaint mixture of occult gifts and an incredible naïveté. His occultism was as genuine as his pomposity. Which reminds me of Stefan George. You know, many Germans consider him the greatest German since Goethe. I never could understand why he should have exercised such an enormous influence. His few volumes of poems could not have done it. To me, of course, they mean very little. I imagine his success was a success of silence. Hardly anybody knew him or ever saw him;

227

he never uttered a word except in his five or six small books; he never received a journalist; he was hardly ever photographed. He was silence personified, and silence impresses us Germans.'

I could not resist the temptation of asking Keyserling whether he knew the British antithesis to the German master of silence: Bernard Shaw. 'The most talkative man in the world', answered Keyserling; 'I know him and I am always greatly amused by him; but even in a private conversation he remains the professional playwright or rather the writer of prefaces to plays. He can never forget that he is Bernard Shaw and that he has to be witty and paradoxical. This becomes tiring. As for real spiritual values, he doesn't even know the meaning of the word spirituality. There is not a spark of spirituality in the whole of Shaw.'

Up till now our conversation had somewhat evaded the questions which should have been put to a man who was first of all a spiritual teacher. The very fact that I had not asked them, and that Keyserling himself had hardly mentioned the subjects that might have been touched upon in this connection, made me wonder whether he could be called a teacher in the sense in which I had understood that word hitherto. We generally think that in order to learn something we have to be given directions of a very definite kind. Questions that I had recently considered not unimportant suddenly appeared to be merely academic. As, however, I was certain that most people would have asked them, when faced by a man like Keyserling, I decided to discharge them at him.

The first question was: 'Do you believe in yoga and meditations?'

'Eastern meditations are almost always useless for Western people. The same applies, of course, to yoga. Certain Jesuit and Freemason meditations may be useful for us Whether to make them, or not, is a purely individual matter which everyone has to decide for himself. For me personally meditation has acquired in the course of years a new meaning. Facing reality in a positive way, and without evading it, is for my active temperament a form of meditation. If I do not shrink from the difficulties of life, but contemplate them, then I consider I have done my kind of meditation. Learning through direct experience, through pain and suffering what your innermost attitude is when facing reality, is the best form of spiritual exercise.'

My second question: 'Do you consider that we should reorganize our sex life, that some sort of celibacy is necessary for spiritual achievement?'

THE LONELINESS OF HERMANN KEYSERLING

'General rules of this kind cannot be given, and one has to be very careful with celibacy. Once again I must repeat that the first thing to do is to find out about one's inner organization. The movement you know what is individual in yourself, then you also know whether to follow the urge of your sex or to suppress it. But remember one thing —things that are by their very nature of a physical kind, have to be dealt with in a physical way.'

The third question: 'Do you consider that the Churches in the Western world are doing their duty and that they are still an important channel for the finding of truth? The American writer Walter Lippmann said in his famous book *Preface to Morals* that "Modern man no longer takes his religion as an account of the real life of the universe". Is this state the fault of the "modern man" or of the modern Church?'

'I am glad that there are Churches. There are a great many people who need them and who can find happiness only through and in a Church. For them Churches must remain. Besides, why destroy them, even if you think you have found something better? One ought never to destroy old institutions because one thinks one has found better ones. This applies to cultural, political, in fact all institutions in communal life. Old and new institutions must live on side by side: the better ones will gradually eliminate those of less value by their very superiority. To many people Churches mean nothing to-day: those people follow other routes in order to find their God. I personally am unable to follow anybody's authority. You may consider that blasphemous or arrogant, but what is the good of pretending that one believes in something if one doesn't! If I acknowledge any individual master at all, it is Buddha: not on account of a special superiority of his teaching, but merely for the fact that he, too, believed in no one else and in nobody's authority but his own. Most of the other teachers speak for someone else; even Jesus Christ spoke not in his own name but in the name of God, his Father. I myself speak only and entirely for myself and in my own name and for that I take the full responsibility. You don't need to listen to me, but, if you do, you must accept that. If people find that they have to follow a particular teacher, Steiner, Annie Besant, Krishnamurti, or Buchman, let them do it. But far be it from me to preach for anybody or against anybody. You must decide for yourself whom you want to follow.'

V

Next evening I dined with the Keyserlings. There were no other guests, and our conversation started with the same intensity and lack of preliminaries as did the morning talks. I could see that something in connection with the passport affair had happened. This affair had become a kind of *leitmotiv* of my stay in Darmstadt, and every new 'act' of my visit began with this particular overture.

'I have received an air mail letter from my lawyer in Berlin written this afternoon. He says that though the responsible ministers in Berlin insist upon my being given back my passport, it's too late to get them to restore it to me. He ends his letter with the words "you will get your *Ausbürgerungsurkunde* (denaturalization papers) at any moment". Well, it seems that to-day is the last day. You will probably have the pleasure of witnessing the arrival of the police to legalize my denationalized status They must appear here before midnight.'

I could not help feeling the melodramatic atmosphere around us. We might have been acting in some detective play. When we sat down to dinner, I asked Keyserling: 'Why haven't you answered all the calumnies and misrepresentations about you which have been circulated by your enemies and which are ultimately responsible for your present state of affairs?'

'I never answer calumnies. It would be fatal against the spirit. If you make no answer to calumnies, they go through your spiritual self like waves, and as though you were non-existent; sooner or later they disappear entirely. On the other hand, if you do answer them, you evoke similar evil powers to the ones used against you, and you will never be able to rid yourself of them.'

Keyserling went on talking. His vitality seemed even greater than usual. He was enjoying his meal, taking huge helpings of every course, except the sweet, of which he never partook. My critical, not to say antagonistic, attitude of thirteen years ago was changing into genuine sympathy. He was an impressive human animal, powerful, vital, active and positive; conceited, arrogant, proud, egotistic and yet generous; childlike, exuberant and almost intoxicating. It was quite obvious that he could only be judged by his own standards, and that it would be futile to pigeonhole him in any of the usual human or philosophical categories. You could disagree with him, you could dislike his manner or his selfcentredness, but you had to admit that he was an exceptional, personality, and that there was an intellectual fertility in him which few people possess. Whether his ideas were right or wrong seemed to me to matter little. It was himself as a personality that counted. He appeared to me to be the very opposite of what he had seemed to be thirteen years earlier. School, labels, theories—all these seemed of little importance. What mattered was Keyserling's own colourful personality.

Conversation during dinner was more personal than during our morning talks. Even the prospects of the alarming visit that awaited Keyserling could not upset him. He was talking of friends, of his ancestral home, of his travels and his children. 'It may amuse you to hear about my first meeting with Spengler, the author of *Decline of the West*. It was in Munich soon after the war and, I believe, Thomas Mann introduced us to each other. Spengler was very pompous and every inch the author of a book of twelve hundred pages. At a certain moment during dinner he turned towards me as though he had just solved the crucial problem of life and said: "Do you know why the German business man is superior to his English colleague? Because, instead of picking up his golf clubs after his work, he sits down to read his Tacitus".' Keyserling roared with laughter, screwing up his narrow eyes and showing his teeth. 'What a knowledge of England and of Germany! Cannot you see all the millions of German business men rushing home in order to settle down to their Tacitus? How typical of Spengler!'

Conversation would have gone on like that endlessly had there not been a few more questions that I was determined to ask. 'What is your method of work?'

'I never make plans for a new book. When my subconsciousness is filled with enough material I suddenly think of a title or perhaps of a date when the book should be finished. I then settle down and write continuously for a number of weeks. I become almost a medium and I hardly realize what the book will be like. Length, plan, number of chapters matter nothing to me, and it is only when the book is ready that I become conscious of all those things, and only then do I begin to introduce them into my manuscript.' It was not difficult to visualize this process of writing: it must have been akin to Keyserling's manner of speech, for the latter obviously was a speaker rather than a writer. You could see how during a conversation thoughts were coming to him from nowhere and how conversation stimulated him to deliver monologue after monologue. You were there only to suggest every now and then a new direction for the conversation to take.

Neither Countess Keyserling nor I drank more than half a glass of wine; Keyserling drank the rest, and also a whole bottle of champagne. When we left the table and settled down in the drawing-room, Keyserling said: 'For many years I did not drink at all. But my active temperament prevents me from sleeping at night. Very often I don't sleep more than an hour at night. When, however, I drink a bottle of wine and a bottle of champagne, I can sleep. A famous doctor in Frankfurt found out the reason for my strange reaction to wine. Wine, instead of raising my blood pressure as it does in the case of most people, lowers it, acting as a sedative. That's why it makes me sleep. You can imagine what stories were invented about me in that connection.' I preferred not to pursue the subject, and Keyserling went on: 'People always invent stories about me, for example, about my health. They don't understand that I never get ill unless my consciousness has to do something against my subconsciousness'.

'What do you mean by that?'

'This spring I was supposed to go on a big lecture tour to Spain. All the seats were sold, but at the last moment I was not allowed to go. I had to remain here, but, when the time for the first lecture arrived, I developed a severe throat disease. When you wrote to me in the spring suggesting that you should come at that time to see me, I had to refuse on account of this throat trouble, which for weeks prevented me from seeing anybody. My throat had been preparing itself for speaking and, when the moment arrived, it simply wanted to speak, and revolted against the enforced silence.'

Suddenly a bell rang. It was well after eleven. Keyserling himself left the room to open the door. Countess Keyserling tried to go on with our conversation, but we could hear voices outside. I must confess that I would not have been unduly surprised if I had heard a shot. Suddenly the door was flung wide open and Keyserling reappeared He was shouting at the top of his voice: 'What did I tell you, what did I tell you? They have sent me back my passport. Look, here it is, without any marks or changes. In the last moment their courage failed them. Look, here it is. Didn't I tell you? My life is always like this. Could any stage producer have managed the affair more effectively?' Indeed, it was astounding I was thankful that Keyserling's worst anxiety was over, and that I had been able to witness this incident of the passport to its conclusion. Keyserling opened another bottle of beer, and forced me to stay for another hour.

VI

Next morning when I arrived at his office I told him that I had decided to leave Darmstadt that very afternoon. I had heard almost more than I was able to digest and, after the astounding experiences of the last few days, it would have been an anti-climax to have lengthened my visit. I also believed that I was beginning to perceive the meaning of Keyserling's position and 'destiny' in this decisive period of his life. 'After our various talks during the last few days,' I said, 'I can imagine what your aims are to-day; but I would like to hear them from you directly. I remember the social flutter you caused some years ago, and I can see how different things have become. I would like to know what you have to say about it.'

For once Keyserling's answer did not come like a bullet. He poured some black coffee into a low, red lacquer cup, which always stood on the table, and his face, like that of an Eastern autocrat, assumed a softness which made it most attractive but which only rarely illumined it. More slowly than usual he said. 'You have seen the worries I have to go through; you can picture for yourself how difficult the last years have been. The main chapter of my new book which I am finishing now is called "Loneliness". It is not by accident that I had to write so much about that subject during these months. But you have seen how cheerful I remain. Have I ever struck you as being gloomy or depressed? Obstacles, as you know, only make me stronger. The effect of the experiences of the last few years, however, has been to make me withdraw more and more into my shell. I begin to see that the outside world, people, things, events are nothing but the attempt to keep us from losing ourselves in the much more lively, more exciting, more bewildering and more important world of our inner selves. The older I grow the more this seems to me the chief use and meaning of the outside world. Withdrawing into my inner self I find enough to keep me busy and happy for the rest of my days'. He paused for a second, which he only rarely did, but after having taken another sip of coffee he continued: 'My goal can only be to radiate spiritual reality. I don't want to convince anyone; people must come of their own free will as you have come, or they must ask me to visit them to deliver a lecture.

233

FULFILMENTS

Spirit cannot radiate through compulsion or even persuasion. Therefore, I never try to persuade people; they must accept my words as I put them or not at all. I don't believe in argument when we deal with spirit. Spirit can only act in an atmosphere of perfect freedom. Spirit has nothing to do with your brain or your intellect, which can be forced to do this or that. The elements of spirit are faith and courage. It needs tremendous courage to lead a life conceived by the spirit. And you can achieve its deepest realization only if you base it on faith. I have understood fully only in the last few years that spirit is the highest and purest realization of faith and courage.

'To come back to your question about my success after the war—I can only say that it wasn't my success, but a success forced upon me by other people. It was a success of fashion and therefore quite unreal. To-day you will find my name as a philosopher and a teacher mentioned but little in Germany. Society has for the most part deserted me. Look at this office: the remains of the "School of Wisdom". And yet to-day I feel that I am having real success and real influence. To-day individual people come to me to ask my advice or just to listen to me. Such contacts mould people, create spiritual readjustments. Men in responsible positions, who have achieved worldly success, arrive here a thousand times gloomier than I have ever been, worried, frightened about the country's and their own future; but they find me serene, buried in my work, writing new books, facing life as it comes, and without constructing abstract theories. Most of them leave me cheered and strengthened. This is more important than any books I have ever written or am ever likely to write.

'I am willing to receive anyone and to help him personally, because that is the only way one can help people. Through personal contact, personal radiation of the spirit. The success of ten years ago was sham. It is to-day that matters.'

I looked round me. The smallness and simplicity of the room—the unpretentious furniture, the bare writing table—suddenly became particularly striking, and I began to understand that spirit can best be realized if the outer shell is broken. In his present loneliness Keyserling seemed to radiate something that had remained hidden while he was enjoying his spectacular successes. Now it seemed to matter little whether or not chance would allow him once again to lecture to great crowds and impress fashionable audiences. What mattered most was that Keyserling himself had realized that only spiritual

234

radiation from man to man could change people and give them a vision of truth. Thirteen years previously I had met in Darmstadt a self-centred celebrity. To-day I was parting from a man whose courage and serenity could not fail to be impressive. This indeed was a fulfilment.

I felt very grateful when I got up to shake hands with Keyserling and say good-bye.

VII

I heard a few months after my visit to Darmstadt that the German Home Secretary, Dr. Frick, wrote to Keyserling personally to tell him that he had officially cancelled all the decisions of the local authorities in Darmstadt. A few days later the *Government Gazette* published a declaration officially restoring German citizenship to Keyserling and his sons. In November 1934 Keyserling was invited to deliver a public lecture in Berlin.

Once again Keyserling could go abroad. The congress in Spain, that he had had to cancel in the spring, could take place early in 1935. After the congress, Keyserling lectured all over Spain and later on in Italy and in Paris, and his tours were a great success. He was acclaimed wherever he went. Joan Estelrich, the great Catalan poet and historian, expressed the opinion of his country when he wrote: 'Our cultural life is inspired in these weeks by the presence and the lectures of Count Keyserling. He is a true champion and a knight of the spirit. . . . In these days of mass activities and equality he preaches the value of personality. In these days of machine work and imitation he emphasizes the importance of creativeness. In these days of social and economic preoccupations he acknowledges the spirit.'

The inner fulfilment seemed to be finding its external reward.

CHAPTER II

THE TESTAMENT OF RUDOLF STEINER

I

When I set out to find for myself the "Testament" of Rudolf Steiner I knew that the object of my pursuits had not died with its maker. Though I had not kept up a direct contact with anthroposophy I knew that it had developed from a stage of investigation and discovery to one of practical work and acknowledged achievement.

The Anthroposophical Society had suffered the same fate to which so many movements crystallized round one man have been submitted. After Steiner's death it had split into two sections. The more official section, with its headquarters at the Goetheanum at Dornach, was led by Steiner's widow and the famous Swiss poet, Albert Steffen, the other included some of Steiner's closest friends and several of the leading personalities in the movement.

But anthroposophy had become too important a movement to be affected by personal disagreements, and was being absorbed even by people who had no direct contact with it as a movement.

The Anthroposophical Society, too, was growing steadily; to-day there is hardly a country without its branch. Though the membership may be just under 20,000 the number of people connected with anthroposophy must be many times greater. In New Zealand, in Java, in South Africa, and even in Honolulu there are either branches of the Society, or anthroposophical farmers, doctors, educationists.

There were small anthroposophical groups in England even before the war, but a society was not established till after Steiner had delivered a series of lectures in this country during the summer of 1923. The countries in which his ideas had most effect were Germany, Switzerland, Holland, Austria, Czechoslovakia. It is difficult to say how far they have invaded English life, but, if books are at all a reliable measure of the popularity of a doctrine, Steiner must be far more widely known in England than is indicated by the infrequent appearances of his name in the press. Steiner's own literary legacy is enormous. Close on a hundred of his books have

236

been translated into English—some of them volumes of many hundreds of pages. There are probably few scientists or philosophers who have left a larger bulk of work.

The external growth of the anthroposophical movement showed that it was strong enough at its founder's death to withstand even the dangers of organization and discipleship. In a way the rapid growth of the movement is surprising. Steiner himself insisted over and over again that such a manysided doctrine as his could not be forced like a hothouse plant. Hence his aversion to all forms of self-advertisement. Unlike Annie Besant, he was not a showman and was opposed to propaganda. It was not without significance that the founder of anthroposophy was not a German but an Austrian. Many of the most valuable elements in Germany's spiritual and cultural life originated not in Germany but in the countries surrounding her.

II

I went first to Dornach to the Goetheanum, and found there everything exactly as I had expected it: a huge impressive building—a monument in cement to its dead creator—studios, laboratories, devoted discipleship and scholarly research work. But I preferred to cut my time for studying the Goetheanum, and to go farther in my search of the living testament of Steiner.

Except for my visit to Dornach and my much later visits to several of Steiner's former friends and pupils, I expressly abstained during my journey through Central Europe from arranging any meetings with anthroposophists, and preferred to wait and see whether I should come across their activities in the ordinary course of events Though I only spent a short time on the Continent my luck was extraordinary, and I realized that anthroposophy had become one of the few spiritual movements of our time that have penetrated into almost every field of human activity.

I went first to stay with someone on a country estate not far from Berlin. I arrived late at night, but before taking me up to my room my host said: 'By the way, I hope you won't mind a guest who is coming here to-morrow for the day. I had invited him before I knew that you were coming to Germany—so I couldn't put him off. But I am sure you'll like him. He is a young minister.'

I forgot all about the minister till his arrival after breakfast next morning. He had a frank and intelligent face, and had preserved a boyish spontaneity, which expressed itself in sudden bursts of laughter. He was minister at one of the Christian Community churches which had been established in connection with anthroposophy, and he left one in no sort of doubt as to his devotion to his profession. There was something impressive in his idealism, which made me feel that, if all the ministers of his church possessed his burning faith, Steiner's Christian Community might indeed improve the spiritual life of Germany.

It was a warm, sunny day, and we spent most of it walking in the park, the while Herr M. discoursed to me on one of the last chapters of Rudolf Steiner's testament.

'How was it', I asked, 'that Steiner who was against the establishment of a new church, and who always emphasized the fact that anthroposophy is not a religion and does not want to create dogmas, became head of such a church?'

The Herr Pfarrer flushed. 'That is not true', he exclaimed, and his words tumbled over one another in his eagerness to dispel my ignorance. 'I fear you have utterly wrong notions of our church and of its history. You must have been as misinformed as the rest. The doctor always insisted that he was not establishing a new church.' (Steiner was always referred to as the "doctor".) 'He was only the adviser and "spiritual inspirer" of a church created by professional theologians of their own desire.'

'How, then, did it all begin?' I interrupted.

'I am glad that you offer me a chance of giving you a brief history of our church', replied the young minister. 'Some two years after the war small groups—comprising both laymen and ministers—formed themselves in various towns. These people realized that the Evangelical church was losing its influence, and were therefore anxious to infuse new vitality into it. They had no connection with one another, but several of them had heard of Steiner's extraordinary pronouncements on Christianity. In 1921 some of them visited him. When they asked him if he believed in the possibility of a religious revival through deeper spiritual knowledge, Steiner affirmed that he did, and promised to give them definite instructions, provided they visited him as a whole group. The young men—for most of them were men of between 20 and 30—assembled in June at Stuttgart, where Steiner gave them his first "Lecture Course for Theologians". He promised that if they would find, say, ten times as many young men genuinely anxious for the future of the church, and willing to work seriously for its reformation, he would tell them more. Such a group collected in Dornach, and Steiner gave them six lectures which contained perhaps the profoundest things said in our time about religion. You may have heard how impressed orthodox theologians were when Steiner spoke to them about Christ.'

'Yes, Friedrich Rittelmeyer writes about that in his book on Steiner,' I answered.

"Rittelmeyer was present at many of those lectures. In fact Rittelmeyer had always been the head of our church—not Steiner. But to come back to my account—these young men were so deeply moved and shaken in their traditional beliefs by what Steiner said in his lectures that they decided to form a new religious community, based on Steiner's revelations. The widow of the German poet Christian Morgenstern invited the young men into her house, or rather put at their disposal the stables in her country place, and it was there that the new constitution of the church was evolved after many weeks' hard work. Though Steiner approved of it, he went on repeating that he must be considered merely as an adviser and spiritual mediator of the new church. His main concession was that, by the laying on of hands, he ordained, at an inaugural ceremony in September 1922, Dr Rittelmeyer who, as you probably know, had been for years one of the leaders of the Evangelical church in Germany and one of the most distinguished preachers of our day. Afterwards Rittelmeyer ordained a number of young ministers who wished to serve the new religious community.'

'What is new in your church?'

'The doctor was asked one day to explain the difference between anthroposophy and our creed. He answered: "Anthroposophy addresses itself to man's need for knowledge and brings knowledge; the Christian Community addresses itself to man's need for resurrection and brings Christ."'

'In what sense am I to understand this?' I asked.

'We try to disseminate that magic reality which Christ has instilled into every church. In most churches that power has been cloaked with so many obscure forms and ceremonies that it has become unintelligible, no matter how willing the congregation may be to take an active part in it. In our church we try to make everything, including the language, clear. Our religious service helps to penetrate

239

to the very roots of religion. We use no Latin: we use the language of the country in which the service is being held. Our congregation is conscious of what is happening during the service, it collaborates with the minister, and is not lulled into lazy self-contentment. I don't think you can say the same of the congregations of most of the older churches.'

III

After my visit to Berlin, during which I had tried to find the new German gods, I proceeded to the Rhineland to stay with a friend. Though towns may furnish us with more facts and give us a more varied picture of existing conditions, it is on the land that we meet with those ambitions and beliefs which in the cities are concealed beneath a veneer of official pronouncements.

The chief hobby of my friend at whose house I was going to stay was the cultivation of a magnificent garden with fruit, flowers and vegetables in profusion. On previous visits I had always been taken soon after my arrival for a walk through it. Since I arrived just before dinner it was arranged that I should see the garden next morning. 'You'll find great changes in the garden', my friend said; 'it is cultivated in an entirely different manner. I run it on biological-dynamic methods.'

'What methods?' I asked.

'The methods discovered by Rudolf Steiner. Many of the more advanced landowners and gardeners in Germany apply them nowadays. I shall tell you no more. You can judge for yourself to-morrow morning.'

The real surprise came during dinner. My friends had two children, and the little boy had been suffering from mastoid. Since the house was in the middle of the country the doctor had to come a long way from town, and it was generally arranged that he should stay for lunch or dinner. In fact, he was to dine with us that very evening. My hostess said that she was anxious for me to meet the doctor, who had succeeded in his treatment of her children where specialists from Cologne had failed. He applied anthroposophical methods, and he was at the head of a hospital for children in a neighbouring town.

I was not favourably impressed at first, for his voice and manner were unpleasantly Germanic in their impatient and arrogant tone; but during dinner I had to admit that in his knowledge of human

240

nature he far surpassed the average German doctor. His professional success proved that his knowledge was not merely theoretical.

'I had been a doctor for almost fifteen years,' he said, 'before I discovered anthroposophical medicine. Naturally I was very sceptical at first, and I looked upon it as a new form of quackery. Then I read one of Rudolf Steiner's lectures to doctors, and was amazed at his deep insight into the very essence of medicine. That induced me to read more about anthroposophy and Steiner. Eventually I decided to undergo a proper anthroposophical training, and I worked for over a year like a young student. I think I can claim that since then my understanding of the human body and the human being is deeper than that of my colleagues, who base their knowledge on the usual medical study and experience alone.'

IV

Next morning my friend took me round the garden. At dinner the night before I noticed how good the home-grown vegetables had been. Yet the determination to remain impartial made me, if anything, more sceptical than I should normally have been, even when my friend bade me compare the flowers, fruit and vegetables grown according to the new methods with those near by which, for reasons of experiment, were still cultivated in the ordinary way. My friend took me to a section of a field where tomatoes had been grown. Those grown under the old methods in one corner were much smaller than the others.

'Do you know the reason for this difference?' my friend asked. 'The bigger tomatoes were sown exactly forty-eight hours before full moon; the others were sown at some other time.'

'Is this the only difference?' I enquired incredulously.

'Yes, otherwise they have been treated in exactly the same way. Sowing in accordance with planetary constellations is one of the many new methods revealed by Steiner.'

I was shown that not only human beings but animals also noticed the superior quality of food grown according to Steiner's methods. 'Since we have begun to manure and cultivate some of our fields by the new method,' my friend explained, 'neither cows nor sheep will graze on other fields. As it takes time to reorganize all the fields, it has become something of a problem to satisfy our "gourmet" cattle.' The same was true of the chickens: since they had been fed on food grown in the new manner, they were most reluctant to eat ordinary food.

V

When I arrived back in England I immediately settled down to an intensive study of anthroposophy in ordinary life. England with her slowness in adopting new methods and her mistrust of 'foreign improvements' was hardly the ideal country for such investigations. On the other hand, the very conservatism of English life, by preventing any exaggerated enthusiasm, would show the intrinsic value of the new method.

The strong position of theosophy in England impeded the growth of anthroposophy. While on the Continent many who were once theosophists had begun to follow Steiner, in England only few such conversions had occurred. Theosophy was emphatically a British movement; its leader had been for many years an Englishwoman and its European headquarters were in London. In spite of all this I soon discovered that anthroposophy had entered deeper into English life than was at first apparent.

It is impossible to give exact figures as to the present state of the anthroposophical movement in Great Britain. The number of farmers, educationists and doctors who are adopting Steiner's method is constantly increasing. Even the sales of Steiner's books are growing; and yet his books are written in a style which does not make for easy reading. Mr. H. Collison, Steiner's English translator, told me that 'the doctor' would make no concessions of style in the translation of his books. Mr. Collison had suggested that it would be helpful in places to simplify the English version, since the English mind was not trained in the same way as the German. Steiner replied that such a concession to the laziness of a reader would be a departure from truth. He considered that to make his books easier to read would be an unworthy concession of truth to personal profit. He preferred to wait till the books became popular on their own account.

VI

I was anxious to see if I should find in England the remarkable results of Steiner's agricultural theories which I had found on the Continent, for the climatic and agricultural conditions of the two countries differed considerably from one another. As far as I could judge, after visiting several English farms run on anthroposophical lines—mine is, of course, not the opinion of an expert farmer—Steiner's methods had been carried out in this country with similar results.

Steiner called his agricultural discoveries the biological-dynamic method. One might say that, beginning with the name 'anthroposophy', most of the terminology of the movement is particularly cumbersome; but, as Steiner would never allow the slightest distortion of truth, the necessity for these names becomes evident. He could not possibly descend to the modern fashion of concocting slick and easy names that had but little connection with the fundamental truth of the object. In calling his agricultural system the 'biological-dynamic method' he acknowledged that life is a manifestation of forces: so if we want to influence these forces we must work dynamically.

Steiner formulated his agricultural methods as lately as in 1924, a year before his death. Though his method required a revolutionary change in one of the most conservative of human activities, it was widely accepted within a few years. Steiner himself warned his followers that his suggestions could not produce much result in anything much under four years. Nevertheless there are to-day on the Continent over a thousand farms, landed properties and market gardens run according to his ideas. Even in Great Britain, the last European country to follow up Steiner's suggestions, several farms have introduced his method.

Steiner expounded his agricultural ideas at a special series of lectures to a gathering organized by a leading agricultural expert, Count Carl Keyserlingk, who controlled a number of landed properties in Silesia. Steiner's lectures were arranged for professional agriculturists only, and they are the basis of his whole biological-dynamic method. The experts attending these lectures were so impressed by them that an experimental circle was founded in order to test them. Soon afterwards similar bodies were created in various parts of the country. To-day there are some two thousand experimental stations, gardens and farms, all over the world.

Steiner's agricultural methods are based on his acknowledgement of the earth as a living organism, not unlike a human being, and the need for it to be treated accordingly. Intimately related to this is his warning that humanity will probably die of starvation within the next hundred years if it does not abandon the use of agricultural remedies containing chemical poisons. He drew the attention of his listeners to the generally acknowledged fact that most of the soils in the so-called civilized countries are sick as a result of the use of artificial manures which, incidentally, have not been invented to help agriculture but to use up the superfluous wastes in chemical production. Our soils have become so encrusted, solidified and sour that they can be kept healthy only by heavy doses of lime.

The *New Statesman and Nation* published in 1932 an article on Steiner's agricultural methods, and admitted that his thesis of the death of the soil was a scientific truth. 'Steiner's theory', it read, 'was that we are stimulating the earth and its products to the detriment of both. . . . Agriculturist and horticulturist keep the earth in a state of feverish and unhealthy activity. . . . At first his ideas were treated with contempt, but of late there has been no lack of medical evidence in their support. . . . It is impossible in the face of the evidence to avoid an uneasy feeling that the modern stimulus of production is accountable for the spread of disease in the vegetable, animal and human kingdom. . . .' Before concluding his article the writer asks the important question: 'Is it not reasonable to suppose that there is a limit to the stimulus that may be applied to the lands for the forcing of crops?'

Legitimate agriculture and medicine are constantly giving us new proofs that the intrusion of chemicals into agriculture in the form of ready-made manure, sprays, bug killers and fertilizers destroys both the quality of the soil and of the products grown on it. The Swiss Cheese Federation, one of Switzerland's most important economic bodies, decided that no cows were to be allowed on pastures situated under trees sprayed with poisonous mixtures, and that none of their manure was to be treated with the usual chemical stimulants, such as iron sulphate or super-phosphates.

Steiner, for whom life and nature are an indivisible whole, regards nature as in a constant state of fluctuation, of evolution—that is, in short, as something dynamic. A farm, or indeed any agricultural unit, is for him an organism with an inner living current. You cannot treat it merely as an economic unity without considering its living faculties. The same inner balance that exists in the human body must be maintained in a farm There should be enough cattle to produce all the manure required, and the amount of pasture and of the various products, such as corn, vegetables and fruit, should be balanced in such a way as to make the farm as self-supporting as possible under modern conditions.

Steiner demands an even more subtle form of acknowledgement of the living character of a farm. Suppose someone buys an old farm and tries to modernize it. He pulls down an old barn, builds a garage, cuts down some trees and rearranges his fields. In its long existence the farm has developed its individuality and has become one body of which the different fields, buildings or trees are the various limbs—and a limb cannot be cut away without a disturbance of the inner balance which will prove detrimental to the whole. The fields, trees or plants will probably yield less. Such a method can only be avoided if the new owner tries to enter into the ancient spirit of the farm, if he lives in it long enough to be imbued with its individuality deeply enough to understand both its visible and its invisible unity and its inner equilibrium. Only then will he begin to know where improvements should be introduced, where the farm is 'tired' of an old tree, where it requires the replanting of a field. Some old- fashioned farmers, 'born' with a genius for their job, feel instinctively those hidden relations and necessities of their farm. Steiner's followers do not base their knowledge on such instincts (possessed only by a few), but on scientific discoveries. These discoveries were initiated by Steiner, and developed later on by farmers themselves and in special laboratories.

VII

How can the earth be saved from premature death? The answer of the biological-dynamic method to this is: By intensification of its living qualities and by elimination of all methods that kill it. This applies most of all to the chemical poisons that have been introduced into agriculture in modern times. The soil must not be stimulated artificially, but its natural functions must be enhanced, and this cannot be achieved by introducing dead matter in the form of chemicals

Anthroposophical farmers produce their own manure out of natural remnants to be found on the farm, such as animal dung, vegetable remnants, old foliage, bones and other natural refuse. Out of such remnants large compost heaps are built, and such plants and herbs are added to them as have beneficial effects upon our health. Steiner indicated that the following six plants should be used for that purpose: dandelion, yarrow, nettle, valerian, camomile and oak rind. The qualities of those plants are strengthened by a special preparation, and their use engenders in the soil the same chemical processes that are caused by artificial manure, but instead of being forced upon the soil suddenly, those processes grow in it organically. There is no sudden stimulation, no sudden shock as with ready-made manures, the natural faculties of the soil are intensified. Special sprays are used for the prevention of diseases, the principal one being made of silica. But it, once again, is not used in an artificial but in its natural form as part of equisetum tea. Every farmer should himself understand the production of these manures and sprays.

Scientific examination has shown that soils treated in this way contain much more of the microbes necessary for the working of a soil than is usual, whilst their products contain far fewer of the harmful microbes than are found in other products.

Once we realize that the soil and the farm, with everything that lives and grows on it, are living organisms and parts of a far greater macrocosm, we must acknowledge the relations between them and other parts of the universe. Not only are the four seasons, the sun, the wind, and the rain parts of the universe that affect the earth and life upon it, the influence of the other planets and of the moon is of equal importance. I was taken over a wheatfield on one of the anthroposophical farms in England. One section of the field was planted exactly forty-eight hours before the full moon and other sections ten and twenty hours later. While the wheat planted forty-eight hours before full moon grew evenly and fully, the rest of the field showed uneven green patches of varying size and thickness.

Steiner would explain to his pupils his own spiritual perception of a new discovery and he would then ask his agricultural collaborators to test it in the usual scientific way. In most cases he also indicated the exact method of the required test. The research work in laboratories always proved that both his discovery and his prescription for the experiment were right; and there is already a huge volume of scientific evidence testifying to the correctness of his perceptions.

Steiner explained why it is better to sow the seed in the afternoon, when the earth is, so to speak, breathing in, and is more inclined to take the seed into her womb; why the watering of plants and the application of manure, especially liquid manure, should be done in the evening; why reaping and harvesting should be done in the early morning hours; why seeds should be sown during the waxing of the moon; why plants, vegetables and flowers remain much fresher when cut in the very early morning; why the influence of the planets and the moon are able to work upon the substances in the earth only when these are no longer in a solid state; in what way the planet Jupiter affects the metal tin, the Moon—silver, Saturn—lead, and the Sun—gold.

There was nothing mysterious in Steiner's indications of the connection of life with the planetary system. Steiner discovered that there is a connection between the rhythms of the various planets and the rhythms that regulate our life. 'They correspond', he once said, 'in the same way that the movements of a clockhand correspond to the course of the sun—though we could hardly say that the sun turned the wheels. The relations point to a common origin but neither is produced by the other.'[1] The establishment of exact relationships between the various rhythms showed the working of inner laws in nature, the knowledge of which was most important in agricultural work.

Steiner's instructions were not limited to plants alone. They dealt with animals, insects, minerals—in short, with all the organisms and their manifold interrelations with agriculture. His investigations even established clear connections between the various planets and the life and work within a beehive.

The practical results of only one aspect of the biological-dynamic method may be illustrated by another quotation from the article written in the *New Statesman and Nation*: 'At X., where there are a few fields, cultivated on the Steiner method,' the writer says, 'I have seen lately fruit and vegetables of outstanding quality, so excellent, indeed, that hard-headed shopkeepers in the nearest large town will pay more than the current market prices for them.'

Though Steiner gave his followers very exact laws, he warned them not to cling fanatically to any given instruction but to establish its truth in their own experience. No two moments in life are equal, he said, no two instances of it can be treated identically. The same freedom of action which he preached with regard to people, he also

[1] *Paths of Experience* (Lecture on the Moon), transl. by H. Collison, 1934.

insisted upon when speaking of the earth, the plants or the animal kingdom.

There is no doubt that in England it will take longer than in many other countries for Steiner's agricultural methods to be adopted as a whole. The need is at present not so great as in most European countries, for the dampness of the British climate counteracts the deleterious effect of chemicals upon the soil, which, too, unlike the soil of many European countries, has not been forced to yield more than is good for it. The conservatism of the English farmer, ever suspicious of innovations, prevented much harm coming to the soil. The English farmer was one of the last to adopt the method of chemical cultivation.

VIII

Steiner's medical principles were presented to professional physicians in two courses of lectures in 1920 and 1921. Some of these discoveries were not entirely new—though they had been neglected for centuries Steiner's aims in medicine were to restore 'in a new form the old condition where the art of healing was bound up with the spiritual knowledge of man and the world'. 'In the mysteries,' Steiner said, referring to the ancient mysteries, 'these two were connected and this connection must be regained.'

The first practical and visible result of Steiner's lectures to doctors was the foundation by the Dutch woman doctor, Ita Wegman, of a clinical and therapeutical Institute at Arlesheim in Switzerland, which became the base for Steiner's further medical investigations. In later years clinics of a similar kind were founded in other countries.

One of Steiner's most important discoveries in the field of medicine was the acknowledgement of a threefold dynamic order in man. Man comprises for Steiner three different systems: a nervous system, which is the seat of consciousness and includes all nervous functions and all functions of sense; a metabolic system which includes man's unconscious functions, such as digestion with its many processes resulting in the formation of blood; and a rhythmical system which functions between the two. The rhythmical system is centred in the heart and the blood, and expresses itself in breathing and in the circulation of the blood.

Such a division can, of course, be applied to the living man alone. In Steiner's dynamic order the nervous system is the basis of our thought; the rhythmical of our feelings; and the metabolic of our will. The nervous system builds up our spiritual consciousness but destroys organic life. We see its example in the constant destruction by thought of the smallest entities in the brain, or in the using up of the retina in the eye through the process of seeing. The metabolic system builds up our unconscious faculties and our formative powers. Thus a living organism is for Steiner a current in which constant creation and constant destruction take place. These two forces produce a necessary balance, and that balance is responsible for all the rhythm in life.

Steiner's medical theories resulted in the establishment of what might be called a new medical science, new, that is, in the method of diagnosis, therapy and the production of medicines.

Steiner formulated exact methods of diagnosis, based on clairvoyant examination, but not limited merely to doctors with certain spiritual faculties and open to any medical man. Steiner insisted that the examining doctor should consider the original mental and organic state of the patient, and should retrace in his diagnosis the course of the illness step by step. The process of healing, too, should be a backward reconstruction of the illness, till the original normal state is reached.

In his medical discoveries Steiner went one step further than Goethe's famous discovery of the formative powers in a plant, known as the *Urpflanze*. Just as Goethe had found that the leaf holds the secret of the whole plant, Steiner recognized that in each individual part of the human organism the same formative life powers act that are responsible for the whole. Exactly as the seed contains already all the elements of the future tree, so does every individual organ disclose the dynamic faculties of the entire body.

Founding his medical discoveries on his truly cosmological knowledge, Steiner established the natural connections that exist between the various human organs and plants, animals and minerals. By doing this he indicated the way of anthroposophical therapy.

The truth of Steiner's medical 'visions' was proved in practical investigations, and it became the basis even of a new pharmaceutic science.

IX

The anthroposophical farmer had to abstain from using artificial manure; the anthroposophical doctor must have at his disposal entirely new medicines. Man is an image of the macrocosm. Corresponding laws and powers act both in man and in nature. In order to make use of those laws in medicine they must be co-ordinated and their relationship must be established.

Anthroposophical doctors claim that they not only remove illness or pain but that they heal. Many of the pharmaceutical products as used nowadays do not heal the patient but merely kill the disease. Even among ordinary doctors it is admitted more and more that such remedies can leave within the body harmful effects that are bound to show themselves sooner or later. Though the actual illness has been destroyed, the foundations of a new one may have been laid.

In establishing the cosmological connections between the organs and functions of the human body and the corresponding minerals, plants and animals, anthroposophical pharmacy adopted a number of the herbs, plants and minerals, and even methods of healing, to which people resorted centuries ago. In anthroposophical pharmacy an attempt is made to produce the medicine in accordance with the processes in the human body for which the medicine will be used. A certain medicine will be manufactured at the exact temperature of the human blood, and others in the same rhythm which operates in the organs for which each of them is meant. Thus anthroposophical pharmacy acknowledges the direct relationship existing between the living forces in nature and the working of the human body. The manufacture of anthroposophical medicines may be called a living process, that of ordinary medicines a mechanical one.

Medical-pharmaceutical laboratories were established by Steiner's medical collaborator, Dr. Ita Wegman. Similar establishments have been founded since in most of the capitals of the world, and even non-anthroposophical doctors are beginning slowly to employ their medicines.

Anthroposophical medical science claims to have discovered a number of remedies for various diseases that have hitherto seemed almost incurable. A number of ordinary doctors have accepted anthroposophical remedies for malaria and consumption. Of other anthroposophical cures the most important are those for anaemia, seasickness and rheumatism. Rudolf Steiner's doctrine that man's mind cannot be ill because it is of a divine nature and that only the body in which the mind is placed can be responsible for the

disease, produced new methods in the treatment of mental disturbances.

The most important discoveries seem to be those made in connection with the treatment of cancer. Steiner saw and comprehended
the connection between cancer and the phenomenon of mistletoe
blossoming forth at the place where a tree develops an unnatural
growth. A tumour is a parasite which absorbs many of the life forces
of a body; the mistletoe sucks out the living forces of a tree and stores
up within itself those powers that originally belonged to the tree.
Steiner showed the deeper relation between the two, and advised
his medical assistants to work out his suggestions scientifically.
This resulted in an entirely new cure for cancer. Most of the cancer
cases treated by the Anthroposophical Centre at Arlesheim were
those that had been abandoned by ordinary doctors, and in many
of them the new method proved successful. And yet for a number of
years the cure was severely handicapped by a technical difficulty
which was not overcome till 1933. Steiner suggested that special
mixtures of the various mistletoe juices required for the injection
ought to be mixed under conditions in which the influence of the
speed of the earth could be eliminated A mixing instrument had
to be constructed in which the speed of the earth could be outbalanced by the speed of the instrument It took over ten years for
science to produce a steel strong enough to withstand the terrific
centrifugal force created by the speed of the container in which the
mixture was to be made.

Some of the anthroposophical scientists claim to have discovered
means of diagnosing cancer in the human blood long before the
disease is localized or the patient is even aware of it himself. It is
claimed that these blood examinations combined with the mistletoe
injections have already produced results which are more striking
than those of any other method. Several medical journals have
begun to write of those cases.

X

I had heard and read much of Steiner's educational system and
was particularly anxious to see one of those establishments in which
his combined educational and medical methods were practised. I am
referring to that most difficult form known as the curative education
of under-developed children. On account of paralysis, idiocy, epilepsy

or some similar disease such children have to be specially treated. The main home for curative education in England is situated in a large park in Clent, not far from Birmingham, and was founded by an admirer of Steiner's methods. The cures are based on Steiner's educational instructions and on a therapy and medicinal treatment established by anthroposophy. Several of the sixty or seventy children whom I saw had been pronounced incurable and had been at the home only a few months. They had so far recovered as to be singing songs round a Christmas tree, some of them were playing instruments and others were beginning to read and write or paint little pictures. Orthodox doctors considered the results achieved in this home as verging on the miraculous.

To carry out Steiner's educational principles the teacher must have considerable medical knowledge. Steiner bases his educational work on the conviction that at the ages of seven, fourteen and twenty-one fundamental changes take place in the human being. They are expressed by the cutting of the second teeth, puberty and the attainment of full growth.

Steiner established the theory of an inter-dependence of these turning points in the life of the child and its corresponding spiritual phases, and the growth and change in its physical organs. According to him, the whole life process in a child up to seven is occupied in building up the head and the nerve centres; after the second teeth it is occupied more with the chest system, the breathing and the circulation of the blood, and from the age of fourteen upwards it develops the child's metabolism. According to Steiner, 'until the change of teeth the human body has a task to perform upon itself which is essentially different from those set for other periods. . . What has been neglected before the seventh year can never be made good.' Out of such considerations come instructions for the teacher. 'In this period,' Steiner says, 'moralizing and appeals are useless. . . . Whatever goes on in the surroundings of the child will be imitated. . . . The child is first wholly sense organ. Sense perceptions are closely bound to the child's emotions and will . . . there is a unity of body, soul and spirit. This is why it is impossible for a child to keep still when it notices anything. It functions in all its faculties at every stimulation. The adult person transplants sense experiences first into thought and transforms them into knowledge; the child acts instantly.' For a child up to seven the example of the teacher is of paramount importance.

THE TESTAMENT OF RUDOLF STEINER

Steiner gave many interesting examples of the effect of a teacher upon the child. 'If the choleric temperament of the teacher', he once wrote, 'expresses itself too vehemently it gives the child a shock which can have results later. . . . It appears in the years from forty-five to fifty as digestive troubles. . . . Other temperaments in the teacher can be equally devastating in disorganizing the nervous system, creating illnesses of the breathing and blood circulation.'

Steiner showed with particular clearness the connection between faults of education and rheumatism in later life. He made the important pronouncement that for a country as a whole to contain a large percentage of rheumatic people denotes faults in its educational system.

In Steiner's opinion, the child can be influenced from without only after the age of seven. It begins to dream vaguely and sees life as a sequence of pictures. Therefore emphasis should be laid on the use of pictures, images, fairy tales. Imagination should be guided 'A child until the change of teeth', Steiner said, 'expresses its soul life most strongly through the movements of the limbs. Afterwards it lives more in the rhythm of its breathing and blood circulation. It instinctively responds to everything presented in rhyme, rhythm and measure.' This is where special emphasis is laid on eurhythmy.

Music, painting, drawing, modelling, woodwork are applied in anthroposophical education always in accordance with the particular stage of spiritual and physical development. Steiner showed what connections exist between the various forms of painting and the character of the child. 'Choleric children like vermilion and bright yellow and express their temperament happily and healthily if they are allowed to play about with these colours for a time', Steiner instructed anthroposophical teachers. 'Melancholic children love pale lilac and a rather deeper blue and grow more cheerful if they are allowed to express their more sober natures with these colours. The sanguine child's painting is characterised by the repetition, with rhythmic modifications, of some particular motive; while phlegmatic children express themselves in large patches of a single colour. Painting also discovers morbid conditions, such as digestive disturbances. . . .'

The above example shows us a fraction of Steiner's educational theories. But there was nothing autocratic in his instructions to

253

teachers: they were suggestions rather than strict rules, and the teacher had to modify them according to the individual case.

In 1919 the 'Waldorf School' in Stuttgart was inaugurated. It was the first practical example on a big scale of Steiner's educational ideas. In pre-Nazi days, with over a thousand pupils, it was the biggest school in Germany. It is interesting to read the description of some aspects of the school which was given by the Government official who was sent to inspect it on behalf of the Ministry of Education. 'I must put on record', says the official inspector, 'the fact that the college of teachers with its high moral standard and intellectual attainments gives the Waldorf School its peculiar quality. A staff of teachers in such a close bond of union, working in the same spirit and filled with the same warmth of enthusiasm, cannot but bring their feeling of unity to daily expression. . . . The literary scholars and humanists are introduced by the mathematicians and scientists to the domain of mathematics and science . . . and the humanists help the scientists. . . . The whole of the professional work of the teachers is filled with and upborne by the same spirit . . . such as could scarcely be found in the same degree in any other school in the land.'[1]

There are anthroposophical schools in seven other German towns[2]; also in Switzerland, Austria, Norway, Sweden, England and the United States. There are curative homes for children in a number of countries, and there are special classes for teachers and doctors at the Goetheanum at Dornach and in Arlesheim.

XI

The field of anthroposophical activity which least impressed me was art. This is not surprising. Steiner's perceptions could open the doors to a wider and truer knowledge in many fields; but they could not create artists or replace lack of genius by a deeper understanding of truth. I came across anthroposophical pictures which may have been painted with greater consciousness than other pictures; but they lacked vigour in their design and their colouring was sentimental. Altogether they were too theoretical to be impressive. I have no

[1] *The Free Waldorf School at Stuttgart*, by F. Hartlieb, 1928. (English translation, edited by H. Collison.)
[2] All these schools as well as other anthroposophical institutions in Germany have been closed down by the Nazis.

doubt, nevertheless, that a great artist could improve his work greatly by the understanding gained through such ideas as those disseminated by Steiner.

Other anthroposophical artistic work, such as furniture, decoration or jewellery exhibited a similar lack of individuality, and a degree of precosity. Artistic creation depends too much upon personal talent to advance very far through a penetration into spiritual truth, no matter how deep.

In literature Steiner's influence produced, in addition to his own important and moving mystery plays, much better results. Some of the finest work of the leading Swiss poet Albert Steffen and of Christian Morgenstern, one of the most interesting German poets before the war, have been inspired directly by Steiner's ideas.

His political and economic principles had found their expression in his *Threefold Commonwealth*, mentioned in an earlier chapter. Many of his ideas have since then been adopted all over the world. They have been changed and distorted, and yet there are many instances of modern political or economic legislation based on ideas similar to those published by Steiner fifteen years ago. These ideas were undoubtedly in the air, and sooner or later they had to be adopted. We find distorted versions of them in the Corporative State of Mussolini; we find them in the weakening of the political strengthening of the economic ties between England and her Dominions; and we find them especially in the many readjustments in the economic structure of the world caused by the world crisis.

Even in Steiner's lifetime there were experts who realized the importance of his political and economic ideas. Soon after the publication of his *Threefold Commonwealth*, the *Hibbert Journal* published an article about it, written by a distinguished scholar, J. S. Mackenzie, a professor of Logic and Philosophy, and one of the leading Scottish authorities on these subjects. Professor Mackenzie, who admits that Steiner's ideas deserve 'very serious consideration', compares them with those of Plato's *Republic*. Plato and Steiner have certainly much in common. Prof. Mackenzie analyses Steiner's ideas even from the point of view of their adaptability in Great Britain, and he finds that they might be suitable for this country. He states in conclusion that Steiner's leading principles are a 'real contribution to social theory' and 'of the highest value'.

FULFILMENTS

XII

The variety of subjects described in this chapter contain only a part of the discoveries and principles left by Rudolf Steiner as his testament. It would need almost an Encyclopaedia to give a full picture of his work. Only those among his activities that are already establishing themselves in modern life have been touched upon here.

Mr. D. N. Dunlop, the founder and head of the World Power Conference, one of the great international organizations of our time, expressed the opinion of many people when he said that Rudolf Steiner's 'spiritual science embraces the whole wide sphere of the Heavens above and the Earth beneath'. He summed up Steiner's work in the following words: 'He has brought the knowledge of the spirit into practical application in the world of men in the spheres of philosophy, sociology, science, art, religion, medicine, education. . . . Rudolf Steiner's wisdom revered the traditions of the past, illuminated the problems of the present, pointed forward to the possibilities of the future.'

Professor Mackenzie's important analysis of Steiner's political ideas and Mr. Dunlop's eulogy are exceptions rather than the rule. Only very few unbiased and serious articles about Steiner have appeared in the press. The reader is justified in asking how it is possible that a man like Steiner should be still so little known, and should play so comparatively small a part in modern life. The main reason is that only new teachings which are fundamentally of a traditional kind can gain an immediate response. A revolutionary teaching that requires an entirely new conception of all aspects of science, and that affects every branch of our life, cannot possibly be established in one or two generations.

If Steiner had not based his doctrine on an open acknowledgement of the spirit, and if he had explained his occult perceptions in a way more acceptable to the physical sciences, the world at large would have followed him much more readily. Had his doctrine required less effort on the part of the individual, had it been presented in a less scientific form, many more people would have tried to adopt it. Had Steiner been less of a fanatic with regard to truth, had he allowed himself in any way to compromise, his success would have been instantaneous.

Those who study Steiner seriously and dispassionately are not surprised that the acceptance of his ideas should still be limited to a comparatively small group, and that they should have revitalized only a few thousand acres of soil. Steiner insisted over and over again that a movement like anthroposophy had to develop organically and slowly, and that it could not be forced in its growth. For Steiner, who believed with St. John that 'a man can receive nothing, except it be given him from heaven', knew that in forcing spirit we distort truth, and that this is a real offence against heaven.

CHAPTER III

KRISHNAMURTI IN CARMEL

I

I had revisited the Continent where my search had begun; I had seen Keyserling again, and I had learned what had become of Steiner's grandiose visions of a truer world. But I anticipated no change in any of the teachers I had been in touch with more keenly than the one that had taken place in Krishnamurti. I wrote to Eerde in Holland, asking him when and where I could visit him. I waited for an answer for more than three months, and when it eventually arrived I learned that he was just leaving New Zealand after a lecture tour in Australasia, that he was on his way to California, and that he would not be back in Europe for another eighteen months. A journey to California meant a great sacrifice of time and money. Nevertheless I decided to go all the way to the Pacific Coast to learn how Krishnamurti had changed since the days when I stayed with him at his Dutch château, and especially since the dissolution of his organization. Krishnamurti's Californian home was at the Ojai Valley, not far from Hollywood.

When I decided to visit Krishnamurti in California, I hoped to get incidentally a glimpse of the spiritual atmosphere in the country in which he now lived. I had seen enough of America to know that Romain Rolland's description of what was most striking in American life still held good: '. . . the existence side by side of the hope and the fear of the future, the highest and the most sinister forces; an immense thirst for truth, and an immense thirst for the false; absolute disinterestedness and an unclean worship of gold; childlike sincerity and the charlatanism of the fair.' A desire for spiritual knowledge lived side by side with the most blatant materialism.

When I arrived in the United States in the autumn of 1934 I soon noticed that the disappointment and the growing mistrust of purely material salvation, resulting from the economic disasters of the last few years, had created in many people a hunger for things of the spirit. There was a distinct awakening of the spirit not unlike that which took place in Germany in the immediate post-war years. This was not surprising. Few forms of experience are more conducive to

258

spiritual understanding than suffering. The failure of most of the deities—politics, finance, industry—to satisfy their worshippers was bound to attract attention more and more to the power of the spirit —the only power that had been left unexplored.

It was, then, not without significance that Krishnamurti was to be found in the American scene. He was not the first teacher from India to exercise a spiritual influence over American thought through personal contact. Almost half a century before him young Vivekananda, the great Indian teacher and disciple of Ramakrishna, had visited the United States, had impressed the Parliament of Religions in Chicago in 1893 more than any theologian, philosopher or churchman, and had influenced William James, the great American philosopher. The peculiar form of spiritual truth, as it is perceived by the East, was no longer unknown to the American public. After the teachings of Ramakrishna and Vivekananda, the message of Krishnamurti was transplanted to American soil at one of the most critical and thus spiritually most propitious times in the evolution of American civilization.

II

As my time was limited, I decided to travel from New York to California by aeroplane. I had never flown before, and though the speed of over two hundred miles an hour meant little to me, I was strangely moved when seventeen hours after we had left the icy atmosphere of New York we landed three thousand miles farther west, at Hollywood's airport, Glendale, bathed in a brilliant sun and encircled by mountains with snowy peaks.

No-one awaited me—a depressing arrival. When I telephoned I was told that Krishnamurti was not at Ojai but at Carmel, where he had been staying for the last few weeks. But I was assured by the voice at the other end that I would like Carmel, which was not very far from San Francisco, much better than Ojai.

After I had got over my first disappointment, I was glad to be going to Carmel. I remembered Carmel from a previous visit to California, and I anticipated that it would offer more possibilities of quiet and concentration than Ojai with its proximity to Hollywood.

I left Hollywood in the evening in pouring rain. I had to leave the train at Monterey, and I telephoned from the station to Krishnamurti to inform him of my arrival. Half an hour later a car pulled up in front of the station and Krishnamurti jumped out.

FULFILMENTS

III

I had not seen him for a number of years. There was still the graceful slenderness of appearance, but the face had no longer its former boyish smoothness. Seven years ago he had radiated nothing so strongly as beauty and, though already older, he had looked a youth in his early twenties. Now the cheeks seemed hollower, and under the eyes there were deep shadows. Silver threads ran through the thick black hair, and the lines of the face betrayed, perhaps, some hidden worry or conflict—or was this merely the evidence of increased maturity?

We drove out to Carmel, which was several miles away. It had stopped raining, and the countryside was emerging from its drabness. In the morning sun the plains were green and golden and the hills and mountains purple and violet.

Since all the rooms were occupied in the little hotel in which Krishnamurti was staying, he took me to a larger one near by. My hotel was situated in the very midst of huge pines, on a hill overlooking the sea. Except for the diningroom and the lounge, the hotel consisted of a number of small huts, scattered in the woods. This was a particularly attractive way of living. You had your own hut with its little front porch, and your own grounds. Pines, shrubs and innumerable plants grew between the various huts, situated on different levels. The effect was pleasing and picturesque, and you could work or relax in your room without being disturbed by any of the other hotel guests.

After I had taken a look round my new home and expressed my delight with it, Krishnamurti said· 'I don't quite know what you want from me, or whether I'll be able to satisfy you. How do you propose to proceed?'

'Let us just be together as much as possible, if you can bear it', I answered. 'We will talk, and things will probably develop automatically. I came here to pick your brains and to ask you many indiscreet questions', I added, not quite as a joke.

Krishnamurti promised to visit me that afternoon, when we would go for a long walk and have our first conversation; in the evening we would dine together, and I would meet the people among whom he lived.

We were both very fond of walking, but heavy clouds gathered during the afternoon, and when Krishnamurti came to fetch me

KRISHNAMURTI IN CARMEL

it rained so hard that we had to remain indoors. Between the trunks of the pines outside my window you could overlook the sea covered with the white combs of hurrying waves. I was slightly nervous at the thought of our first conversation. The lack of common daily experiences tends to make such a conversation artificial.

In several books and in many articles attacks had been launched against Krishnamurti, and, as far as I was aware, he had not answered them. There was, for example, the question of his attitude with regard to the claims of a second Christ made on his behalf; again there was the question of his finances and of his private life. I considered that our conversation could serve no useful purpose while there remained a doubt in my mind as to Krishnamurti's absolute honesty of purpose.

I said, without looking him straight in the face: 'I am afraid my first question will seem tactless to you. But I have not come all this way to enjoy a polite conversation with you or to plunge into abstract philosophical discussions. I came to find out the truth. I want to be able to tell my readers that I believed what you have told me, and therefore the first thing I ask of you is absolute frankness and honesty. Otherwise I shall feel that my whole journey out here will have been in vain. I may perhaps formulate my request by quoting the relevant passage from a biography of Mrs. Besant by Theodore Besterman. This is what the author has to say about you: "Mr. Krishnamurti is now in a position in which he is able to do much good, the message he is bringing to the world is one which is badly needed; if he can succeed in inducing a large and influential number of people to adopt these views and to act on them, the benefit conferred on the world would be incalculable. But Mr. Krishnamurti must realize that, as an advocate of truth in the largest sense, he must himself act the Truth. He has been very frank, but he must be franker still. Up to 1929 Mr. Krishnamurti's life was entangled in a complex network of far-reaching claims. Mr. Krishnamurti must tell us the truth about these things, however painful it will necessarily be to discuss his past friends in public."'

Krishnamurti took my hand with an almost passionate gesture, and said: 'Now listen. No apologies are necessary. You can ask me anything you want, the most tactless, the most intimate questions. There is no privacy in my life, and everyone may hear any detail that may interest him. Let us put our whole relationship on that basis, and it will save us a lot of unnecessary trouble. Ask anything you want—go ahead.'

I decided to begin with a point, the best formulation of which I found in the same book by Mr. Besterman. It dealt with Krishnamurti's authorship of a short mystical book, which he was supposed to have written as a little boy, but under the direct guidance of the 'master' preparing him for an 'initiation'. I went on: 'This is what Besterman says about one of your earliest "crimes": ". . . he must tell us the truth about the authorship of such books as *At the feet of the master*, which appear under his name. . . . I must say in the plainest terms that so long as Mr. Krishnamurti does not speak to us frankly about these years before 1929 he will never obtain the ear of intelligent and educated people. . . ."'

Krishnamurti became pensive for a second and said: 'People have asked me that question before. Some of them were satisfied with my answer, others weren't. For anyone who does not know me well it may be difficult at first to accept my answer. I am bound to say a few words about myself before I can answer your question. You must have noticed that I have got an extremely bad memory for what one may call physical realities. When you arrived this morning I could not remember whether we had met two, three or ten years ago. Neither can I remember where and how we met. People used to call me a dreamer and they accused me, quite rightly, of being desperately vague. I was hopeless at school in India. Teachers or friends would talk to me, I would listen to them, and yet I wouldn't have the faintest notion what they were talking about. I don't recollect whether I used to think about anything in particular at such moments, and if so, what about. I must just have been dreaming, since facts failed to impress themselves upon my memory. I remember vaguely having written something when I was a boy educated by Bishop Leadbeater, but I haven't the slightest recollection whether I wrote a whole book or only a few pages. I don't know what Leadbeater did with the pages I wrote, whether he corrected them or not, whether they were kept or destroyed. I don't know whether I wrote of my own accord or whether I was influenced by some power outside myself. I wish I knew. I don't claim to be a writer, but it seems to me that no-one can ever tell whether a writer is directed by a power outside or just by his own brain and his own emotions. I would very much like to know the hidden subtleties of that complicated process which is called writing. I, too, would like to know the facts about the writing of the book *At the feet of the master*. I can still see myself sitting at a table and writing something that did not come at all easily to me. I must be some twenty-five years ago.'

'How old are you now?'

'I can't tell. In India age matters less than in the West, and records of age are not kept. According to my passport I was born in 1897. But I can't vouch for the accuracy of this.'

The atmosphere seemed by now intimate enough for what I considered the most difficult question to put to him. I personally attached little importance to it, but I knew that people interested in Krishnamurti were always discussing it. 'Many people are sceptical', I said, 'with regard to you because you have never denied the claims made on your behalf. You have never got up and said clearly: "All this talk about my being the World Teacher is bunkum, I deny the truth of it." '

'I never either denied or affirmed that I was Christ or anybody else', Krishnamurti replied. 'Such attributions are utterly meaningless to me.'

'But not to the people who come to listen to you', I interrupted.

'Had I said yes, they would have wanted me to perform miracles, walk on the water or awaken the dead. Had I said no, I am not Christ, they would have taken this as an authoritative statement and acted accordingly. I am, however, against all authority in spiritual matters, against all standards created by one person for the sake of others. I could not possibly say either yes or no. You will probably understand this better after you have been with me for a few days, and after we have had several talks. To-day I can only say that I consider my own person of no special importance, Christ or no Christ. What matters is whether what I say can help people or not. Any confirmation or denial on my part would only evoke corresponding expectations on the part of the people. When I visit India people ask me: "Why do you wear European clothes and eat every day? You cannot be a true teacher. If you were one, you would be fasting and walking about in a loincloth." My answer to this can only be that everyone teaches what it is his particular duty to teach and that everyone has to lead his own life. It does not follow that because Gandhi wears only a loincloth and Christ walked on the water, I must do likewise. The labels for my personality are irrelevant. But there was another reason as well for never denying clearly the claims made on my behalf. It was regard for Dr. Besant. Had I said

263

that I was not the World Teacher, people would have cried, "Mrs. Besant is a liar!" My categorical denial would have harmed and hurt her. By saying nothing I did spare her without harming anyone else.'

'Why did you go on lecturing even after renouncing your organization?'

Krishnamurti seemed surprised. 'I never thought of that', he said after a short pause, 'I went on lecturing out of habit, I suppose. I was made to do it since my boyhood, it became a sort of tradition with me, and I just went on doing it. I suppose I was never quite conscious in those days of what I was doing. It is only in the last few years that I have become fully aware of all my daily actions and that I no longer act as though walking in a dream.'

'I believe you, Krishnaji, but do you think my readers will?'

'I can help neither you nor them if they won't. I am not hiding anything from you, I am telling you the whole truth. I presume that people with a strongly developed sense of facts and a good memory must find me exasperating. But I cannot help that.'

I had never spoken to Krishnamurti since he had given up his huge organization, and I was anxious to know more about that momentous decision. Then we should be able to turn to more important matters.

'When did you decide to give up that organization which had been built up for you, and to renounce all your earthly possessions? And why really did you do it?' I asked. 'Was it in 1929 that you spoke about it for the first time?'

'No, a year or two before. But I did not feel clearly about it till 1929. I talked to Rajagopal[1] about it, we had long discussions, and eventually I spoke to Dr. Besant about my decision. She only said: "For me you are the Teacher, no matter what you decide to do. I cannot understand your decision, but I shall have to respect it." For a certain time she appeared to be rather shaken, but she was a splendid woman and at last she seemed to agree with what I was doing. I gave up my organization because I came to realize beyond all doubt that anything of that sort must be hindering if you want to find truth. Churches, dogmas, ceremonies are nothing but stumbling blocks on the road to truth.'

'But you go on lecturing even to-day, don't you?'

'Indeed I do. I feel more than ever that I can help people. Of course I cannot give them happiness or truth. No-one can. But I

[1] Krishnamurti's best friend and late executive head of The Order of the Star.

264

can help them to discern a way of approaching truth. Last year I went to Australia, and at times I had to speak to ten thousand people. In a few months' time I shall probably go on a lecture tour to most of the South American countries.'

I had intended to question Krishnamurti about his financial situation and the moment seemed particularly appropriate. 'Do you make much money during those tours?'

'None at all,' Krishnamurti answered, 'though they pay my expenses.'

'There are so many stories regarding your financial situation,' I said, 'that it would make it easier for me if you could enlighten me about it. Some people accuse you of having accepted large fortunes left to you by a number of very rich people in England and America —it is said, in short, that you are practically a millionaire.'

Krishnamurti laughed. 'Do you know what I possess? A couple of suits, a few books, a few personal belongings—and no money. There are a few kind friends who help to keep me alive. They ask me to stay with them, they pay my modest expenses when I travel. Take Carmel for example: I stay at my hotel as the guest of an old friend who has got a house in the neighbourhood and who knows that I love working here. If I had money I should give it away as I did once before. My needs are so small that what I receive is ample. If no-one gave me anything I should just work for my living.'

'I am glad we have cleared up that point', I said; 'from now on I need no longer feel like counsel for the prosecution, and we can spend our time on things that really matter.'

'Then let's start straight away and go and have some dinner', Krishnamurti exclaimed, getting up. 'We dine early here, not like you in England. I generally go to bed soon after nine, and get up in the morning before six.'

It was quite dark outside, and we drove slowly to Krishnamurti's hotel. The road took us higher and higher over cliffs and through pine woods, while from deep below came the thunder of waves breaking against the rocks. The road was narrow and steep, and there were many sharp corners. On one side there seemed to be a deep precipice. 'I don't drive very much these days', Krishnamurti said as his hand lay rather vaguely on the steering wheel; and he added with a chuckle: 'I hope you insured your life before you left England?'

FULFILMENTS

IV

The weather was glorious next morning, and I went to fetch Krishnamurti for a walk. We had not gone very far when we reached a clearing in the huge pine trees high up on the hills, with an endless view over the picturesque coastline. We decided that it would be easier to talk sitting down. Krishnamurti sat down in Eastern fashion with crossed legs on the heather-covered ground. I had already worked out a plan which would enable us to talk every day about certain definite subjects, hoping that this would help us not to lose ourselves and that it would introduce a certain structure into our talks.

'What is your message to-day?' I began.

Krishnamurti's answer came in a very definite tone: 'I have no message. If I had one, most people would accept it blindly and try to live up to it, merely because of the authority which they try to force upon me.'

'But what do you tell people when they come and ask you to help them?'

'Most people come and ask me whether they can learn through experience.'

'And your answer is?'

'That they cannot.'

'No?'

'Of course not. You cannot learn spiritual truth through experience. Don't you see? Let us assume that you had a deep sorrow and you learned how to fight against it. This experience will induce you to apply the same method of overcoming grief during your next sorrow.'

'That does not seem wrong to me.'

'But it is wrong. Instead of doing something vital, you try to adapt a dead method to life. Your former experience has become a prescription, a medicine. But life is too complicated, too subtle for that. It never repeats itself; no two sorrows in your life are alike. Each new sorrow or joy must be dealt with in that particular fashion that the uniqueness of the experience requires.'

'How can that be done?'

'By eliminating the memory of former experiences; by destroying all recollection of our actions and reactions.'

'What remains after we have destroyed them all?'

266

KRISHNAMURTI IN CARMEL

'An inner preparedness that brings you nearer truth. You never ought to act according to old habits but in the way life wants you to act—spontaneously, on the spur of the moment.'

'Does this apply to everything in life?'

'It does. You must try to eliminate from your life all old habits and systems of behaviour, because no two moments in any life are exactly similar.'

'But all this is only negative, and I don't find anything positive at all in your scheme of things.'

Krishnamurti smiled and moved nearer me: 'You don't need to search for the positive; don't force it. It is always there, though hidden behind a huge heap of old experiences. Eliminate all of them, and truth—or what you call the positive—will be there. It comes up automatically, You cannot help it.'

I pondered over his words for a while, then I said: 'You have just used the word "truth". What *is* truth, according to you?'

'Call it truth or liberation or even God. It is all the same. Truth is for me the release of the mind from all burdens of memory.' This definition was new to me, but before I could say a word Krishnamurti went on: 'Truth is awareness, constant awareness of life within and without you. Do you follow?' His voice became almost insistent.

'I do, but please explain to me what you mean by "awareness" ', I replied.

Krishnamurti came even closer to me, and his voice became even more persuasive. 'What matters is that we should live completely at every moment of our lives. That is the only real liberation. Truth is nothing abstract, it is neither philosophy, occultism nor mysticism. It is everyday life, it is perceiving the meaning and wisdom of life around us. The only life worth dealing with is our present life and every one of its moments. But to understand it we must liberate our mind from all memories, and allow it to appreciate spontaneously the present moment.'

'I take it that by spontaneous appreciation you mean an appreciation dictated solely by the circumstances of that very moment?'

'Exactly—there can be no other spontaneity of life; and that is precisely what I call real awareness. Do you understand?'

'I do, but I doubt whether such awareness can really be expressed in words. . . . I think it can only be understood if we actually experience it ourselves. No description can possibly do it justice.'

267

FULFILMENTS

Krishnamurti did not answer immediately. He was lying on the ground, facing the sky. 'It is so', he said slowly; 'but what is one to do?'

'What indeed, Krishnaji? I wondered what you really meant when you told me yesterday that you tried to help people by talking to them. Can anyone who has not himself gone through that state of awareness of which you speak comprehend what it means? Those who possess it do not need to hear about it.'

Krishnamurti paused again, and I could see that he was affected by the turn our conversation had taken. He said after a while: 'And yet this is the only way one can help people. I think that one clarifies people's minds by discussing these things with them. Eventually they will perceive truth for themselves. Don't you agree?'

I knew that Krishnamurti disliked all questions that seemed to arise out of mere curiosity or to depend upon abstract speculation, but I nevertheless asked him: 'Don't you think that the limits of time and space must cease to exist once we establish within ourselves a constant awareness of life?'

'Of course they must. The past is only a result of memories. It is dead stuff. Once we cease to carry about with us this ballast there will be no time limits with regard to the past. The same is true in a slightly different way with regard to the future. But all this talk about seeing into the future or the past is only a result of purely intellectual curiosity. At every lecture I give half a dozen people always ask me about their future and past incarnations. As though it mattered what they were or what they will be. All that is real is the present. Whether we can look into the to-morrow or across continents is meaningless from a spiritual point of view.'

'Don't you think that conscious perception through time and space can be very valuable? Don't you think that the results obtained by Rudolf Steiner's occult perceptions are really helpful to humanity?'

'I have never studied Steiner, and I wish you would tell me more about him. All I know about Steiner comes from Dr. Besant's occasional remarks I think she had a great admiration for Steiner's unusual gifts, and was sorry that their relationship had to be broken, but I never studied him properly As for occult perceptions, for me they are not particularly spiritual: they are merely a certain method of investigation. That's all. They might be spiritual at times, but they are not always or necessarily so.'

'You have never read any of Steiner's books?'

KRISHNAMURTI IN CARMEL

'No, nor have I ever read any of the other philosophers. . . .'

'But Steiner was not a philosopher', I interrupted.

'Yes, I know. I only meant writers of a philosophical or similar kind. I cannot read them. I am sorry, but I just can't. Living and reacting to life is what I am interested in. All theory is abhorrent to me.'

Although noon was at hand and it was growing very hot, Krishnamurti suggested a walk towards the sea. 'Are you writing anything at present?' I asked him when we reached the road going down to the sea.

'Yes, I am preparing a book. But it is nothing consecutive—just a book of thoughts.'

'What about your poetry?'

'I feel poetry, but somehow I cannot write it at present.'

'What books do you read? I remember that at one time you used to read a great deal, and that you liked choosing your friends especially from among artists and writers.'

'What books does one read?' Krishnamurti answered, slightly embarrassed.

Questions about his personal habits always seemed to make him uncomfortable. I noticed this repeatedly during my visit at Carmel. Though he derived every detail of his teaching from personal experiences, and preferred talking about it in a personal way, it seemed to me that he withdrew himself, as it were, whenever I put questions that were not connected directly with his mission in life or that dealt with such matters as his personal tastes and habits. Discussion for the satisfaction of intellectual curiosity seemed to cause him discomfort. This was not any result, I believe, of what is usually called natural modesty. It was rather as though he tried to remain perpetually on a plane of inner awareness, and felt uneasy whenever he had to switch over to a plane of intellectual discussion. But he loved ordinary conversation about topical subjects, politics, music, the theatre or travel. It was only when the outside world was brought into direct intellectual relationship with his personality that he shrank away from such interrogation.

'I am not a specialist of any kind', said Krishnamurti, in answer to my original question. 'I read everything that seems interesting—Huxley, Lawrence, Joyce, André Gide. . . .'

'Did you really mean what you said when you told me that you never read philosophy?'

FULFILMENTS

'Goodness me, yes! What should I read philosophy for?'

'Perhaps to learn from it.'

'Do you seriously think you can learn from books? You can accumulate knowledge, you can learn facts and technicalities, but you cannot learn truth, happiness, or any of the things that really matter. You can read for your entertainment, for thousands of other reasons, but not to learn the essential things. You can only learn from living and acknowledging the life that is your very own. But not from the lives of others.'

'Does that mean that in your opinion nothing can ever be learned from books, from the experience of others?'

'I shall refrain from saying definitely yes, though I feel inclined to do so. The knowledge of others only builds up barriers within ourselves, barriers that stand in the way of an impulsive reaction to life. Of course it is easier to go through life learning from the experience of others, leaning on Aristotle, on Kant, on Bergson or on Freud; but that is not living your life, facing reality. It is merely evading reality by hiding behind a screen created by someone else.'

'Do you consider this to be true of religion also?'

'I do. Religions offer people authority in place of truth; they give them crutches instead of making their legs strong; they give them drugs instead of urging them to push out along their own paths in search of truth for themselves. I fear none of the churches to-day has very much to do with truth.'

'Do many, among the thousands who come to listen to you, ask you questions about religious matters?'

'Most of them do. There are three questions that crop up over and over again, and no meeting is complete without them, whether I speak in India, in Australia, in Europe or in California. I deduce from their popularity that they must deal with the three most urgent spiritual problems of modern man. They are questions about the values of experience, of prayer and of religion in general.'

Krishnamurti had already given me his opinions of experience and religion, so I only asked: 'What is your attitude towards prayer?'

'Prayer in which you ask God for something is in my opinion utterly wrong.'

'Even if you ask God for help to achieve the awareness you were talking about?'

'Even then. How can anything be spiritual—and prayer, I take it, is supposed to be something spiritual—that asks for a reward? This is not spirituality but economics, or whatever else you like to call it. In spiritual truth things just are; but there can be no requests, promises or rewards. Things happen in life because they simply have to happen. A reward can never be anything else but fixed, stationary, if you understand what I mean. Spiritual life, true life, must be always moving—fluctuating, alive.'

'But cannot prayer be just a bridge along which we move towards the inner awareness?'

'It can, but that is not what people generally understand by prayer. What you now mean is simply a state of real living, of inner expectation. This identifies us with truth. Do you see the difference?'

'I do, and I therefore presume that you deny all "crystallized" forms invented by man for the attainment of truth, such as meditation, yoga or other methods of mental exercise.'

'Yes, it is so. How can you expect to achieve something which is constantly fluctuating through a method that, in your own words, is crystallized—or in my words, dead? People often come to me and ask me about the value of meditation. All I can tell them is that I see no reason why they should meditate on one particular subject, instead of meditating on everything that enters their life, because it seems to me that deliberate concentration on one particular thought, eliminating all others, must create an inner conflict. I consider it wiser to meditate on whatever happens to enter your mind: whether it be about what you will do this afternoon or as to which suit you will put on. Such thoughts are as important—if attended to with your full inner awareness—as any philosophy. It is not the subject of your thought that matters so much as the quality of your thinking. Try to complete a thought instead of banishing it, and your mind will become a wonderful creative instrument instead of being a battlefield of competing thoughts. Your meditation will then develop into a constant alertness of mind. This is what I understand by meditation.'

I remembered Keyserling's answer to my question on meditation, and was struck by the similarity of the views held by these two so different men. 'Keyserling', I said, 'quite recently told me something of much the same sort. He said that for him meditation was nothing else but facing reality as it came along.'

'I agree with him in that respect. You can find truth only by your own constant awareness of life. You must not try to live up to somebody else's standards, because inevitably those of two different men can never be really identical.'

271

FULFILMENTS

'Does this mean that you believe in the absolute equality of men?'

'Of course I do, though not in the way Communism understands it. Because I preach equality of races, religions and castes, Communists think that I preach Communism. American Communists often come to visit me at Ojai and say: "We believe in you because you preach the things that we do. But why don't you join our party?" They don't understand that I am not only unable to join their party, or any other party, but that I cannot possibly agree with their methods. You can achieve equality among men only by greater knowledge, by deeper understanding, by better education, by making people grasp what life means. How can you do this if the leaders themselves don't know, if they themselves behave like automatons and preach their particular gospels not from an inner awareness of life and its necessities—which means according to real truth—but by repeating over and over and over again certain formulae invented by others. You cannot achieve equality by taking their possessions away from people. What you must take away from them is their instinct of possessiveness. This does not apply only to land and money, a factory or a sable coat. It also applies to a book, to a flower, to your wife, your lover or your child. I don't mean to say that you must not have or enjoy any of these things. Of course you must! But you must enjoy them for the sake of the joy they transmit, and not for the feeling of pleasure that their possession gives you. This fundamental attitude has to be changed before anything else can be done. Nothing can be altered by taking things away from the rich and giving them to the poor, thus developing their feeling of greed and possessiveness.'

V

When we met again we no longer pretended that we were going for a walk but went straight to our pine-shadowed resort on the hill. It was an ideal place for conversation—not a single human being passed it all through the day and the view was exalting. The only noise was that of the sea breaking on the cliffs. I no longer felt intimidated by the subjects on which I had considered it my duty to question Krishnamurti; I knew that I could speak freely about everything; and I felt that the moment had arrived when I could question him about sex.

272

KRISHNAMURTI IN CARMEL

Life in England had taught me to assume that sex was of much smaller importance than I had believed it to be in the days when I lived on the Continent. I had learned to treat sex in the way one treats poorer relations or in the way Victorian society treated women's legs: pretending that they do not exist and never mentioning them. Such an attitude may provide a temporary solution, and it is probably of practical value in all the more conventional circumstances of life. But it does not solve the essential problem. It brings no happiness, nor does it release any of those forces that sex, properly and honestly expressed, ought to create. Hypocrisy, or rather make-believe in matters of sex, may be laudable in the face of certain necessarily superficial aspects of the life of a community; but hypocrisy can never be more than merely a means of escape—it shirks the facing of reality. Hypocrisy pushes sex behind hundreds of screens, each one of which can hide it for only a short while, without doing anything to solve the essential underlying problem. Among the few people who find sexual satisfaction in perfect love the sex problem does not exist —but such people are few. The majority are not capable of regulating their sex impulses in a satisfactory way. Listen to the cases in the police courts of any country; ask your medical friends; invite your married or unmarried friends to tell you the whole truth about themselves, speak seriously to educationists—and you will find out this sad reality for yourself.

I asked Krishnamurti whether he thought it wrong for people with a very strong sexual impulse to give way to it. 'Nothing is wrong if it is the result of something that is really within you', was his answer. 'Follow your urge, if it is not created by artificial stimuli but is burning within you—and there will be no sex problem in your life. A problem only arises when something within us that is real is opposed by intellectual considerations.'

'But surely it is not only intellectual considerations that cause many people to believe the satisfaction of a strong sex urge to be wrong, even if it is too strong to be suppressed.'

'Suppression can never solve a problem. Nor can self-discipline do it. That is only substituting one problem for another.'

'But how do you expect millions of people, who have become slaves of sex, to solve the friction between their urge and that judicial sense which tries to prevent them from giving way? In England you will find fewer people openly ruled by sex, but consider America; consider most of the countries of the continent of Europe; consider many of the Eastern nations—for them their sex needs are a grave problem.'

I noticed an expression of slight impatience on Krishnamurti's face. 'For me this problem does not exist', he said; 'after all, sex is an expression of love, isn't it? I personally derive as much joy from touching the hand of a person I am fond of as another might get from sexual intercourse.'

'But what about the ordinary person who has not attained to your state of maturity, or whatever it should be called?'

'To begin with, people ought to see sex in its proper proportions. It is not sex as a vital inner urge that dominates people nowadays so much as the images and thoughts of sex. Our whole modern life is propitious to them. Look around you. You can hardly open a newspaper, travel by the underground or walk along a street without coming across advertisements and posters that appeal to your sex instincts in order to sing the praises of a pair of stockings, a new toothpaste or a particular brand of cigarette. I cannot imagine that so many semi-naked girls have ever before walked through the pages of newspapers and magazines. In every shop, cinema and café the lift attendants, waitresses and shopgirls are made up to look like harlots so that they may appeal to your sex instincts. They themselves are not conscious of this, but their short skirts, their exposed legs, their painted faces, their girlish coiffures, the constant physical appeal which they are made to exercise over the customer do nothing but stimulate your sex instincts. Oh, it is beastly, simply beastly! Sex has been degraded to become the servant of unimaginative salesmanship. Someone will start a new magazine and, instead of racking his brains for an interesting and alluring title-page, all he does is to publish a coloured picture of a girl with half-opened lips, suggestively hiding her breasts and looking altogether like a whore. You are being constantly attacked, and you no longer know whether it is your own sex urge or the sex vibration produced artificially by life around you. This degrading, emphatic appeal to our sex instinct is one of the most beastly signs of our civilization. Take it away, and most of the so-called sex urge is gone.'

'I am not a moralist', Krishnamurti added after a pause; 'I have nothing against sex, and I am against sex suppression, sex hypocrisy and even what is called sexual self-discipline, which is only a specific form of hypocrisy. But I don't want sex to be cheapened, to be introduced into all those forms of life where it does not belong.'

KRISHNAMURTI IN CARMEL

'Nevertheless, Krishnaji, your world without its beastly sex appeal will be found only in Utopia. We are dealing with the world as it actually is, and as it will probably be in days to come, long after you and I are gone.'

'That may be so, but it does not concern me. I am not a doctor; I cannot prescribe half-remedies; I deal simply and solely with fundamental spiritual truth. If you are in search of remedies and half-methods you must go to a psychologist. I can only repeat that if you readjust yourself in such a way as to allow love to become an omnipresent feeling in which sex will be an expression of genuine affection, all the wretched sex problems will cease to exist.'

He looked up for a few seconds and then gave a deep sigh. 'Oh, if you people could only see that these problems don't exist in reality, and that it is only yourselves who create them, and that it is yourselves who must solve them! I cannot do it for you—nobody can if he is genuine and faithful to truth. I can only deal with spiritual truth and not with spiritual quackery.' His voice seemed full of disillusion and he stopped and lay back on the ground.

I began to understand what Christ must have meant when He spoke of His love without distinction for every human being, and of all men being brothers. Indeed, the omnipresent feeling of love (in which sex would become meaningless without being eliminated) seemed the only form of love worthy of a conscious and mature human being. Nevertheless I wondered whether Krishnamurti himself had reached that stage of life-awareness in which personal love had given place to universal love, in which every human being would be approached with equal affection.

'Don't you love some people more than others?' I asked. 'After all, even a person like yourself is bound to have emotional preferences.'

Krishnamurti's voice was very quiet when he began to speak again. 'I must first say something before I can give you a satisfactory reply to your question. Otherwise you may not be able to accept it in the spirit in which it is offered. I want you to know that these talks are quite as important to me as they can possibly be to you. I don't speak to you merely to satisfy the curiosity of an author who happens to be writing about me, or to help you personally. I talk mainly to clarify a number of things for myself. This I consider one of the great values of conversation. You must not think therefore that I ever say anything unless I believe it with my whole heart. I am not trying to impress, to convince or to teach you. Even if you were my oldest friend

275

or my brother I should speak in just the same way. I am saying all this because I want you to accept my words as simple statements of opinion and not as attempts to convert or persuade. You asked me just now about personal love, and my answer is that I no longer know it. Personal love does not exist for me. Love is for me a constant inner state. It does not matter to me whether I am now with you, with my brother or with an utter stranger—I have the same feeling of affection for all and each of you. People sometimes think that I am superficial and cold, that my love is negative and that it is not strong enough to be directed to one person only. But it is not indifference, it is merely a feeling of love that is constantly within me and that I simply cannot help giving to everyone I come into touch with.' He paused for a second as though wondering whether I believed him, and then said: 'People were shocked by my recent behaviour after Mrs. Besant's death. I did not cry, I did not seem distressed but was serene; I went on with my ordinary life, and people said that I was devoid of all human feeling. How could I explain to them that, as my love went to everyone, it could not be affected by the departure of one individual, even if this was Mrs Besant. Grief can no longer take possession of you when love has become the basis of your entire being.'

'There must be people in your life who mean nothing to you or whom you even dislike?'

Krishnamurti smiled: 'There aren't any people I dislike. Don't you see that it is not I who directs my love towards one person, strengthening it here, weakening it there? Love is simply there like the colour of my skin, the sound of my voice, no matter what I do. And therefore it is bound to be there even when I am surrounded by people I don't know or people whom I "should" not care for. Sometimes I am forced to be in a crowd of noisy people that I don't know, it may be some meeting or a lecture or perhaps a waiting room in a station, where the atmosphere is full of noise, smoke, the smell of tobacco and all the other things that affect me physically. Even then my feeling of love for everyone is as strong as it is under this sky and on this lovely spot. People think that I am conceited or a hypocrite when I tell them that grief and sorrow and even death do not affect me. It is not conceit. Love that makes me like that is so natural to me that I am always surprised that people can question it. And I feel this unity not only with human beings. I feel it with trees, with the sea, with the whole world around me. Physical differentiations no longer exist. I am not speaking of the mental images of a poet; I am speaking of reality.'

When Krishnamurti stopped his eyes were shining, and there was in him that specific quality of beauty which easily appears sentimental or artificial when described in words, and yet is so convincing when met with in real life. It did not seem magnetism that radiated from him but rather an inner illumination that is hard to define, and that manifests itself as sheer beauty. I now experienced the feeling we sometimes have when confronted by strong impressions of Nature. Reaching the top of a mountain, or the soft breezes of early spring, with the promise of daffodils and leafy woods, can produce occasionally such states of unsophisticated contentment.

VI

Krishnamurti had told me a lot during the few hours on the hill, and I felt on our walk home that I must first digest it all, and that it would be wiser to remain by myself for the rest of the day.

I read during the afternoon the pamphlets that Krishnamurti had given me, and that contained his recent lectures at Ojai and in Australia. Though I recognized in these many of his fundamental beliefs, I was struck again by the words in which he expressed to an Australian audience that it is essential to eliminate the I, the ego, in order to see truth. 'Happiness, or truth or God cannot be found as the outcome of the ego. The ego is to me nothing but the result of environment.' I wondered whether the people at large could grasp this idea. Weren't they always taught that they have to develop their ego, their personality, before they can hope to achieve anything important in life? Would it not be wiser if Krishnamurti proceeded step by step, teaching that inner awareness could be found only gradually and after long and slow preparation?

That was my first question when we settled down next morning under the pines overlooking the ocean. 'Mrs. Besant once said to me,' Krishnamurti answered, ' "I am nothing but a nurse who helps people who are unable to move by themselves and who are in need of crutches. This I consider to be my duty. You, Krishnaji, appeal to people who do not need crutches, who can walk on their own feet. Go on talking to them, but please let me speak to those who need help. Don't tell them that all crutches are wrong, because some people cannot live without them. Please, do not tell them to refuse to follow anyone on whom they can lean."'

'What was your answer?' I interrupted. 'I think Mrs. Besant's request was very fair.'

'I said to her: "I cannot possibly do what you are asking me. I consider that any definite method or advice is a crutch, and thus a barrier to truth. I simply must go on denying all crutches—even yours." Do not blame me for having been so cruel to a woman of eighty, to whom I seem to have meant a great deal and whom I always loved and admired.'

'I see your point, Krishnaji; nevertheless I question its wisdom,' I said. 'The majority of people are neither independent nor conscious of themselves—that's why they need help. Your attitude might be considered cruel. Your duty is, I take it, to help people and to help as many as you can. Doesn't that mean that you have to consider the overwhelming majority of people?'

'I cannot possibly make distinctions between a majority and a minority; for it is wrong to assume that there is one truth for the masses and another for the elect. All people are spiritually equal.'

'But even Jesus Christ had to differentiate. He first gave His message to a small minority before it could become public property.'

'Is it really so? He gave it to anyone who was willing to accept it. Whether He spoke directly to twelve or to twelve thousand people does not alter this. He spoke of universal things that affected everyone in the world, no matter what their racial, religious, intellectual or social standing. He never appealed to a minority only.'

'But wouldn't you consider it wiser to prepare people slowly for a truth that requires such a thorough inner readjustment? Only a few people are ripe for the necessary inner revolution.'

'These few matter. Those who genuinely search for truth, who study it from every angle, who test it and open themselves to it, will find it easy to live in constant inner awareness. Preparing people for it would mean compromising. And a compromise is a bargain between truth and untruth. How can you expect me to preach untruth—no matter in what form—after having found truth? I am not a quack. I am only concerned with spiritual truth.'

'So what should the people do who cannot walk through life without crutches?'

KRISHNAMURTI IN CARMEL

'Let them go on using them—but I shall have nothing to do with them. People who need a sanatorium must not come to me.' Krishnamurti came nearer to me and took my hand, as he would sometimes do when in despair at my inability to see his point; and then he said: 'You must understand that I can only talk to people who are willing to revolutionize themselves in order to find truth. You cannot find truth by living on a special emotional diet or by using an elaborate system of mental exercises.'

I began to see that no compromise was possible and that Krishnamurti could only offer truth with all its revolutionary consequences or else no truth at all. In spite of this I said: 'I think you are right; but yet I ask myself, How can truth, as conceived by you, be communicated to the masses?'

The same expression of sadness came into Krishnamurti's face that I had noticed before when I questioned him on that point. He began to speak slowly, as though talking to himself 'I, too, often ask myself, How? When I speak in India more than ten thousand people will come to a meeting to listen to me. Thousands come to listen to me in America—thousands in Europe—thousands in Australia.[1] I know that most of them come simply out of curiosity or for fun, and only a few because they are trying to find something which they haven't found elsewhere. How many of them return home happier or richer? . . . And yet I know that I must go on doing it. One can help people only by talking to them, by discussing truth with them.' He stopped for a moment and then turned towards me: 'As you know, I abhor the whole idea of discipleship and all the futility of a so-called spiritual organization; yet at times I wonder whether I shouldn't prepare a few helpers who might be able to enlighten those people who won't listen to me because of my former notoriety as "the messiah". They might listen to my "pupils" who have no past to live down. I must confess that it makes me sad that I cannot help as many people as I should like to.'

We got up, and Krishnamurti insisted upon accompanying me halfway towards my hotel. The sea was stretched at the bottom of the steep road, on one side of which was a private garden full of red, blue and yellow flowers and mimosa trees covered with thick clusters of golden blossoms. Beyond the garden hills rose swiftly towards the

[1] In the summer of 1935 I received a letter from Krishnamurti, from Rio de Janeiro, in which he wrote: 'I gave here two meetings in a football stadium, as ...ere was no theatre large enough to hold the crowd.' Each time twenty thousand people attended his meeting.

279

sky. Though the sun was shining, a faint haze lingered over the sea. November was approaching, but the light, the heat and the vegetation suggested July. When we reached the bottom of the road we separated, and I walked on by myself along the coast, Krishnamurti turning back up the hill. I looked round after a minute and saw him walking very slowly; his head was hanging down and his shoulders drooping—his shoulders looked narrower than ever before. I felt like running back and saying something to him—but I did not do it.

VII

What effect had Krishnamurti's message on those who had had no proper preparation for it or no chance of daily conversation with him? I wondered whether they found it very hard to grasp, and whether they felt it beyond their powers. Now the moment had arrived to learn something about the reactions of other people.

Carmel seemed particularly propitious for such a task. There were at Carmel not only those average Americans who would react to Krishnamurti's message in the usual, that is to say, emotional rather than critical way, but also people with pronounced capacities for the understanding and criticism of it. Carmel was not what might be called a 'colony'. It was not the Capri of English novelists and Russian religious 'maniacs'; it was not the defenceless Positano upon which descended soon after the war hordes of German and American painters; it was not the Swiss Ascona in which Germanic dreamers were following many and varied gods; it was not even one of those fishing villages along the Mediterranean coast which, discovered by a fashionable Anglo-American dramatist or novelist, are turned overnight into a centre of international frivolity. Carmel was one of those faintly baroque survivals, scattered here and there under the pines and cedars along the coast, of California's Spanish past. An antique church stood outside the miniature town with its main street called Ocean Avenue, its big drugstore in which everything could be bought from hot sandwiches to detective novels and chewing gum; there were shops in one-storey houses, faintly reminiscent of colonial architecture. There was even an art gallery, run by a few ladies and dedicated fearlessly both to music and to pictorial art. Once a month the big white room of the art gallery would be transformed into a concert hall, with a miniature stage and many rows of little chairs. Musicians from all over the world, in need of

280

KRISHNAMURTI IN CARMEL

a short rest during their American tour, would stop in Carmel for a couple of days on their journey between San Francisco and Los Angeles, and would give a recital in the white exhibition room with its modern pictures and its host of eager listeners. The residential houses were in smaller side streets, and lay in the midst of little gardens, adorned by hibiscus and fuchsias of unusual size. The woods and plains round Carmel had so far escaped suburbanization. One or two houses were built on some romantic promontory, over-hanging the sea and commanding a limitless view of sky and coastline.

Though Carmel had become the home of many creative person-alities, its life had not been deadened by an intellectual or artistic unity of purpose. Yet the presence of Krishnamurti seemed to be producing an as yet little visible common link, affecting the com-plexion of the community. Carmel has not become a Krishnamurti colony. Nevertheless his presence seemed to have focused the atten-tion of the inhabitants of Carmel and of the neighbouring Dal Monte, Monterey and Pebble Beach. I was assured that even in the shops in Ocean Avenue people talked much less of Mr. Roosevelt or of the latest Hollywood scandals than of Krishnamurti.

Many of the inhabitants have approached Krishnamurti directly —some no doubt to satisfy a curiosity awakened by the man's former notoriety, a few out of a religious need, and the greatest number perhaps because they were personally attracted by him. This class seemed by far the largest, and it represented most of the social and intellectual figures in the life of Carmel.

VIII

Among these people I met Robinson Jeffers, one of America's greatest living poets. Although he was not interested in 'spiritual movements' or religious teachers, so that the name of Krishnamurti had meant nothing to him before they met, Robinson Jeffers was so attracted by Krishnamurti's personality that the two men soon became friends. I was anxious to talk to Jeffers about Krishnamurti, and I gladly accepted an invitation to visit him and his charming wife.

They lived right on the coast in a house built by the poet's own hands from the cobblestones that lay about on the beach. He had brought them thence stone by stone until he had built the house— an unaided labour of five or six years. He spent another two years in erecting a medieval-looking tower in the garden, constructed also from stones found on the beach. This tower had a steep and spiral flight of steps, and on its top you entered a tiny and unexpected room, with panelled walls, a comfortable bench and a superb view, looking across the beach towards the sea. The sound of the waves, the dark outlines of the rocks—from the grey stones of which the tower and the house had been built—the wind and the salty freshness of the atmosphere made you think of Cornwall.

I spent an afternoon in the small tower room, talking to my host about Krishnamurti. A log fire was burning in the small fireplace, and California seemed very far away. Robinson Jeffers was reserved and shy, and his persistent silence almost suggested an inner fear that a spoken word might destroy images maturing in his poet's brain. He was wearing khaki breeches and leggings, and but for his dreamy eyes, and the great tenderness in the expression of his mouth, he might have been an English farmer. Both his wife and his friends had warned me that I should have to do most of the talking, but once or twice I succeeded in making him speak. 'For me', he said in a slow and hesitant manner, 'there is nothing wrong in Krishnamurti's message—nothing that I must contradict.'

'Do you think his message will ever become popular?'

'Not at present. Most people won't find it intelligible enough.'

'What struck you most when you met him for the first time?'

'His personality. Mrs. Jeffers often makes the remark that light seems to enter the room when Krishnamurti comes in, and I agree with her, for he himself is the most convincing illustration of his honest message. To me it does not matter whether he speaks well or not. I can feel his influence even without words. The other day we went together for a walk in the hills. We walked for almost ten miles and as I am a poor speaker we hardly talked at all—yet I felt happier after our walk. It is his very personality that seems to diffuse the truth and happiness of which he is always talking.' Robinson Jeffers lit his pipe, which had gone out, and then again sat watching the flames in the grate.

'Do you think Krishnamurti's message is so matured as to have found its final formulation?'

'It may be final, but I wonder whether it has quite matured yet. It will be mature when its words are intelligible to everyone. At present there is a certain thinness in them. Don't you think so?'

'I quite agree. I confess that at times I simply don't know how to write about him. Whatever I put on paper sounds unconvincing and makes Krishnamurti appear the very antithesis of what he really is: it makes him look conceited, a prig or a complacent fellow. In writing, his arguments are irritating and his logic unconvincing. And yet they sound so true when he uses them in conversation. It is almost impossible to describe him, for so much depends upon his personality, and so little upon what he says.'

'Yes, it is almost impossible to describe certain personalities.'

'I think this may be mainly because Krishnamurti's intellectual faculties have not developed quite as completely as the spiritual side of the man. After all, intellectually he is still a youth. Most of his life has been spent in the theosophical nursery. Most of his ideas were stifled in those days. Many teachers impress us by their knowledge; Krishnamurti does it by his very person, which he gives to his listeners and which inspires them, and not by his particular brand of wisdom.'

'I suppose it is so', replied Jeffers in his slow, quiet way. 'Others will have to find a clear and convincing language to express his message. After all, it would not be the first time that the followers of a teacher have had to build the bridge across which a new message can reach the masses.'

I met several people in Carmel and also in other parts of America who expressed similar opinions. Some of the inhabitants of Carmel told me that they were unable to grasp Krishnamurti's message or that they failed to see its practical value—but all of them confessed that he gave them a feeling of happiness and calm that they had never known before.

On Sunday afternoons anyone who wished could come to the hotel at which Krishnamurti stayed, and there join in a general discussion in the big lounge. I was more amused than impressed by these discussions, in which purely personal questions were asked, often irrelevant, or prompted merely by intellectual curiosity. I told Krishnamurti what I thought, but in his opinion he could help people to find truth for themselves if he and they evolved the answers together. Perhaps twenty, perhaps two hundred people would attend these Sunday discussions which created a nucleus for Krishnamurti's message in California.

It was always Krishnamurti's personality that most of all impressed people. They felt that here was a man who lived his teaching even more convincingly than he preached it. I was told that when

FULFILMENTS

Krishnamurti entered America he was granted a limited time of residence there. It was suggested to him, however, that, if he cared to state in his passport that he entered the country as a teacher, he would be allowed more favourable conditions. Friends urged him to describe himself, for the sake of his own convenience, as a teacher; but Krishnamurti refused to do so. An official acknowledgement of his status as a teacher would have produced many of those misleading implications which he had cast overboard when he dissolved all his organizations. Krishnamurti's decision may seem pedantic, but it was the only possible step which could accord with his personal attitude towards truth.

IX

At the end of a week, spent almost constantly in Krishnamurti's company, I felt that I could formulate my own opinions about his teaching. What were the main points of his message? Truth can only be the result of an inner illumination, and this can only be enjoyed by one who fully recognizes the many-sidedness of life. We find truth through permanent inner awareness of our thoughts, feelings and actions. Only such an awareness can free us automatically from our shortcomings, or can solve our problems without our striving to force the solution of them. Life becomes a reality through a loving self-identification with every one of its moments, and not through our habitual and mechanical pursuits. No sacrifices of an ascetic or similar kind are necessary, for our former limitations are eliminated automatically by full living.

It was not difficult to see that Krishnamurti's message was more or less the same as that of Christ, of Buddha or indeed of any genuine religious teacher. All he demanded from people was that they should live a personal life of inner awareness. This, possible only through love and thought, opens to us the doors of truth. In such a life none of our self-created shortcomings—envy, jealousy, hatred and possessiveness—can exist.

The problem of how far Krishnamurti's language could be understood seemed to me of paramount importance, and I decided to talk to him once again about it. It was one of my last days in Carmel, and I was walking with Krishnamurti. 'I have been talking to all sorts of people who have met you,' I said, 'and I have tried to discover whether your teaching is as convincing to them as it is to me. Many consider it most difficult, and it makes me sad that they should find

284

it so hard to understand what seems to me the simplest truth. I wonder why God should have made it appear so complicated?' I sighed, but Krishnamurti only smiled: 'It is not God, but ourselves. It seems complicated because of our power of free choice.'

'Free choice?' I interrupted in surprise.

'Indeed, it is only our free choice which creates conflicts in our lives; and conflicts are responsible for deterioration. By free choice we begin to build up handicaps and complications which we are forced to drive out one by one if we are to make our way towards truth.'

'Then we should despair, according to you, just because we have been given the faculty of free choice? Would it be better if we were as the animals, which simply follow their dark fate and do not know what free will means?'

'Not at all. Only the unintelligent mind exercises choice in life. When I talk of intelligence I mean it in its widest sense, I mean that deep inner intelligence of mind, emotion and will. A truly intelligent man can have no choice, because his mind can only be aware of what is true and can thus only choose the path of truth. An intelligent mind acts and reacts naturally and to its fullest capacity. It identifies itself spontaneously with the right thing. It simply cannot have any choice. Only the unintelligent mind has free will.'

This was rather an unexpected account of free will. 'I have never come across this conception before,' I said; 'but it sounds convincing.'

'It can be nothing else; it simply is like that.'

I had noticed on various occasions before that he never seemed conscious of the novelty of some of his pronouncements or of the unexpected result of a conversation He never discussed for the sake of discussion or for my sake but in order to clarify for both of us the problem under discussion. The reason why he had to expose himself to the accusation of evasiveness became clear to me. Only truth found through collaboration joined with personal effort can have any meaning at all.

Suddenly Krishnamurti stopped: 'Many things became clearer for me since we started our daily conversations. I meant to tell you the other day that after one of our first talks I had a particularly vivid experience of inner awareness of life. I was walking home along the beach when I became so deeply aware of the beauty of the sky, the sea and the trees around me that it was almost a sensation of physical joy. All separation between me and the things around me ceased to exist, and I walked home fully conscious of that wonderful unity. When I got home and joined the others at dinner, it almost seemed as though I had to push my inner state behind a screen and step out of it; but, though I was sitting among people and talking of all sorts of things, that inner awareness of a unity with everything never left me for a second.'

'How did you come to that state of unity with everything?'

'People have asked me about it before, and I always feel that they expect to hear the dramatic account of some sudden miracle through which I suddenly became one with the universe Of course nothing of the sort happened. My inner awareness was always there; though it took me time to feel it more and more clearly; and equally it took time to find words that would at all describe it. It was not a sudden flash, but a slow yet constant clarification of something that was always there. It did not grow, as people often think. Nothing can grow in us that is of spiritual importance. It has to be there in all its fullness, and the only thing that happens is that we become more and more aware of it. It is our intellectual reaction and nothing else that needs time to become more articulate, more definite.'

X

I was leaving Carmel next day, and when we reached our favourite spot under the pines on the hill I knew that this would be our last talk together. Farewells often bring words to my lips that I might feel shy of using in less exceptional circumstances But Krishnamurti's presence summoned up my emotional faculties without making me feel a fool. 'Krishnaji,' I said as I took his hands between my own, 'my visit is coming to an end. I am very grateful to you for these wonderful days. Nevertheless I must talk to you once more about something which we have discussed many times.'

'What is it? Don't feel shy—go ahead.'

'I appreciate your point of view that your mission is not to act as a doctor and that you cannot prescribe spiritual pills for people. But once again: How do you expect to help others? I know you want them to live their lives in such fullness as to become truthful, and so truthfully as to be able to give up possessiveness, jealousy and greed. But such an inner revolution requires a strength possessed only by few. You have achieved it, and you are standing on a mountain top on which you can live in a state of unity with the world that

286

amounts to constant ecstasy. But you forget that we all, millions and millions of us, live in the vast plains at the foot of the mountain. Few could endure a life of continuous ecstasy. It would burn them up, it would destroy them to live in that permanent awareness which is essential. I can see it as a goal; I can see that it is the only life worth living; but I don't see that we are mature enough for it.'

Krishnamurti came quite near me—as he had often done before —looked deep into my eyes and said in his melodious voice: 'You are right They live in the plains and I live, as you call it, on the mountain top; but I hope that ever more and more human beings will be able to endure the clear air of the mountain top. A man infinitely greater than any of us had to go His own way that led to Golgotha; no matter whether His disciples could follow Him or not; no matter whether His message could be accepted immediately or had to wait for centuries. How can you expect me to be concerned with what should be done or how it should be done? If you have once lived on a mountain top, you cannot return to the plains. You can only try to make other people feel the purity of the air and enjoy the infinite prospect, and become one with the beauty of life there.'

This time there was no sadness in Krishnamurti's voice, and in his eyes there was a light that was love, compassion, sympathy, and that had often before moved me. Not the faintest sign of hopelessness was in him when we rose to walk slowly up the hill to the house in which he lived. The sun was setting, and ribbons of green and pink clouds were stretched across the full length of the sky. Night comes quickly in these regions, and in a few minutes the light would be gone.

XI

We shook hands and I descended towards the beach as I had done every day since my arrival at Carmel. It seemed quite natural on this last day of my visit that the whole of Krishnamurti's life should unfold itself before me. Is there another life in modern times comparable with his? There have been many masters and teachers, yogis and lamas whom their followers worshipped. But none of them had been torn out of an ordinary existence to be anointed as the coming World Teacher. None of them had been accepted by the East and the West, by the oldest and the youngest continent, by Christians, Hindus, Jews and Moslems, by believers and agnostics. Neither Ramakrishna nor Vivekananda had been brought up and educated

287

for their future messiahship; neither Gandhi nor Mrs. Baker Eddy, neither Steiner nor Mme. Blavatsky had known such a strange destiny. Neither in the records of Western mystics nor in the books of Eastern yogis and saints do we find the story of a 'saint' who after twenty-five years of preparation for a divine destiny decides to become an ordinary human being, who renounces not only his worldly goods but also all his religious claims.

It was quite dark and the first stars were beginning to appear. The attention was not distracted by the lights and colours and shapes of the day. The mysterious pattern of Krishnamurti's remarkable fate was becoming clearer, and I began to understand what he had meant when he said that till a few years ago life had been a dream to him and that he had scarcely been conscious of the external existence around him. Were not those the years of preparation? Were they not the years in which the man Krishnamurti was trying to find himself, to replace that former self through whom Mrs. Besant and Charles Leadbeater, theosophy and a strange credulity, acted for over twenty years?

Indeed, was not Krishnamurti's a supreme story? The teacher who renounces his throne at the moment of his awakening, at the moment when the god in him has to make way for the man, at the moment when the man can begin to find God within himself? Have not even the years in which his spirit lingered in dreams been full of a truth that as yet is too mysterious to be comprehended by us?

CONCLUSION

THE LIVING GOD

'There can be no doubt that the scientist has
a much more mystic conception of the external world than he had in the last century.'
SIR ARTHUR EDDINGTON.

I

The number and popularity of the various men and their
teachings described in the foregoing pages must seem surprising
to many readers. Mysticism, occultism and similar movements
have always existed, but for centuries they were the private domain
of Eastern or religious recluses, of small esoteric schools, occasionally
of saints, frequently of fanatics. To-day the situation is different.
Many of the people given up to these researches are scientifically
schooled; and the subjects of their investigations are no longer the
privilege of little sects of initiates who jealously guard them from
the eyes of the world, but are open to everyone anxious to learn.
The legitimate sciences, though reluctantly, are beginning to take
them more seriously than they did twenty or thirty years ago, and
the dividing line between the two is in many instances no longer
visible.

Sir James Jeans, quoted at the beginning of this book, is by no
means the only modern scientist who has to admit the existence of
the world of the spirit. Scientists all over the world are beginning
to do the same. One of the most distinguished in England, Sir
Ambrose Fleming, the perfecter of the two-electrode thermionic
valve, and thus one of the fathers of modern wireless, declared in
January 1935, in his presidential address to the Victorian Institute
and Philosophical Society of Great Britain, that 'the origin of man
is to be looked for in the creative power of a self-conscious Creator'.
Sir Ambrose admitted that the Biblical miracles cannot be regarded
as superstitions. 'The bodily resurrection of Christ', said the eminent
scientist, 'is one of the most certainly attested facts in human history;
but if so, it certifies all previous Biblical miracles. . . .' Sir Ambrose
went so far as to attack 'those sections of enlightened clergymen'

who 'deny the possibility of miracle or exceptional action on the part of Deity', and who assume that 'no events have ever happened or can happen which are outside of our present limited experience of Nature'.

Equally startling are the pronouncements of Sir Arthur Eddington in his American lectures in 1934 at Cornell University. After putting the weighty question, 'Why should anyone suppose that all that matters to human nature can be assessed with the measuring rod?' he asserts 'that the nature of all reality is spiritual', and thus acknowledges a power that no scientist in the last century would have considered worth serious examination. Sir Arthur Eddington represents an entirely new spirit in science, for he confesses 'that the scientist has a much more mystic conception of the external world than he had in the last century', and that he 'is not sure that the mathematician understands this world of ours better than the poet and the mystic'.

The most revealing conclusion that I reached in the course of fifteen years of spiritual investigation is that all genuine teachers are trying to find the same truth. Differences are caused only by the differences in their states of consciousness, in their origins, or in their methods. One of them, like Keyserling, may appeal above all to the imagination; Gurdjieff employs a most complicated system, and Krishnamurti's influence derives almost entirely from the beauty of his personality; Ouspensky approaches truth like a surgeon, and Rudolf Steiner like a scientist who is also a mystic. But they are all trying to find—and then to sow the seeds of—the same truth.

As Krishnamurti said: 'There is no-one who can give us truth, since each of us for himself must discern it.' Teachers can only encourage the efforts which we make for ourselves when they have pointed out to us the way.

I shall not deal in the following pages with those matters that may have enriched my mind without influencing my character. They can be studied in the writings of the teachers themselves. Only that knowledge will be expounded which was confirmed over and over again by daily life, for only such knowledge is of real use Truth is not what we keep in a bottom drawer for Sunday but what can affect every moment of our existence. It is unfortunate that most religions are presented in forms so dogmatic that they can no longer exert much influence on conduct in life.

THE LIVING GOD

II

The principal command of all teachers, irrespective of their race, creed or method, is that a man must 'know himself'. Thus the elimination of conventions and habits becomes one of the fundamental spiritual laws. The prophet who took the visitor round the Temple of Apollo at Delphi always pointed first to the inscription over the entrance: 'Know thyself'. Plutarch in his treatise 'On the E at Delphi' states: 'The prophet said to the visitor, "Fix these words in thy memory, for they hold the key to all wisdom." ' Only through self-knowledge can we hope to understand the world as it actually is and not as it appears through the veils of our imagination. The Greeks with their distinctively spiritual consciousness clearly perceived the reason for that paramount truth. In their opinion, 'Only one Being exists always and fills eternity—that is God, who gives life to all things and who dwells within man. This is why Apollo says to his worshippers "Know thyself." '[1]

The knowledge of oneself is the knowledge of the world inside us, and the road to truth and thus to God is shortest when we search for Him within ourselves. Eventually we shall detect Him also in the outside world, in a tree perhaps or in another person. Once we have caught a glimpse of truth we comprehend that the inner union with God is nothing else but a life of the cardinal Christian virtues. It was one of the most revealing moments of my life when I grasped for the first time that the life within, the life of the spirit, is identical with the life as realized to the fullest by Jesus Christ.

III

There was a period in my life when meditation and contemplation seemed the most suitable methods for approaching truth. Many people of the present day have such a mistaken conception of that method that it may be useful briefly to expound it.

Meditation and contemplation are not identical, though closely related to each other. Neither requires special gifts or knowledge, and both are open to everyone. While meditation is deep thinking about one particular subject with the elimination of all other thoughts, contemplation is absolute unification with the subject—

[1] Schuré, *From Sphinx to Christ.*

not of the intellect only but of the whole of our being. Both meditation and contemplation begin with ordinary concentration as we know it in daily life.

The first essential thing is to calm the rush of our thoughts and to establish as much peace within as possible. I have mentioned in an earlier chapter that it is easier to meditate in certain postures of the body, and that no system has developed that technique better than *hatha* yoga. Though genuine yoga, even if learned in the East, is not of much avail to Westerners, we may deal with its subject briefly, if only to dispel certain fantastic notions existing about this method of self-advancement. Besides *hatha*, or yoga of bodily control, there are: *raja* yoga, which develops mainly our consciousness; *jnana* yoga, which employs chiefly the intellect; *karma* yoga, which works through right action; and *bhakti* yoga, which is the yoga of religion and love. The differences between the various yogas are often indiscernible, and at times one may act according to the commandments of yoga without actually following any yoga system. Thus, Miraben, Gandhi's English disciple, answered when I asked her what particular yoga Gandhi followed: 'The mahatma does not follow any yoga. His whole life is yoga of service and sacrifice. For him, as for Christ, or for Buddha before him, spiritual exercises consist in serving the lowest and the poorest, sacrificing himself constantly on their behalf.' And yet Gandhi's life could be described as *raja* yoga, which demands service and self-sacrifice.

In *hatha* yoga the adept learns the many difficult postures which help him to certain spiritual attainments. Both the bodily and the breathing exercises of *hatha* yoga start simply and end with such remarkable achievements as standing on one finger or stopping the breathing for a number of minutes. The most widely known posture, or *asana*, as it is called in India, is the simple one of Buddha, with the right foot resting on the left thigh, and the left foot on the right.

It must not be assumed that it is essential to adopt *yoga* methods to succeed in meditation. In fact, only a few Europeans have ever had genuine success in *yoga*. But there are also Western *asanas*, such as those prescribed by religious brotherhoods or secret societies. In fact, the Christian posture of kneeling to pray is an *asana*.

Even Western postures are not essential for meditation or contemplation. Everyone must try for himself what bodily position makes him feel most at ease and enables him to forget his body. It may be the lotus posture of Buddha, the kneeling attitude of the

Christian religion, or perhaps the ordinary positions of lying flat in bed or sitting in a chair.

The question of what to meditate about is much simpler than many people assume. There are, of course, special sentences, formulae and prayers specially prepared and given by responsible teachers. It is, however, quite enough to meditate about anything from a tree in blossom to a kind action.

Intellectual or mental concentration and meditation are only the first step. Eventually we must transplant the meditation from the brain to the breast, and later on the subject of our meditation must fill out the whole of our being. By that time we shall have reached the stage of contemplation.

Even after the earliest attempts we discover that such an inner identification produces within us lightness. We see the solutions of our problems more clearly than we have ever done before, and we feel as though we were nearer something of great significance. At the beginning we must be content if the meditation lasts no longer than a minute, and the contemplation only a second or two. After persistent attempts and much patience the state of inner clarification and calm can be achieved at any given moment, and it will then become the underlying current of our whole day. We eventually discover that we have established within ourselves a link with guiding powers, hidden from us before, and leading finally to an unmistaken realization of God.

Before taking leave of the subject of meditation it must be emphasized that all exercises done on a basis of yoga require a personal teacher, cannot be learned from a book and are only taught in the East. Ordinary meditation and contemplation, as sketched in these pages, can be done by everyone, but can only serve as a help and cannot be treated as the main current of our spiritual life.

In the Western world we find in our prayer an exercise comparable to yoga; and, not unlike yoga, prayer can be more helpful if we know how to pray. Prayer, like any other form of spiritual concentration, can be degraded to a mechanical action, or even worse, to a mere superstition. We should never pray for anything that we might be able to achieve through our own effort, we should never pray for a selfish reward; we should never pray for anything that may (even indirectly) harm someone else. But we might pray for enlightenment regarding things that we cannot possibly reach with our intellect, that are unselfish or essential for the performance of a good deed.

FULFILMENTS

Unbelievers often say: 'If God knows everything, He also knows my needs, and therefore it is superfluous to pray.' Though God knows everything He may not wish to impose His will or His help upon us as long as He has not been asked for them. Let us take for an illustration the case of a poor man who has a rich friend, aware of the poor man's need and willing to help. As long as the poor man does not approach him to ask for help, the rich one may find it difficult to impose his help upon him. It is, in a way, the same with prayers. A prayer is an invocation by which we tell God that we have exhausted all means of solution, and that we find ourselves forced to beg Him for help.

Besides prayer for personal assistance, there is also prayer for the sake of others. When Rudolf Steiner was asked during the war how one was to pray for the safety of those on the battlefields, he replied that one ought to send out helpful thoughts to the guardian angel of the person in question rather than to the person directly. People who pray to God, usually believe in some kind of spiritual hierarchy. The guardian angel is not a superstition of uneducated minds but a deep conviction which existed in all religions for thousands of years, and which, in more spiritual epochs than ours, was treated by prophets and thinkers alike with the greatest reverence. When asked how to pray to the guardian angel, Steiner answered that we should try to visualize the angel as standing above the person, pouring out light and holding in his hands the radiating star which represents the higher individuality of the person. This radiating star has been mentioned by Plutarch in his *Opera Moralia* as that part of the human spirit that is not tied down to any of our organic functions, and that is thus connected with eternity even during our lifetime. According to Steiner, we should send out our loving thoughts to the vision of the angel carrying the star and enveloping the person we are praying for with light.

IV

Neither prayer nor contemplation can replace life, for in their own sphere they are like exercises taken for physical fitness in theirs. Exercises alone cannot give us health if the rest of our life is not wholesome.

I shall try to describe how I attempted to live, even when faced with great difficulties in daily life, on a basis of truth and thus in accordance with the fundamental laws of God. A theoretical God, approached on Sundays alone, is no God at all. He is only real if He directs every moment of our life and if we learn by experience that He does it better than anyone else.

The God in whom we believe only in moments of happiness matters less than the One who proves Himself to us in moments of misery Let us assume that we are faced with a difficulty far exceeding our power of solution. It may be the loss of a beloved person, the destruction of our fortune, the danger of losing our job, betrayal by the person we trusted most, a scandal endangering the whole of our future, a situation that evokes our most violent jealousy. The worst thing to do on such occasions is to cling desperately to that which we are losing. The problem is how to face the new situation without breaking down. Some people get drunk, others take a drug, or go on a cruise or try to forget by doubling their work. All these expedients may be helpful for a while, since they prevent us from brooding over matters that we cannot change; but they bring only temporary relief.

Truth alone can provide the real cure. We must try to accept the new situation as it really is and without succumbing to it. The first thing to do is to establish for ourselves the facts of the new situation without viewing them through the tears of grief or resentment. We must meditate upon it point by point, and we must not allow hypocrisy to invade our thoughts. We may know that we ought to face the new situation in a spirit of goodwill and love, but it is no good to pretend that we are loving if we are not. Such an admission of the facts of the new situation and of our real emotions makes for truthfulness. If we proceed to think with honesty our thoughts become creative and reveal those methods which we should adopt.

Just as we cannot contemplate with our brain alone, so must this process of thinking be different from the intellectual 'everyday' thoughts, and must be done with the whole of our being. And yet we must never lose the consciousness that we are thinking, that we are identifying ourselves with something outside ourselves. Such a method of thinking is the 'yoga of action' of which Keyserling spoke to me. It is, if done persistently and conscientiously, the vital 'thinking' which in Steiner's opinion creates within us 'spiritual eyes'. We cannot force events that depend upon people, things and conditions beyond our control; but it is in our power to open doors within, through which we can discern the right road.

FULFILMENTS

Some people excuse their inability to think by pretending that they prefer to rely on their instinct. What they call instinct is in most cases a half-confessed wish magnified by the imagination. The word imagination is used in this chapter in the way Ouspensky uses it. It does not describe creative imagination, but that uncontrollable power within us that distorts truth, that runs away with our thoughts and leads us to unproductive day-dreams. There exists a power called instinct, which means the natural faculty for seeing truth without taking refuge in thought. In Eastern teachings, based on the doctrine of *karma*, instinct is often regarded as the result of right thought in our previous incarnation.

People with a genuine instinct are able to arrive at the right conclusions without having to go through the whole process of thinking, unavoidable for those without instinct. Reliance upon instinct may, however, be dangerous, for in most cases we mistake imagination for instinct. Constructive and contemplative thoughts, on the other hand, leave little room for errors.

It must be understood that identification in thought is not the same thing as the clinging to a problem in an uncontrolled, emotional way. The latter is the reverse of facing reality Ouspensky calls it destructive imagination, others call it mental self-abuse. The method of thinking referred to in these pages must be done with the exclusion of our imagination and, though dispassionately, yet with the passion of our whole being. Sorrowful pondering over grief destroys thought, and is a submission to negative emotions.

V

It is necessary to break the continuity of the narrative at this point and to investigate the part negative emotions[1] play in our lives, for it is impossible to attain any perception of truth if we give in to them. If people realized the harm they do themselves by allowing negative emotions to linger within them, there would be little evil in the world. Hatred, jealousy, envy, sorrow, greed, resentment do not exist in the region of spirit which is truth; but the lying faculties of our imagination make them swell beyond all proportion.

---

[1] No philosophical or psychological system defines the destructive power of negative emotions more clearly and convincingly than the one propagated by Ouspensky.

THE LIVING GOD

Negative emotions destroy an amount of life energy of which the ordinary person has no conception. A few minutes' lingering over negative emotions uses up more energy than man requires for a fully active life of twenty-four hours.

There exists a machine measuring that waste: it is formed by our knowledge of ourselves, and it begins to function the moment we register honestly our reactions to either negative or positive emotions. Hatred, jealousy and grief muddle both our thoughts and our feelings. The more we allow them to rule us the more complicated life becomes, and in the end we are so tied up within that no escape seems possible. We feel worn out, irritable and deeply ashamed of ourselves. If, on the other hand, our negative emotions are replaced by positive ones, if, for example, we meet the person responsible for our troubles lovingly and openly, we feel freer and happier. Solutions will suddenly come as though from nowhere, and where there was muddle there is now simplicity and light. The necessity for the elimination of negative emotions is an economic as well as a spiritual law.

The most harmful of all such emotions is fear. Fear destroys both the vision of truth and the power of right action. If humanity could overcome fear there would be hardly any unhappiness left in the world. Few sayings seem to me more helpful than that of an Eastern sage: 'It is better to be good than to fear evil.'

Just as negative emotions stand in the way of wisdom and produce stupidity, so does love create wisdom. Of course it is difficult to change a feeling of dislike into one of love. The easiest way to achieve this is either through deep thoughts, in the course of which we discover that our negative feeling was useless, or in fact only a phantom of our imagination, or through prayer, in which we include the person we believe we most dislike. At the end of an honest prayer of such a kind the former uncomfortable feeling disappears and the difficulty, created by the person for whom we had prayed, becomes of less significance. Only daily thought or daily prayer of such a kind can produce a lasting transformation, for fundamental changes are not worked by sudden miracles but solely by constant daily readjustment. If we find it impossible to pray, then it is best to cut short our lingering in negative emotions, and to force ourselves time after time to think about something entirely different.

FULFILMENTS

VI

From the moment a difficulty in life has been honestly 'thought over', the direction for right action discloses itself. Nevertheless we must not pretend that Christ or God Himself sends us His direct guidance when we just shut our eyes and keep the pencil ready to write down His orders. It is rare that creative thought—necessarily of a divine nature—falls into our lap. We have to evolve it ourselves, by working our way up towards it. There is Grace, but it rarely comes without effort. Emotional willingness is not enough to force Grace to come. Grace is like the sun and the rain. They perform the miracle of transforming the seed into the plant, the flower and the fruit, but they cannot do it while the soil is unploughed and the seed unsown.

VII

The method of facing difficulties described in the preceding pages became real to me only after life itself confronted me with a problem of such magnitude that I simply had to translate my knowledge into action if I did not wish to break down.

I was on my way back from Krishnamurti in California. Three days before leaving New York on the homeward voyage I received a letter announcing that sudden and entirely unforeseen circumstances were to change the whole basis of my life. I was suddenly faced with the prospect of giving up my home, which had become almost a part of me, and, what was much more painful, of abandoning a most precious relationship in my life. On top of everything else my financial foundations were shaken, and there was hardly one part of my life that did not suffer injury. Both my personal and my professional life were affected. It was by far the heaviest blow I had ever suffered. Things that I used to take for granted were suddenly gone, and I was faced with the prospect of founding an entirely new existence. I could do nothing to alleviate the blow, and had to start on my return journey without being able to make the slightest move. Three hours after the fatal letter had arrived I was still sitting on the bed in my room at the hotel, repeating to myself thoughtlessly over and over again that all this was only a nightmare and that soon I should wake up. What frightened me most was that many of my spiritual convictions had been built up on certain premises that were now being broken in pieces. For the three days before my departure I went through life as a man who was dazed.

The first morning on board ship I decided that the new situation simply had to be faced, no matter how painful it was. If all my spiritual knowledge, gained from many years' study, was of no avail at such an important crisis, then it was nothing but a lie. The situation required a translation of knowledge into action.

The illumination—I can find no less pretentious word to describe the experience—came during the very first morning. It did not come like a sudden miracle but it grew slowly out of a determined effort during a three hours' walk round the deck of the ship. My effort might have been less successful had I not just been staying with Krishnamurti, and had my spiritual determination not been strengthened through his influence. During my long walk round the deck at first I was anxious to eliminate all ill feeling, resentment and self-pity, and to produce within myself an atmosphere of detachment in which there would be room for honest thinking. After that I tried to face my new situation in the manner described earlier in this chapter.

I noticed that a change was taking place within me. I had not found a solution for those problems that were, as I knew, beyond my powers, but I no longer worried about them. The fear that had for the last few days been dragging down each of my thoughts was gone, and for the first time I slept all through the night. While previously thoughts of my difficulties would give me acute distress, I could now observe them dispassionately, as though I were dealing with the problems of someone else.

Such an enlightenment can, as a rule, be produced only by a thrust sharp enough to pierce the crust of habit and convention. Real joy and real pain can both open doors through which we perceive truth. Great sorrow shakes us and awakens faculties that can discriminate between reality and illusion—a shock caused by great joy evokes a feeling of gratitude so deep that all petty feelings and conventional ideas melt away therein. But neither sorrow nor happiness by itself can bring a solution to our worries. We must make an effort to find it. When happiness or sorrow becomes chronic, then it becomes dangerous. Permanent sorrow is produced by the exaggerated pictures of our imagination; the longer we allow ourselves to dwell in that state the further we drift from truth. Permanent happiness tends to make most people selfish, oblivious of truth, uninterested in anything outside their own happiness.

FULFILMENTS

By the time I arrived back in England I understood fully what Krishnamurti had meant when he spoke of the necessity of suffering for the attainment of truth.

The inner freedom that I had found did not make me forget my difficulties once and for all. It was still hard to get used to the idea that so many things that had contributed to my happiness were lost. But the new inner freedom gave me a much deeper sense of happiness, and the things I was losing had no longer their former meaning to me. I had many times to fight over again my battle of that first morning at sea, and each time my victory gave me new strength to grapple with newer difficulties. Eventually it almost became like light streaming into a room without anyone drawing the blinds.

VIII

Though I had always suspected that success can be gained only if we act not for the sake of success but for the sake of whatever we happen to be doing, I had never been able to live that truth in daily life. I often pretended to myself that I did certain things merely for their own sake, but deep down I knew only too well that I was constantly watching the chances of success. The new inner 'illuminations' enabled me at last not only to preach but to live the gospel of 'doing for doing's sake'. I made my decisions not with regard to their possible success but merely because contemplative thought I had revealed them to me. And it became obvious to me that if acted absolutely in such a way and without any regard for a possible success, then that success was sure to follow automatically.

Even more startling was another discovery. My first misfortune, of which I had been notified by the letter I received in New York, was only the beginning of a long series of worries that followed one another almost daily after I arrived home. I was struggling constantly between giving in wearily and going on translating my spiritual knowledge into action. It was an incessant fight between hopelessness and faith, between resignation and the belief in a higher justice and higher necessity. But the continuous efforts to face reality were bringing new glimpses of truth almost every day and they disclosed to me eventually the last and most important stage of how to act in conformity with truth. No teacher and no study could have given me that last realization.

With a thrill deeper than any I had ever experienced, I perceived at last the most successful way of finding a solution for difficulties that defy all our own resources. It was the way of Christianity as it was shown to us originally before it was cheapened by dogmas, compulsion, self-righteousness and mechanization. I understood at last what it meant not to force events but to let them solve themselves. It was not evasiveness nor was it fatalism but merely trust in the inevitable victory of truth, in the power of God. It was the admission of the superiority of the divine method over even the cleverest method invented by the human brain.

Even people who believe that God acts from within us often find it difficult to 'locate' Him. There is only one answer to this—God's most evident instrument within us is our conscience. Whenever our intellect is unable to point the way we must listen to our conscience. It must be understood, of course, that conscience should be employed only as a 'controlling station' for actions directed by us, and as a 'power station' only when the decisions do not depend on ourselves.

What is conscience? It is the guardian of the very best within us.

Often we think that it is within our power to alter in our favour the trend of events by preventing or forcing certain incidents. This applies most of all to the countless decisions that depend upon others. The surest way to act in such circumstances is to obey the commands of our conscience.

Of course, even our conscience has become mechanical in its action. We have, therefore, to find our way back to it, and this can best be done through contemplative thought. After having reached our conscience—and not that imaginary conscience which is only the result of upbringing, social environment and traditions—we ought to listen to it instead of obeying the commands of our brain. We must forget all about the possible success or failure of our action and try to realize our highest ideals.

At first such a method will seem hopelessly idealistic and lacking in all contact with daily life And yet to act according to our highest ideals is the only method that does not fail even in the most complicated entanglements of our life. Driven by fear and lack of faith, we try to affect the trend of events more than we are entitled to, and we give God no chance to play His part. Hence the confusion we achieve whenever we are faced with a truly complicated situation.

Trust in the wisdom of higher powers does not exclude discrimination. Lack of discrimination leads to fanaticism, and the fanaticism of righteousness is as far removed from truth as its opposite. A life directed by our conscience with the help of discrimination can never deteriorate into fanaticism. In fact, it is in the noblest lives that we find measure and discrimination. 'A man's heart', I once read in a book of Eastern wisdom, 'does not lie to him—it is always the brain that lies.' This is one of the deepest of truths. When we state that the convictions of the heart are more valuable than those of the brain, we naturally do not refer to decisions of a purely intellectual or mechanical kind.

The commands of the heart can be followed only if they are supported by courage and faith. Courage is necessary so that we may be able to abandon fear; and faith so that we may trust God Had not Keyserling told me in Darmstadt that spirit was for him the result of courage and faith? What he called spirit someone else calls truth or God. (People who object to the word God may replace it by any word that expresses in their opinion the directing impulse of life, such as 'the absolute', the 'sense of life', or the 'central power station', or any other of the fashionable names.)

IX

My new inner awareness allowed me to make several un-expected spiritual discoveries. One of them was that nothing in life happens accidentally, and that every individual grief I had suffered had been a needed 'lesson'. I also understood that it was rather 'kindness' on the part of fate that put me through all my trials, and that gave practical effect to my former theoretical 'lessons'.

The sceptic will say: 'If you believe that everything in life works according to a plan, then it should be possible to discover the plan by some logical system. If this be so, life ought to be rational, and yet we know that it is not so.' Indeed, life is not rational, not con-sistent with reason and logic. Rational systems can explain the ex-ternal manifestations of life only. The system by which life as a whole is run is not rational but spiritual, and cannot be compre-hended by intellectual means. Mystics, spiritual teachers, certain types of thinkers, poets or artists catch glimpses of it. The founders of religions, the prophets, such seers as the Delphic pythia, some of the Christian saints, men like Plato, Paracelsus, Jakob Boehme, Steiner, one or two of the great Jewish rabbis, poets like Blake,

THE LIVING GOD

Goethe, Wordsworth, painters like Raphael *see* a spiritual structure where other people try to comprehend it with their brains.

The pattern created by the spiritual system is what we call destiny or fate. The more and the harder we try to wake up and to see truth, the more the pattern of fate reveals itself. Accidents exist only for the blind. But the doctrine of fate must never deteriorate into fatalism; for, besides fate or, as the East calls it, *karma*, there is also, not exactly free will, as we wrongly call it, but freedom of understanding.

Let us for a moment consider the two directing powers called fate and free understanding Fate is the power that carries us along through life and that we cannot escape: it embraces such different elements of our existence as the century in which we were born, our race and nationality, our intellectual and social class, our physical features, our good and bad qualities. We cannot escape fate, but we can work in conformity with it. That is where freedom comes in. We are free to comprehend the facts given by fate, and to discriminate according to our intelligence. Our comprehension and our discrimination shape our will. Both fate as it is given to us, and freedom of understanding as we use it, work together and can never be separated. They are like the horizontal and vertical faces of the steps in a staircase—the one cannot exist without the other.

One of the first people in recent history to perceive clearly the difference between free will and free understanding was Rudolf Steiner. Only a few people before his time discovered that it is not the will that is free but our power of understanding that sets our will in motion. Summing up, we can say that fate and personal freedom act side by side, as the divine and the human powers within us. For it is wrong to assume that God's knowledge of our future necessarily determines it. Seeing something is not the same thing as coming to a decision about it.

X

The truth of the above experiences was proved to me by my own power of understanding; and afterwards by the way life responded to my actions and showed me that the doctrine of fate and freedom was not an intellectual theory but a truth confirmed almost daily by facts. I had always felt that there was a direct connection between our conduct and the way fate treated us. But the proofs of such a connection were too vague to be accepted intellectually. The main difficulty in the establishment of a definite law was that my actions

303

and the apparent answers of fate were separated by intervals of time too long to allow me to discover the link between the two.

This changed fundamentally once I began to make a real effort to allow truth to direct my actions. The difference between the working of fate in the earlier and the later days was a difference both of visibility and of speed. Whereas the missing link had formerly been almost indiscernible, now it was becoming clearer every day. Occasionally I could almost foretell in what way fate would react to my own movements; and at times these reactions would take place within twenty-four hours. The laws evolved from my experiences could be summarized thus: (a) The more consciously we act in life, the more clearly the pattern of life is revealed; and (b) The better we know what is right and wrong, the more quickly does fate act.

I understood beyond all doubt that both good and bad thoughts, emotions and deeds evoke corresponding reactions on the part of fate. I do not call good and bad what are considered as such by conventional morality, but what we are told by the voice of our conscience and by the very best within ourselves. (The best within ourselves always commands not only a truthful but also a loving attitude in which there is no room for negative emotions. Thus truthful action must always be also loving action. In the realms of the spirit truth and love become almost identical.)

Let me illustrate my last discovery by an example. Suppose I should try to achieve a certain success by a subtle lie, a pronouncement that was not quite fair to another person, an attempt to influence someone in a manner that could be defended intellectually but would not withstand the judgement of conscience. Formerly I often succeeded in my aims, without incurring any punishment from fate. Since, however, I began to see the meaning of truth, retribution would come almost immediately and so unmistakably that there was no doubt of the direct connection between my misdeed and its punishment. Even if I achieved success at first something would happen the next day to turn it into failure. If, on the other hand, I acted in accordance with my better self, success was inevitable. This was true not only of my actions but equally of my most secret thoughts and emotions. There was no escape from conscience: if I tried to cheat it, fate immediately retorted by punishing me.

The greater our knowledge the greater our responsibility, and we are forgiven our sins as long as we do not know that we are sinning; the moment we are conscious of the lie that every bad deed implies, we no longer have the right to sin. If fate is kind, it warns us by sending punishments without delay. If we go on committing such sins as thinking evil, lying to others or to ourselves, revelling in negative emotions, the punishments become heavier. Eventually we realize that we shall ruin ourselves unless we cease to sin.

XI

In the introduction to this book there is the sentence: 'Conditions to-day would be different if the men who directed our destinies had been driven more by conscious faith than by the forces of scepticism. . . .' The reader will understand now that no Utopian idealism was aimed at in those words. The existing political, economic and social muddle and the deep dissatisfaction of individuals are a result of the universal lie that forms the basis of modern life. Instead of beholding the truth as it is, the nations and their leaders accept the distorted pictures of their own imagination. Instead of approaching the difficulties before them in a spirit of truth and love, they approach them filled to the brim with negative emotions, with fear, jealousy, pride, with determination to employ all kinds of intellectual tricks. They accept hasty conclusions and are satisfied with half-thoughts Their attitude is one in which intellect and emotions do not collaborate intelligently but fight independent battles, struggling with one another. How can anything be achieved in the world if the men who are supposed to direct it employ every method except the right one; if they organize politics, economics and the social life of countries before even attempting to organize *themselves*; if they expect the nations to trust them, and yet themselves have no faith in God or in any higher intelligence than their own? It seems a miracle that the world can survive this general spiritual anarchy.

I have often heard people say: 'What is the good of my being decent if everyone round me cheats? If others consented to be decent, I too would behave decently.' For all it is worth, such a remark forms one of the most popular excuses for most misdeeds and follies. The answer to it is that we should not behave decently for ethical purposes or to convert others, but merely for our own sake. By living in accordance with the highest within ourselves we may deprive ourselves of the weapons of that astuteness that we suspect our enemies of employing, but we submit ourselves to an intelligence that is more efficient than that of the cleverest of our enemies. Instead of trying

U   305

to force events that are beyond our powers we replace the brittle arms of our limited intellect by mightier weapons.

Far be it from me to preach ethics of one sort or another. All I am attempting is to show from personal experience that we ought to act according to the noblest elements within us merely for the sake of solving our difficulties more efficiently. A life lived in that way is not a life of negative submission, of lazy expectancy, or responsibility eschewed. It is a life of much wider consciousness and of constant inner activity in which spiritual inertia plus physical activity have been replaced by constant awareness plus physical economy.

And this is the only life in which the God within us can cease to be merely an abstraction. It is a life in which the God within us emerges from the shadows of our ignorance, and steps forth to become the living power that commands all our life. It is the God that makes of every day a Sunday. It is the only living God.

BIBLIOGRAPHY

It is almost impossible to compile the full bibliography of a book which narrates experiences stretching over more than fifteen years. Besides, the men described in this volume are approached in a personal rather than in an intellectual way. Thus, though I have read most of the publications about them, there may exist several books that have escaped my attention. Even so, the following list covers most of the important publications that are mentioned in this book, or were helpful in its writing.

PART ONE: THE UNKNOWN CONTINENT

INTRODUCTION: 'TRUTH IN KENSINGTON GARDENS'

The quotations from Dean Inge are taken from a book *English Mystics* (Murray) It is a collection of lectures delivered as far back as 1906. It is one of the most lucid books on the subject and it gives some of the profoundest and yet clearest descriptions of true mysticism known to me. *Preface to Morals*, by the popular and brilliant American critic and publicist, Walter Lippmann, is a provocative book about the attitude of modern man with regard to spiritual truth.

CHAPTER ONE: 'WISDOM IN DARMSTADT'

The most thorough English book on Keyserling is *Introduction to Keyserling* (Jonathan Cape) by Mrs. Mercedes Gallagher Parks. It is a very conscientious analysis of Keyserling's writings, but deals very little with their author. There are several French books about Keyserling. The most important are *La Sagesse de Darmstadt*, a critical study by Ernest Seilleire, and *La Philosophie de Hermann Keyserling* by Maurice Boucher. The Italian Filippo Burzio published two volumes of *Portraits* in which we find much about Keyserling's philosophy. A brilliant though sarcastic portrait of Keyserling has been painted by the American author Will Durant in his *Adventures in Genius*.

307

BIBLIOGRAPHY

Among Keyserling's own works *The Travel Diary of a Philosopher* was the most widely read and is still one of the author's most entertaining books. *South American Meditations* (both published by Cape), which came out more than ten years later, is considered by Keyserling his *magnum opus*. It is more difficult to read than the *Diary*, but is full of stimulating ideas and an altogether typical work of its author For my own liking it is somewhat too long and too redundant—but these are peculiarities of Keyserling's style.

Chapter Two. 'Episodes in Modern Life'

As far as I know, there are no books in English on Stefan George. Since I am dealing with George from the purely personal point of view, I have resisted the temptation to find out how far English literary scholarship has penetrated into the mystery of George's personality and poetry. I found the most useful among German books *Stefan George* by the late Friedrich Gundolf, one of George's closest pupils, who became in his later years the famous professor of Literature at the University of Heidelberg. Faithful to George's doctrine of secrecy in personal matters, it gives only the faintest outline of his life, but provides a very profound—though at times cumbersome—analysis of his work. *Die Ersten Buecher Stefan Georges* by Eduard Lachmann is a much simpler, less important and yet scholarly study of George's poetry. (Both books have been published by Georg Bondi, Berlin, George's own publishers.)

Bô Yin Râ, or rather his doctrine, has been described at some length in Felix Weingartner's *Bô Yin Râ* (Rhein Verlag, Basle, 1923), and Bô Yin Râ the man—in a biographical sketch compiled by Robert Winspeare (published in 1930 by R. Hummel, Leipzig). The most instructive of the various publications on Bô Yin Râ is the German pamphlet *Weshalb Bô Yin Râ?* by Koeber-Staehlin. (Bô Yin Râ's books have been published by Koebersche Verlagsbuchhandlung, Basel.)

Chapter Three: 'Occult Truth'

Books on Steiner are mostly dedicated to individual aspects of anthroposophy. A general study dealing with the whole of h.. life and doctrine does not exist, and the two chapters in this volume seem to be the first attempt of that kind. But no books about Steiner are as enlightening as his own. His literary legacy is so enormous that only some of his most important books can be quoted here. Among them are *An Outline of Occult Science, Knowledge of the Higher Worlds* (which gives Steiner's method for the development of second sight); *Christianity as a Mystical Fact* (an important contribution to the mystery of the life of Jesus Christ), *Philosophy of Spiritual Activity* (one of the earliest books revealing the new *Weltanschauung*, crystallized later in anthroposophy), and, above all, his autobiography *The Story of My Life*, which ends unfortunately with the year 1912. This somewhat difficult book gives the story of Steiner's inner development rather than an account of his life, and it unfolds the logical way that led step by step to the final establishment of anthroposophy. Steiner's attitude towards the war and his relationship with General von Moltke are described in a German volume consisting mainly of documents and of Steiner's own pronouncements and articles. It was published in 1933 under the title *Rudolf Steiner während des Weltkriegs*. A moving account of Steiner is given by Friedrich Rittelmeyer in his *Rudolf Steiner Enters My Life* (George Roberts, 1929). This little book about the friendship of the two men discloses incidentally the charming personality of its author. Of a similar character are the two personal books by the Swiss poet Albert Steffen *Begegnungen mit Rudolf Steiner* and *In Memoriam*, which gives a poignant picture of Steiner's death.

Edward Schuré, whose *Les Grands Initiés* and *From Sphinx to Christ* are quoted in this chapter, was a French mystic and writer on metaphysics who died only a few years ago. Though certain readers may find it difficult to accept the author's enthusiasm, which at times seems to sweep him off his feet, they will acknowledge Schuré's knowledge of ancient mysticism and of Greek mythology, and the soundness of many of his spiritual perceptions. Schuré was deeply impressed by Steiner's insight into the world of the spirit and especially by Steiner's Christology. The origin of certain principles of clairvoyance propagated by Steiner can be found in that mysterious little book *Nuptiæ Chymicæ, Christiani Rosenkreutz, Anno 1459*, by Valentin Andreae, published in 1604. It is a purely esoteric book and is bound to disappoint readers unprepared for such fare

BIBLIOGRAPHY

PART TWO: THE ENGLISH ADVENTURE

INTRODUCTION: 'THE ENGLISH SCENE'

New Country (Hogarth Press) is an interesting collection of essays, poetry and fiction by some of the representatives of English literature of the last few years. Those interested in the British Israel Movement will find its comprehensive story and its principles in *Notes and Queries on the Origin of British Israel* by Helen Countess of Radnor (The Marshall Press, 1925).

CHAPTER ONE: 'THE THRONE THAT WAS CHRIST'S'

A serious book on Krishnamurti is *Krishnamurti* by the French author Carlo Suaré (published in 1932, Edition Adyar, Paris). Very interesting are the rather outspoken chapters about Krishnamurti in Mr. Theodore Besterman's brilliant biography *Mrs. Annie Besant* (Kegan Paul, 1934). There is a biography of Krishnamurti by Lilly Heber (Allen & Unwin, 1931), containing some useful information, but too uncritical and chaotic to be of great value. The ordinary reader will find little satisfaction in the large volume of theosophical literature on Krishnamurti: it is altogether too credulous and un-critical. Few modern personalities have roused the curiosity of the press more than Krishnamurti, and articles about him have appeared constantly for twenty-five years, though only a few of them are above the level of sensationalism.

The choice of Krishnamurti's own writings—prose or poetry—must be left to the individual taste. They are all written rather in the same Eastern lyrical strain, and are far less impressive than Krishnamurti's spoken words. His writings have been published by Allen & Unwin, London, and the Star Publishing Trust.

CHAPTER TWO: 'PORTRAIT OF A "PERFECT MASTER" '

I am told that the former editor of *Everyman* is preparing a biography of Shri Meher Baba. The best and most complete account of Baba in existence can be found in Paul Brunton's exciting *A*

BIBLIOGRAPHY

Search in Secret India (Rider, 1934). There have been many articles about Baba, good and bad. In December 1934 *John Bull* published a most damning article in which Baba was accused of what amounts to financial fraud. *John Bull* called him 'a rather curious financial adventurer', and concluded with the words 'we suggest that the "fake" messiah might be regarded as an undesirable alien and be refused admission to this country'. Certain publications by Baba's own followers, such as the *Meher Gazette* published in India, are too childish to be taken seriously.

CHAPTER THREE· 'THE MAN WHOSE GOD IS A MILLIONAIRE'

I found the most useful among the many publications on Dr. Buchman *Oxford and the Groups* (Basil Blackwell, Oxford). This book is the composite work of twelve different authors and it analyses Buchmanism in connection with such different subjects as education, religion, the universities, social problems. The writers try to be impartial: they praise where praise is due and condemn where criticism seems justified. It is an important contribution to the history of Buchmanism. The amusing book *Saints Run Mad* (John Lane, 1934) by Marjorie Harrison is somewhat biased. The author associated intimately with the Oxford Group Movement and studied it seriously though dispassionately. In her entertaining book, to which the Bishop of Durham has written the foreword, she gives us firsthand glimpses of some of those aspects of Buchmanism that an ordinary 'sinner', unaccustomed to the wanton ways of the groupers, may find hard to believe. The most famous book on Buchmanism is *For Sinners Only* by A. J. Russell—the account of the conversion of a journalist to Buchmanism. For several years the Groups regarded this chatty narrative as a kind of official history of their movement. It is only since they realized the harmful effect of that book on all thinking people that they have ceased to identify themselves with it. More serious is *What is the Oxford Group?* by the 'Layman with a notebook' (Oxford University Press). It is a survey of the principles of the Groups. *Why I believe in the Oxford Group?* by Jack C. Winslow (Hodder & Stoughton, 1934) is rather more primitive. There exist a great many other books and pamphlets written by members of the Oxford Group Movement. Most of them repeat the same stories, argue with the same arguments and betray

BIBLIOGRAPHY

the same cheerful credulity which we find in every member and every activity of the movement. A detailed account of the unfortunate misdeeds of a Buchmanite is given in *Up for Murder*, A Selection of famous South African Murder Trials, by Benjamin Bennett (Hutchinson & Co.). The book *Le Grand Secret* mentioned in this chapter is one of the few valuable modern books on occultism by Eliphas Levi, the French occultist of the last century whose real name was (the Abbé) Alphonse Louis Constant.

CHAPTER FOUR: 'MIRACLE AT THE ALBERT HALL'

George Jeffreys published two books *Healing Rays* and *Pentecostal Rays* (Elim Publishing Company). The former of the two contains a few personal statements about the beginnings of the author's remarkable career. On the whole, both books are simple biblical studies, in which Jeffreys tries to establish a faultless link between the fundamentalist principles of his own doctrine and that contained in the Bible.

CHAPTER FIVE: 'WAR AGAINST SLEEP'

There is no better way of approaching Ouspensky than by reading his two books *Tertium Organum* and *A New Model of the Universe* (both published by Kegan Paul). They are important contributions to modern thought, and no-one interested seriously in the subjects treated in this volume should miss reading them. Though the *Model* is a more scientific and much longer book than the more entertaining *Tertium Organum*, I should give preference to it: it is more important and more startling in its scientific discoveries and deductions.

CHAPTER SIX: 'HARMONIOUS DEVELOPMENT OF MAN'

The letters by D. H. Lawrence quoted in this chapter appeared in *Lorenzo in Taos* (Martin Secker) by Mrs. Mabel Dodge, a most interesting American, who was Lawrence's hostess in New Mexico, and who is considered one of the most stimulating personalities in American intellectual circles.

BIBLIOGRAPHY

PART THREE: FULFILMENTS

Introduction: 'Aryan Gods'

The only book mentioned in this chapter is *Der Mythus des XX Jahrhunderts* (Hoheneichen Verlag München, 1934) by Alfred Rosenberg, who, besides being the head of the Department of Foreign Affairs of the Nazi Party, is also the cultural leader of the Nazi movement. Next to Hitler's *Mein Kampf* the *Mythus* is the most important book of the Nazi ideology. It is a review of the whole history of civilization written from the aspect of race purity and the superiority of the German nation. The number of historical facts contained in this book is enormous—but they are supported by a knowledge that is muddled and distorted. Western readers accustomed to the acknowledged traditions of scholarship will find Herr Rosenberg's arbitrary and fantastic deductions too childish for serious consideration. But his book illustrates vividly the low level and the perversions of the Nazi minds even among their 'intellectual' leaders.

All the important books in connection with Keyserling and Krishnamurti have been described in the first part of this bibliography.

Chapter Two: 'The Testament of Rudolf Steiner'

The many branches of anthroposophical science either created by Steiner himself or since developed by his followers have been expounded in numerous publications. Steiner laid down his principles in books and lectures, in which he dealt with every branch of anthroposophy. His most instructive pronouncements on Education can be found in *The New Art of Education, The Education of the Child* and the two series of lectures *Lectures to Teachers* and *Essentials of Education*. His ideas on medicine are contained in his *Fundamentals of Therapy, Outline of Anthroposophical Medical Research* and *Four Lectures to Doctors*. Steiner always tried to stimulate his pupils to work independently along the lines suggested by him, and thus to obtain individual results. The records of these results are contained in innumerable publications that have appeared since his death. Important among them are the books by Dr. L. Kolisko about biological, chemico-astronomical and physiological discoveries made by her in laboratory work. Her publications, which are purely scientific and cannot in consequence be very fully appreciated by the lay reader, contain truly revolutionary evidence of the connections between planetary rhythms and biological life. One of her most important books is *Working of the Stars in Earthly Substances* (2 volumes). Many of Dr. Kolisko's books are profusely illustrated with photographs showing the novelty of hundreds of experiments made by the author.

There exist various publications by Steiner's medical followers, such as the writings of Dr. Werner Keelin, who specializes in the cancer cure originated by Steiner, or the writings of a more general kind by Dr. Ita Wegman. Since anthroposophy treats the world as a whole, many anthroposophical books cannot be pigeonholed according to subjects. Thus a book by Dr. Guenther Wachsmuth, *The Etheric Formative Forces* (2 volumes), covers most of the subjects of anthroposophy. It is a work of scientific character, yet comprehensible enough to be enjoyed by anyone. Other important anthroposophical authors are Dr. Johannes Stein, Dr. Carl Unger, Dr. Ehrenfried Pfeiffer, Ernst Bindel, Dr. E. Vreede and George Kaufmann.

There are innumerable publications about every branch of anthroposophy. In most countries in which there are anthroposophical farmers there exist corresponding agricultural publications. In England an Anthroposophical Agricultural Foundation publishes a quarterly magazine *Notes and Correspondence* and pamphlets on various agricultural subjects.

There are two main English centres for the publication of anthroposophical literature: The Rudolf Steiner Publishing Co., and the Anthroposophical Publishing Co.

CONCLUSION: 'THE LIVING GOD'

The quotations from Edward Schuré are taken from the chapter 'The Hellenic Miracle' in *From Sphinx to Christ*. Plutarch's quotations come from his *Opera Moralia*, especially the treatises 'On the E at Delphi' and 'On the Cessation of Oracles', one of the most metaphysical of Plutarch's writings.

BIBLIOGRAPHY

On the subject of yoga there exist many books, but very few of those written by Europeans are of much value. One of the best short expositions of yoga is contained in Ouspensky's *New Model of the Universe*, Very interesting are the accounts of firsthand yoga experiences of a European in Paul Brunton's *Search in Secret India*, already mentioned. The author worked for a number of years under Eastern yogis in India. It may be added that, unlike most European authors who boast of their practical knowledge of yoga, Mr Brunton's experiences are entirely genuine.

INDEX

317

INDEX

INDEX

INDEX

Ingram Content Group UK Ltd.
Milton Keynes UK
UKHW020838190423
420422UK00006B/410